Revising Culture
Reinventing Peace

Revising Culture
Reinventing Peace

the influence of
Edward W. Said

edited by Naseer Aruri and Muhammad A. Shuraydi
with an introduction by Richard Falk

OLIVE
BRANCH
PRESS

An imprint of Interlink Publishing Group, Inc.
New York • Northampton

First published in 2001 by

OLIVE BRANCH PRESS
An imprint of Interlink Publishing Group, Inc.
99 Seventh Avenue • Brooklyn, New York 11215 and
46 Crosby Street • Northampton, Massachusetts 01060
www.interlinkbooks.com

Copyright © Naseer Aruri and Muhammad A. Shuraydi 2001

All rights reserved. No part of this publication may be reproduced, stored in a retrieval system, or transmitted in any form or by any means, electronic, mechanical, photocopying, recording or otherwise without the prior permission of the publisher.

Library of Congress Cataloging-in-Publication Data

Revising culture, reinventing peace : the influence of Edward W. Said / edited by Naseer Aruri and Muhammad A. Shuraydi.
    p. cm.
Includes bibliographical references and index.
    ISBN 1-56656-357-7
    1. Said, Edward W.--Views on Arab-Israeli conflict--Congresses. 2. Said, Edward W.--Views on orientalism--Congresses. 3. Said, Edward W.--Views on imperialism--Congresses. 4. Said, Edward W.--Views on culture--Congresses. 5. Said, Edward W.--Views on Arab-Israeli conflict--Congresses. 6. Orientalism--Congresses. 7. Imperialism--Congresses. 8. Culture--Congresses. I. Aruri, Naseer Hassan, 1934– II. Shuraydi, Muhammad A.

CB18.S25 R48 2000
956.04--dc21   00-040713

Davis, Lennard, "Nationalism and Deafness: The Nineteenth Century," from *Enforcing Normalcy: Disability, Deafness and the Body* (London: Verso, 1995): 73–99 reprinted with the kind permission of the publisher.

Printed and bound in Canada

To request our complete 48-page full-color catalog, please call us toll free at **1-800-238-LINK**, visit our website at **www.interlinkbooks.com**, or write to
Interlink Publishing
46 Crosby Street, Northampton, MA 01060
e-mail: sales@interlinkbooks.com

Contents

Acknowledgements   vii

Introduction
Empowering Inquiry: Our Debt to Edward W. Said   *Richard Falk*   x

I Nationalities

Nationality, Disability, and Deafness	*Lennard J. Davis*	2
Imperial Britain & the American Nation	*Deirdre David*	29
Edward Said & the Future of the Jewish People	*Marc H. Ellis*	38

II On Orientalism

Humanizing the Oriental	*Yasmeen Abu-Laban*	74
Angry Beauty & Literary Love	*Timothy Brennan*	86
Orientalism in the Arab Context	*As'ad AbuKhalil*	100

III To Palestine

Toward A Pluralistic Existence in Palestine/Israel	*Naseer Aruri*	120
The Arab Economy in Western Eyes	*Atif A. Kubursi*	134
Peace for Palestine	*John Sigler*	159

Epilogue
Edward Said & His "Beautiful Old House"   *Muhammad A. Shuraydi*   170

Contributors   179
Index   182

Acknowledgments

The essays in this book were all, except the Epilogue, presented in the conference "Culture, Politics, and Peace," honoring the scholarly contributions of Edward W. Said at the University of Windsor, September 19–20, 1997.

Atif Kubursi of McMaster University came up with the idea of honoring Professor Said. He and I formed a committee with Marwan and Nadia Taqtaq and Issam and Wafa Salah, and asked Dr. Naseer Aruri—known in the Arab-American community for his professional dedication, the unambiguity of his political stand, and his personal integrity—to chair the program.

The idea of honoring Professor Said was rooted in the following:

a) As a renowned scholar, political analyst, and artistic/cultural critic of Arab/Palestinian origin, his contributions deserve international recognition and respect.

b) The desire of the Arab-American and Arab-Canadian community to meet Professor Said in person.

c) His unclouded vision and unadulterated stand against the Oslo Declaration of Principles as a "Palestinian Versailles," offering no redress for the victimization of the Palestinian people and obstructing the attainment of a truly genuine and just peace between the Israelis and the Palestinians.

In addition to the original two sponsors of the conference, The Canadian Arab Society of Windsor and the Arab World Fund at the University of Windsor, the conference was co-sponsored by all the major Arab-American and Arab-Canadian community organizations in Michigan and Ontario, and supported by the local business community.

On September 19–20, 1997, more than twenty scholars participated in the four sessions of the conference: "*Orientalism* and Literary Criticism," "Culture and Imperialism," "The Arab World, Palestine, and Islam," and "Palestine, Peace, and the Jews."

The undertaking of this international conference demanded the coordinated efforts of many dedicated individuals, groups, and institutions, locally, nationally, and internationally. Thanking all of them by name is an almost impossible task. It goes without saying that without the invited speakers and their commitment to the thinking of Professor Said, the conference would not have taken place nor would this book have been published. The chairpersons of the fundraising committee, Marwan and Nadia Taqtaq, unselfishly devoted their personal and material resources toward the completion of this honorable project. Their donations, along with those of Atif Kubursi and Fouad Tayfour, are noteworthy. Other members of the fundraising committee, Issam and Wafa Salah, Warren David, Juliet Metri, and the treasurer, Fouad Dabdoub, deserve special thanks.

Phyllis Bennis must be singled out as the one person who played the most crucial part in the process leading to the publication of this collection. Not only did she read every chapter and offer sound critiques, but she also provided substantive copyediting. Her efforts, together with those of Pam Thompson, made it possible for a collection written by authors of diverse talents and disciplines, to stand out as a single and consistent volume. To both, the editors wish to express gratitude.

Thanks also to Verso for their kind permission to reprint part of Lennard Davis' chapter from *Enforcing Normalcy*.

The University of Windsor, in particular the hospitality of the Office of International Affairs and its Director, Dr. R. Julian Cattaneo, are praiseworthy. Members of the planning committee in the State of Michigan and the Province of Ontario were exemplary in their devotion to the successful completion of the project. We are especially thankful and grateful to the dedicated efforts of the conference co-chairperson, Atif Kubursi. Every member of the planning committee is worthy of a sincere "Thank You."

Finally, appreciation is due to Roy Freij, Steve Ghannam, and Debra Peterson of Iris Design, Print & Copy for the production of the commemorative book and the other informational and promotional material used in the conference.

To the professor of a truly just peace, Edward W. Said, who kindly gave two days of his time to be with us, I humbly say: Thank you for the honor of your landmark visit.

—Muhammad Shuraydi
University of Windsor

INTRODUCTION

Empowering Inquiry: Our Debt to Edward W. Said

Richard Falk

A few years ago, while giving talks in several Indonesian cities, I was struck by how often questions were raised during the discussion periods relating to the work and ideas of Edward W. Said. Indeed, anywhere that intellectuals with a progressive or internationalist outlook gather on this planet, there is an awareness and appreciation of the indispensable contributions that Said has made to the life of free and independent inquiry, and beyond this, to a whole style and method of thought that takes ideas and culture seriously as crucially linked to structures of oppression and processes of emancipation.

Said's work is also connected to the confusions of a Janus-faced identity of intellectuals that is so characteristic of this era, that of seeming to belong everywhere and nowhere simultaneously. At least two forms of connection emerge from Said's life and writings. First of all, being uprooted, Said embraces the identity of displacement, and yet addresses the audience of a borderless world. Beyond this, Said is convinced that the "hybridity" associated with displacement is the signature of the age, is at the core of globalization, and is the essence of the capitalist obsession, namely, money.

Such admiration and awareness is, of course, rare, but what makes it particularly remarkable, is that in Said's case it is inseparable from his long and passionate engagement with the cause and tribulations of the Palestinian people, an embattled and frustrating particularity. Sadly, too many of its most committed partisans have long ago had their moral, political, and intellectual energy sapped by such an involvement. Although for Said, his Palestinian origins and horizons are never truly absent, the depth and range of his concerns are such that their Palestinian grounding, rather than being a limiting factor, roots his thought and adds a dimension of authenticity and seriousness that partly explains its extraordinary range of influence.

The Palestinian ordeal, without being in any sense backgrounded, is itself partly transfigured from a struggle with the other to being a tragic

Empowering Inquiry: Our Debt to Edward W. Said

encounter between two aggrieved and victimized peoples. Said's distinctive capacity to exhibit genuine empathy for the ordeal of the historic opponent, Israel and the Jewish people, despite a lengthy period of oppressive Israeli dominance of the Palestinian people, deepens understanding, and creates the moral and psychological space for genuine reconciliation. By so doing, Said escapes the partisan pitfalls of one-eyed comprehension, thereby both humanizing and universalizing this bloody, anguishing, and still far from resolved encounter between these two peoples fated to continue shaping each other's history to such a startling degree. What Said achieves by his approach is an orientation toward conflict that avoids enmity so convincingly as to make dialogue supersede polemics.

Said's worldview is also an outcome of his lifelong work as a world-class interpreter of literature, and more generally as a renowned and versatile cultural figure, whose publications include professional music criticism and whose activities include acclaimed public performances as a concert pianist. His field of scholarly specialization is comparative literature, which studies the manner by which the most adept cultural and imaginative sensibilities of various countries express the most profound human desires, ambitions, and fears. Such studies presuppose an intimacy with foreign languages and modes of thought that blur distinctions between self and other, citizen and alien, native and foreigner. Such close encounters with literary classics, when undertaken with the intention of better illuminating their wider significance, tends toward an appreciation of complexity, and the incapacity of the human mind to comprehend reality in a totalizing manner. It is always beneficial to appreciate great literature from multiple perspectives, and as perpetually open to new readings. The inexhaustible mysteries of meaning is always a sign of a greatness beyond the now. Such interpretative mastery as is characteristic of Said's literary studies exhibits the extent to which understanding is derived and enriched from a variety of perspectives. A student of comparative literature is self-consciously engaged in a continuing process of discovery that is historically and contextually conditioned even if such an interpreter does not have Said's particular personal preoccupations about how the imaginations of the politically dominant and subordinate are intertwined, as well as dialectically related.

This passion for interpretation is reinforced by Said's modernist skepticism about dogmatic claims, partly expressed by his own frequent reiteration of an unwavering commitment to secularism.

He makes this commitment very clear in a wonderful passage toward the end of his 1993 Reith Lectures, reprinted in *Representations of the Intellectual*:

> ... the true intellectual is a secular being. However much intellectuals pretend that their representations are of higher things or ultimate values, morality begins with their activity in this secular world of ours—where it takes place, whose interests it serves, how it jibes with a consistent and universalist ethic, how it discriminates between power and justice, what it reveals of one's choices and priorities. Those gods that always fail to demand from the intellectual in the end a kind of absolute certainty and a total, seamless view of reality that recognizes only disciples and enemies (120).

In so defining a secular stance, Said is distancing himself from the dogmatics of those Marxist (and anti-Marxists) who see the reality of historical laws as the justification for killing fields. He is equally rejecting crusading devotees of religious faith who are prepared to embark on bloody crusades for the glory of their particular god or gods. My own humanism is less assured on these issues, feeling a kinship with William Connolly's fine book, *Why I Am Not a Secularist*, which allows space for spirituality and religious devotion that is neither extremist nor oblivious to the justice claims of the oppressed and the marginal. Said's secularism does not entertain such fence-straddling, being seemingly embattled against the repressive sides of religious truth claims (as exemplified by Said's early and unconditional defense of Salman Rushdie's *Satanic Verses*) and content to operate within the broad confines of a compassionate and engaged rationalism (thereby making the best of the Enlightenment legacy).

As should be obvious, Said is never using complexity and the elusiveness of reality to validate a posture of non-action and ambivalence in the face of injustice and imperial domination. He seeks as much clarity as the integrity of observation allows, and some of his influence is attributable to an insistence that all cultural activity is inevitably bound up with the matrices of power. The walls of ivy offer no place. Along with Foucault and others, Said goes further, suggesting that the vindication of serious reading and writing finally depends on illuminating the disguised, embedded structures of power and privilege. Gaining such knowledge teaches us how to live and act in the world. We are always confronted with the choice of acquiescence or of resistance to the injustices currently associated with the exercise of power.

Said views "the intellectual as exile and marginal, an amateur, and as

Empowering Inquiry: Our Debt to Edward W. Said

the author of a language that tries to speak truth to power" (xvi). In effect, his stance embodies an alignment with those who are in some way, in any way, victimized by agencies of power (state, media, market):

> It is a spirit of opposition, rather than accommodation, that grips me because the romance, the interest, the challenge of the intellectual life is to be found in dissent against the status quo at a time when the struggle on behalf of underrepresented and disadvantaged groups seems so fairly weighted against them"(xvii).

It should be realized, of course, that these sentiments are not generally shared in universities or among most of those with the strongest academic credentials and honors. In such circles, the relentless search for influence and funds, generally leads "intellectuals" to condition their activity by precisely the spirit of accommodation with the powers-that-be that Said is decrying. His impact on cultural studies and the identity of the intellectual, in particular, is so significant because he insists upon commitment to the struggles of the day, and does so with the authority of an eminent literary critic and the experience of a political militant. Said challenges all of us, by arguing that the decisive test of the worth of intellectual activity is how it contributes to human wellbeing, and at the very least, as expressing the willingness to assume an honorable "role of a witness who testifies to a horror otherwise not recorded" (xvii).

It is tempting, yet mistaken, to discount Said's affirmation of the orientations associated with exiles as self-serving, as an abstract endorsement of his own story so brilliantly depicted in *Out of Place*, a memoir of his formative years. This memoir ends with the completion of Said's graduate studies while he was still in his late twenties. As Said carefully notes, his was at all times a privileged exile if measured in purely class terms. Yet from the perspective of personal discomfort in his immediate family circumstances, the sense of being cast out from his place of origin, and his quintessential feeling of cultural hybridity the case is strongly made that Said possesses an authentic voice of marginality that enables him to enter into genuine solidarity with the oppressed. As a valiant and persistent public voice for justice to the Palestinian people, the strength of this voice has prompted death threats from those who have feared and resented his call for justice and true peace. Said has never retreated from his understanding of such controversies even when the pressure to do so has been mounted and his refusal is derided as stubbornness and arrogance.

Undoubtedly, Said's most widely influential book was *Orientalism*, in which he authoritatively depicted a whole way of not seeing the other, thereby facilitating domination and abuse. Although set in the pivotal relationship over the centuries between the West and the Islamic world, the impact of the book was far more general, suggesting the lethal power of constructing the subordinated other in a manner that vindicated the colonialist and hegemonic claims to civilizational superiority of the dominating self. The Orientalists were academic hired hands who made the work of imperial exploitation far easier to swallow at home, and even more damagingly, encouraged the ingestion of the stereotype by "Oriental peoples" themselves. *Orientalism* brilliantly demonstrates the reactionary political consequences of cultural studies supposedly performed according to canons of academic neutrality, but actually serving the cause of imperialism.

Said continued this line of inquiry in his very ambitious *Culture and Imperialism*, which generalizes the argument about the pernicious corruption of academic activity that is not aligned with the victims of injustice. Although concentrating on the literature of the colonial masters, Said extends his analysis in the latter chapters to the historical setting currently unfolding under the rubric of "globalization" and beneath the banner of the special brand of imperial leadership provided by the United States. In the end, Said is arguing with erudition and conviction against all forms of essentialist and reductive knowledge that defines the other, especially the vulnerable other, by culturally and media-coded images and ideas that validate the violent operations of the rich and powerful. In anti-imperial contrast, Said urges readers and writers alike to give their "attention to detail, critical differentiation, discrimination, and distinction." To the extent that this discipline of detail takes hold, Said believes it will produce "a somewhat elusive oppositional mood," which can in due course emerge "as an internationalist counter-articulation"(311).

Said has some strategic concerns about the current use and misuse of knowledge. He insists on the urgency of we in the West looking beyond the labels of "terrorism" and "fundamentalism" in dealing with the peoples and struggles of the East. And further, that both sides of this cultural divide need to acknowledge, and come to understand, the degree to which "all representations are constructed," making it crucial to evaluate each undertaking by asking "for what purpose, by whom, and with what components"(314).

Empowering Inquiry: Our Debt to Edward W. Said

In recent years, this self-imposed demand to remain on the battlefield of ideas, even if surrounded and isolated, has expressed itself particularly in relation to the Palestinian movement itself as it has turned from the clearcut logic of opposition to dispossession and occupation as the battlefield, to the murky domain of diplomacy carried on behind closed doors. Said has opposed the Oslo "peace process" from its inception in 1993, contending that even before the Likud resumed its control of the Israeli government the essential features being proposed were tantamount to a Palestinian surrender, and, centrally, that the underlying disparity of power as manifested by unequal demands could never lead to a genuine and durable peace between the two peoples. It is an irony of monumental significance that Said's books have been banned in recent years by the Palestinian Authority, a mode of suppression that even the Israelis did not rely upon.

Toward the end of *Out of Place*, Said clearly subordinates political correctness to conscience even at the cost of community. While still an undergraduate at Princeton, Said had discussions with a family friend, the widely respected Lebanese diplomat, Charles Malik, in which he distanced himself from the unwavering identities of family, nation, and religious community that he found in this famous man. In a revealing passage Said expresses the sentiment that "would later become so central to my life and work"(281):

> It was in those Washington discussions that the inherent irreconcilability between intellectual belief and passionate loyalty to tribe, sect, and country first opened to me, and has remained open. I have never felt the need to close the gap but have kept them apart as opposites, and have always felt the priority of the intellectual, rather than national or tribal consciousness, *no matter how solitary that made me*" (280) [my emphasis].

It is this extraordinary stance that Said has sustained in the most difficult of situations posed by the initial near universal enthusiasm surrounding the Oslo framework, and of utmost importance in his depiction of the role of public intellectual. As so often, with the unfolding of this geopolitically guided peace process, Said's initial refusal to add his imprimatur of approval, has gathered increased support, even admiration, both from Palestinians who at first went along with Oslo and Arafat, hoping against hope, and from progressives, whether Palestinian or not, who generally thought that what was achieved at Oslo was the best that the Palestinians could expect to get, given the realities of Israeli/US power, and that if they accepted what was offered, it could in time lead to an acceptable Palestinian state.

Another closely related feature of Said's worldview is his uncanny realization that the personal cannot be excluded from the field of knowledge, that subjectivity is the foundation of thought rather than its adversary. In this regard, Said embraces a view of reason that engages the emotions rather than confines itself to a realm of conceptual abstraction traced back to the formative influence of Descartes on the modern mind, and the rejection of modernist claims of certainty that feed tendencies toward "secular fundamentalism." His affinity with the Romantic tradition enables Said to combine the passionate with the rigorous to constitute a powerful type of academic scholarship that sustains a pervasive concern with struggles to overcome suffering and injustice in the lifeworld, whether these manifest themselves in relation to the health of the person or of the body politic. Said acts as both guide and exemplary figure in this troubling birth of a globalizing world, not only helping us to understand the contradictory currents that are flowing by us on all sides, but also illuminating paths of constructive action and attitude that provide firm ground for taking stands and steps forward, especially on behalf of those most marginalized and victimized. As a citizen pilgrim, committed both to place and to the ennobling journey toward a desirable human future, the work and life of Edward W. Said serve us well as inspiration, while providing us with welcome comraderie.

Works Cited
Said, Edward W. *Culture and Imperialism*. New York: Vintage, 1994.
_____. *Out of Place*. New York: Knopf, 1999.
_____. *Representations of the Intellectual*. New York: Pantheon, 1994.

ONE

NATIONALITIES

Nationality, Disability, and Deafness

Lennard J. Davis

"It is true that deaf-mutes of every country have no mother tongue."
—*John Kitto*, Lost Senses (1845)

It might never have occurred to me to write about disability and nationalism had it not been for Edward Said. When I decided to write *Enforcing Normalcy: Disability, Deafness, and the Body,* I was able to think about the project largely because of what I had learned and observed about Edward Said. Not that Said knew much about the subject. In fact, most of what he knew about deafness, he learned from me. Rather, Said had set for me a model for thinking about oppression and nationalism in his writing and in his life. But more to the point, Said's life and my involvement in it changed my own life in ways that allowed me to think of the world I had grown up in, the world of the Deaf,[1] as having a politics and an analysis that I had not heretofore considered.

I first met Edward Said when I was an undergraduate at Columbia University. I took Said's course "Modern British Literature." This was the fall of 1968, a few months after the student strikes of the spring. This was a period of intense politicalization. Said had been on leave during the strike itself, but he found himself returned to a heightened political environment at Columbia. At the same time, Said himself was making a transition from the world of structuralism and hermeneutics to the world of politics and literature. The course he taught would have been strangely unfamiliar to anyone now knowledgeable about Said's work and trajectory. Instead of looking at British literature through the lens of Orientalism or even colonialism, Said's approach was to trace the concept of "egoism" through these works. There was, in short, nothing overtly political in the course, except that we read T. E. Lawrence's *Seven Pillars of Wisdom,* but from the point of view of Lawrence's egoism.[2] We undergraduates, not given to reverence, even laughed about the topic of the course since Said was known to be very "egotistical" in his teaching at that time. We called the class "the Ed Said" show, giving an English pronunciation to the last word, and indicating that the class was about what Ed said and not much more.

A telling moment occurred during one class. A student, not attending the course, came in and wanted to announce a demonstration or some

Nationality, Disability, and Deafness

political event. Said, unused to this kind of disruption, which had become normal during the strike, refused to allow the student to make his declaration. We were all shocked that Said had such "bad politics."

I tell this story to show how long I've known Said, and how he too came to his politics. It was exactly during this period that Said began to see himself as a person who might become a force, a voice, in articulating the point of view of the Palestinians. It is then that he began to write op-ed pieces and to move from his literary training at Harvard and Princeton to formulate his own synthesis. It is funny and telling that when I first met Said, he reminded me of one of my cousins. While I was growing my hair long, sprouting a beard, wearing bell bottoms, wire-frame glasses, and listening to the Rolling Stones, he was dressed conservatively with heavy black glasses of the kind that Michael Caine wore—in short he looked sort of out of it and "square" from my generations' perspective.

Nevertheless I enjoyed Said's class immensely, and I knew that he was someone who could teach me a great deal. What I learned from him at that point was all about the French intellectuals—Roland Barthes and Michel Foucault, among others. I took a further course in graduate school in which we read the works of those critics we would now call structuralists and also read Said's favorites–Vico and Adorno. Indeed, I was so impressed with the introduction that Said gave me, that I went to France and took courses with every structuralist I could get my hands on. A letter of introduction from Said got me into Barthes' course, and I also carried with me some materials from Said that I gave to Foucault, whom I called on the phone and spoke with in my broken French.

As Said got more involved with Palestinian politics, I learned from him about the conflict and the issues. By now, I had done my dissertation with him (which later became the book *Factual Fictions: The Origins of the English Novel*), which was influenced by much of what I learned about Foucault through Said, and also by his own *Beginnings*. Indeed the introduction to my book is called "Toward a Methodology of Beginnings." For ten years, I taught with Said at Columbia. Not only did I teach in the same department, but I lived in the apartment building that Said lived in as well. That building was the one surrounded by FBI agents during the crucial period when Said was involved in negotiations with the President, and during which time death threats were made against him. My apartment was just below Said's study, and in the dead of night when I was up caring for my infant child, at two or three in the morning,

I would hear Said typing on his Selectric typewriter. I was always amazed and infuriated that he was at work when most people were sleeping. He was the kind of neighbor who would always drop in without an invitation but not without a welcome, carrying his coffee mug, and wanting to talk about some event or to share a piece of music he recently stumbled on. His enthusiasm and commitment, then as now, were infectious. I counted myself lucky to be his student and friend.

This is a long way around to explain how I came to write *Enforcing Normalcy*. I grew up in a Deaf family in a Deaf culture in the 1950's, but I never really thought that this constituency had any relevance to politics or culture. I used to say to Said, "You are lucky to have a cause." Of course, I had the cause of any radical in America—anti-capitalism, anti-corporatism, anti-imperialism, and some more anti's. But this visceral connection that linked Said to a group of clearly defined, oppressed people, was something I thought I lacked. I always admired Said's involvement with what he called "the world." His "worldliness," writing for *The Nation* and other periodicals of public interest was what I wanted to do. And I did, but I was aware of a lack.

After I attended a conference for Children of Deaf Adults and met academics who wrote about Deafness, I began to realize that I indeed had a personal connection to an oppressed group, but I was so oppressed myself, as it were, that I was unaware that this marginalized group had any political rights or cultural interest. That is when I thought of Said. I realized that I could do for disability and Deafness what Said had done with Palestinians and the Middle East. That simple thought was a turning point for me. What follows is my attempt to link up disability with nationalism. This chapter of *Enforcing Normalcy* was a direct result of my exposure to ideas about post-coloniality that I had read in Said's work. Without that connection, I doubt I would have written much, if any, of what I have been doing for the past ten years.

Marx saw the body as essentially reified in the processes that came about as a result of the accumulation of capital in the eighteenth century. Marx's nostalgic retro-fit vision in the *Economic and Philosophical Manuscripts of 1848* was of an earlier period, in which the body existed in sensuous relation to the world, inserted into that world, and creating that world through labor. This vision, however romantic, seems to point to a kind of labor that was not easily distinguished from "life." The parameters of the body and its activities were seen as aspects of nature linked to the processes of natural activities and seasons.

One could go so far as to say that disability, in our sense of the word, did not exist in such a world. Of course, impairments existed, but the impaired body was part of a lived experience, and in that sense functioned. It was not defined strictly by its relation to means of production or a productive economy. But by the mid-nineteenth century, the body *an sich* became the body *für sich* and the impaired body became disabled—unable to be part of the productive economy, confined to institutions, shaped to contours defined by a society at large.

In this regard, it is possible to see the way that the disabled body came to be included in larger constructions like that of the nation. We have only to consider the cliche that a nation is made up of "able-bodied" workers, all contributing to the mutual welfare of the members of that nation.

In order to discuss how the concept of nationality fits into a concept of disability, it is first necessary to say what we mean when we speak of nations. It is commonplace to think of a nation as equivalent to various state or governmental groupings. But the question of nation has become vexed in recent years. As one political scientist puts it:

> Where today is the study of nationalism? In this Alice-in-Wonderland world in which nation usually means state, in which nation-state usually means multination state, and in which ethnicity, primordialism, pluralism, tribalism, regionalism, communalism, parochialism and sub-nationalism usually means loyalty to the nation.... (Connor, 48)

As opposed to a governmental entity, Walker Connor suggests that nation should be defined as "a group of people whose members believe they are ancestrally related" (48). This definition allows us to rethink nation as something perhaps divorced from a self-evident entity represented by the flag (for which it stands), an anthem, a collective will. The simplicity with which Edmund Burke speaks of "the men of England" (200) or says "The people of England know how little influence the teachers of religion are likely to have with the wealthy and powerful of long standing...." (201–2) shows us how powerful an idea is the homogenizing power of national hegemony, eliding as it does in this case the particularity of the Scots, the Welsh, the Cornish, the Irish.

The idea of a nation as a governmental entity is further refined by contemporary scholars like Benedict Anderson, Immanuel Wallerstein, Etienne Balibar, Hayden White, and Homi Bhabha, among others, who propose alternative ways of thinking about nationality. Anderson thinks of the nation as a manifestation of print culture. For him, the gradual honing of a group of people into readers of a common language creates the idea of a homogenous organization. So it was readers "connected through print, [who] formed, in their secular, particular, visible invisibility, the embryo for the nationally imagined community" (47). Likewise, Homi Bhabha deconstructs nation and narrative, while Hayden White writes of histories as forms of fictive metanarrative that novelize a nation to itself. Wallerstein prefers to downplay national entities, seeing them as aspects of a world capitalistic system, while Balibar sees nationalism as a self-constructing, destructive set of ideologies, always in a state of flux, but always defining power structures.

This reassessment of nationalism changes the discussion so that groups of people, who see themselves bound by a common language, culture, and narrative are defined as nations or nationalities. This redefinition allows for ethnic and religious minorities to claim national identity, and gender even comes into play, as Sylvia Walby notes, since women must be seen as a distinct nationality within a nation.

Perhaps one of the most concise definitions of nationality is to be found in a somewhat unlikely source—the writings of Joseph Stalin. His 1913 pamphlet entitled *Marxism and the National Question* outlined five features necessary for a group to consider itself a nationality—1) a common language, 2) a stable community, 3) a territory, 4) economic cohesion, 5) a collective psychology and character. Stalin stresses that nationality should not be thought of as something tribal or racial in nature, not something essentialist, but constructed through history, and inextricably connected to that construction is language.[3]

But a nationality alone does not constitute nation, as we can see in the struggles that took place in Eastern Europe and the former Soviet Union. Nationality needs a political dimension. "A nation," Stalin refines, "is not merely a historical category but a historical category belonging to a definite epoch, the epoch of rising capitalism. The process of elimination of feudalism and the development of capitalism was at the same time a process of amalgamation of people into nations" (13). It is this historical development of the agglutinizing of heterogeneous peoples into the modern nation-state that took place in the 18th century as part of the process of increasing bourgeois hegemony, and by extension, of consolidating the idea of nation and the ideology of nationality.

As Benedict Anderson and others point out, the consolidation of national interests was very much involved with the enforcement of a common language on a heteroglossic group of peoples. "Nothing served to 'assemble' related vernaculars more than capitalism, which within the limits imposed by grammars and syntaxes, created mechanically-reproduced print-languages, capable of dissemination through the market" (47). The novel, according to Anderson, was one step in the formation of national entities, yoking as it did images of national character, national language, and progress through structured time. And Edward Said has taken pains to show how novels help construct national identities through normalizing imperialist attitudes toward "others" into narrative form.

In this essay, I want to observe some of the features of this hegemony as it impacts on what I might call the nationality of Deafness, and by extension disability. As I have tried to show, the modern and postmodern redefinition of nation allows for groups of people claiming a community, a language, a common history and culture to assert themselves as nationalities. So ethnic and linguistic minorities may consider themselves nationalities, and while women cannot claim separate nationality, they may consider themselves separately from the total national identity. As Trinh Minh-ha says of women having to choose between ethnicity and gender: "The idea of two illusorily separated identities, one ethnic, the other woman... partakes in the Euro-American system of dualistic reasoning and its age-old divide-and-conquer tactics" (104). Fractionalized groups such as women or the Deaf shared certain features of nationality during a period of national consolidation in Europe in the 18th and 19th centuries.

At first blush, it might seem that deafness should be regarded as a social/medical phenomenon and as such would have little to do with the issue of nation and nationality. However, the issue of a common language is intricately involved in the way the deaf were treated in the eighteenth and nineteenth century, and parallels can be drawn from that experience and the experience of other linguistically divergent groups in colonial settings. Instead of calling the Deaf a nationality, one might consider them as occupying the place of an ethnic group. In fact, Connor notes that the term "'ethnic' is derived from the closest equivalent to *nationem* in ancient Greek, *ethnos*... and as such is quite close in meaning to nation" (55, note 1). Paul Brass places ethnicity within the realm of nationality, and defines an ethnic group as "any group of people dissimilar from other peoples in terms of objective cultural criteria [language or dialect, distinctive dress or diet or customs, religion or race] and containing within its membership... the elements for a complete division of labor and for reproduction..." (19). And, Brass notes, "ethnic identity is itself a variable, rather than a fixed or 'given' disposition" (13). By these criteria, the Deaf can be defined as an ethnic group or a nationality.[4] If an *ethnos* is defined as a culturally similar group sharing a common language, then the Deaf conceivably fit that category.

The issue is by no means a simple one because the relationship between language and ethnicity is not monolithic. As Etienne Balibar points out, ethnicity is derived from two sources: language and race. "Most often the two operate together, for only their complementarity makes it possible for the 'people' to be represented as an absolutely autonomous unit" (96). However, language is also the first ethnic trait to go by the boards, since second generation immigrants typically no longer bear the traces of their parents' accents or even their original language. In America, now, second and third generation Italian-Americans, Jews, or Germans, for example, rarely speak their "native" tongues, although in the past Jews, for example, might have.

In the case of the Deaf, the issue of language presents itself as a defining structure of consciousness in quite a different way from the issues surrounding other disabilities. Unlike blindness or physical impairment, deafness is in some sense an invisible trait. Only when the Deaf person begins to engage in language does the trait become visible.

The Deaf can be thought of as a population whose different ability is the necessary use of a language system that does not require oral/aural communication. Within a nation, they represent a linguistic minority. There are certainly other disabilities that involve a difficulty or inability to communicate (aphasia, autism), but none of these impairments imply the necessity for another language. While the blind have Braille, it is quite clear that Braille is not a language, but merely a way of transcribing whatever language the blind person may know. No one would claim that the blind have a language other than that of their mother tongue. As such, the Deaf can be thought of as a group defined by language difference.

This point perhaps needs some further elaboration. It is commonly thought that deafness involves the inability to use language properly. If only Deaf Americans could speak and understand English, there would be no problem for them or the larger community. Thus, deaf people are schooled arduously in lip reading, speech therapy, and the activities associated with the oral/aural form of communication. However, it is

Nationality, Disability, and Deafness

precisely this focusing on the dysfunctionality of the deaf that constitutes a privileging of aural/oral system of communication. As Balibar writes, "the production of ethnicity is also the racialization of language and the verbalization of race" (104). Because we are interpellated as subjects by language, because language itself is a congealed set of social practices, the actual dysfunctionality of the Deaf is to have another language system. That system challenges the majority assumption about the function of language, the coherence of language and culture. Consequently, the Deaf are, in a sense, racialized through their use of this system of communication. They are seen as outside of the citizenry created by a community of language users,[5] and therefore ghettoized as outsiders.

But unlike other people with disabilities, also ostracized if not ghettoized, the Deaf have a community, a history, a culture; moreover, the Deaf tend to intermarry, thus perpetuating that culture. There is within the Deaf world, a body of "literature" including written as well as signed works, a theatrical/choreographic tradition, academic discursive practices, pedagogic/ideological institutions, and so on. In this sense, the Deaf have created their own "nationalism" as a resistance to audist culture.[6] This level of social organization and resistance has not generally been the case with other physically impaired peoples, although political consciousness and organizing has increased in recent years. A serious body of literature is beginning to develop around the area of disability studies, but the level of community that is part of the Deaf experience has not yet been achieved.

Ethnicity is, one can say, produced by a dialectical process in which a dominant group singles out a minority and ethnicizes them; but reciprocally, minorities can ethnicize themselves in the course of trying to claim privileges and status from social elites. As de Vos says, ethnic identity is the "subjective, symbolic or emblematic use [by] a group of people... of any aspect of culture, in order to differentiate themselves from other groups" (16). If any aspect of culture can form the seed around which an ethnic community can coalesce, certainly the Deaf can be regarded as such. Further, the formation of a group identity is both imposed from outside ("You are disabled: You are Deaf.") and from within ("We are Deaf!" "Deaf Power!"). So the site of ethnicity, as it were, is a contested one in a struggle for who will define the ethnicity of the group, who will construct it.

It is also possible to think of the Deaf as a race, that is, as a group carrying genetic information that affects physical traits and that can be passed down from generation to generation. One could argue that race is itself a product of imperialism—that to consider a people a race based on some inherited trait was something that arose when it became necessary to think of humanity as divided into races. To think of the Deaf as a race is clearly to follow a dubious line of reasoning, but worth considering at least for the sake of argument. There are two senses in which the issue of racism can come into play here. The first would fit in with Colette Guillaumin's insistence on a "broad definition of racism" that would include not just exclusion based on ethnic groupings but on grounds of gender, class, sexual preference, and disability. The second would posit Deaf people themselves as constituting a race on the basis of inherited traits.

To think the latter, one must consider that there are two causes of deafness: one is an inherited trait and the other is impairment caused by disease or accident. If we focus on the former, we can trace lines of inherited deafness, as does Nora Ellen Groce in her study of deafness on Martha's Vineyard. Since the trait for hereditary deafness is a recessive one, the idea of a deaf race is a bit far-fetched. But, many genetic traits, such as those for hair color, eye color, skin color, are considered racial traits because segregation or geographical isolation has forced those traits to remain within a specific population. As Immanuel Wallerstein suggests, "it makes little difference whether we define pastness in terms of genetically continuous groups (races), historical socio-political groups (nations) or cultural groups (ethnic groups). They are all peoplehood constructs, all inventions of pastness, all contemporary political phenomena" (78–79).

Discussions of race have to take into account the historical determinants of race. In other words, the very concept of race is historically determined and can be considered the product of a particular historical period of development. As Wallerstein points out "*race* was a primary category of the colonial world, accounting for political rights, occupational allocation and income" (189). Theories of race became elaborated during the period of greatest imperialism; indeed it is hard to imagine a justification for imperialism without a theory of race. And it is no coincidence that the eugenics movement impacted directly on deaf people.

Eugenics only further emphasizes the connection between disability and racism. As Etienne Balibar notes "the phantasm of prophylaxis or segregation (the need to purify the social body, to preserve 'one's own' or 'our' identity from all forms of mixing, interbreeding or invasion)...

are articulated around stigmata of otherness (name, skin colour, religious practices)" (18). The stigma of disability, of physical (and, in the case of deafness, inherited) traits, creates the icon of the other body—the disabled figure—an icon that needs to be excluded in a similar way to the body marked as differently pigmented or gendered.

This tendency toward prophylaxis, of course, is reciprocally one of the processes by which an ethnic group forms its own existence. Logically, as the Deaf were constructed as a group, institutionalized, and regulated, they perceived themselves to be such a group and acted as such. The very structures that are the equivalent to what Althusser identified as the Ideological State Apparatus—educational institutions, associations, newspapers, language, and even the desire of Deaf people to form their own state—were pinpointed by Alexander Graham Bell as causes for alarm. Bell foresaw the development of these ideological apparati as leading to "the production of a defective race of human beings [which] would be a great calamity to the world" (41). To avoid having a "deaf variety" of humans by discouraging intermarriage, Bell proposed abolishing residential schools, forbidding sign language education, and prohibiting the Deaf from teaching the deaf.[7] These steps are logically a part of dismantling the culture of a non-national or indigenous peoples. They are also part of a discussion that links disability to race, nationality, and ethnicity.

It may be worth noting here that while a biological stigmata must be part of an anti-disability discourse, it might be appropriate to consider the signification of such physical traits. In other words, there may well be an allegorical meaning ascribed to deafness, blindness, lameness, and so on. As Balibar says "bodily stigmata play a great role in its [racism's] phantasmatics, but they do so more as signs of a deep psychology, as signs of a spiritual inheritance rather than a biological heredity" (24). Here, Balibar is speaking of the Jews, whose physical appearance can often be indiscernible, yet paradoxically the more invisible the physicality of the Jew, the more dangerous the infiltration. The mark of circumcision, for example, is one of the most hidden of "disabilities," particularly during the periods when general circumcision of the male public was not the rule. To be a Jew then meant more symbolically than physically, although the symbolic and the physical were joined at the hip. Likewise, the deaf represented, among other things, the idea of moral and spiritual deafness, an inability to hear the word of God, to participate in reason, and in life. Likewise, the blind were morally blind, and the lame inept. The body illustrated those moral precepts to be avoided in the culture. If, as Balibar suggests, much of modern racism derives from early anthropology's tendency to classify with an aim of making distinctions between humanity and animality (56–57), then the deaf and the blind, as well as the mentally impaired and some of the physically deformed, will be seen as more animal, less human, than the norm. Animals are "dumb"; they cannot hear language; they are morally deaf and blind. Thus the "normal" majority can, through this classificatory grid, see itself as most properly human. In studying disability, we must keep in mind the significations of body, the language of deformity as it is encoded by the "normal" majority.

In order to continue the argument that the Deaf constitute a threat to ideas of nation, wholeness, moral rectitude and good citizenship, I must rehearse what I have shown in earlier chapters. That is, first, that deafness appears in the 18th century as a discourse. By this I mean that before the 18th century there were individual deaf people or families of the deaf, or in urban areas even loose associations of the deaf, but that there was no discourse about deafness, no public policy on deafness, no educational institutions—and therefore the deaf were not constructed as a group. Since most deaf people are born to hearing families, the deaf themselves did not see themselves as part of a community unless they were a part of an urban assemblage of the Deaf. It was only by attending the residential schools created in the 18th century that the Deaf became a community. The dramatic rise in the number of deaf schools in Europe—none in the beginning of the century and over sixty by the end—indicates the groundswell that made this new ethnic group self-aware.

The second point is that by the beginning of the 19th century there had developed a standardized language of the deaf that was transnational. That is, sign language had regional variations but was basically a universal language. This language was disseminated through the deaf schools, and the teachers in these schools were themselves deaf. So an educational system evolved that consolidated the deaf into a community.

Thus, the Deaf became a new sub-group within each state throughout Europe, like Jews and Gypsies, they were an ethnic group in the midst of the nation. Though their numbers were small, they still amounted to a linguistic sub-group that increasingly perceived itself as a community with its own history and culture. By Stalin's criteria, all the Deaf lacked to claim nationhood were a territory and economic cohesion. One might

Nationality, Disability, and Deafness

indeed make a comparison with, for example, the Russian Jews who were excluded from Stalin's definition of nationality because they lacked a territory, although the Bund claimed national status for them.

Douglas Baynton shows us that by the 19th century, the Deaf were regarded as foreigners living within the United States, a kind of fifth column in society resisting nationalization. Baynton, quoting from the oralist publication the *American Annals of the Deaf and Dumb* in 1847 described the deaf person, not as afflicted individual, but as a "strongly marked class of human beings" with "a history peculiar to themselves" (221). Baynton concludes that "deaf people were not so much handicapped *individuals* as they were a collectivity, a people—albeit, as we shall see, an inferior one..." (221). Thus, while the audist establishment initially constructed the deaf person as a model inhabitant of the Enlightenment, a citizen in the world of print culture, it came to see deaf people, particularly with their "foreign" sign language, as an ethnic minority with its own history and language that needed to be incorporated into the state and the nation. Educators were concerned that if deaf people "are to exercise intelligently the rights of citizenship, then they must be made people of our language" (229). They insisted that "the English language must be made the vernacular of the deaf if they are not to become a class unto themselves—foreigners among their own countrymen" (229). This was part of a larger argument for the suppression of sign language because it "isolated people from the national community" (217).

Pierre Desloges in writing a book in the 18th century defending sign language is actually defending his nationality, if you like, from the hegemonic attempt to take away the native language of the Deaf. We have seen that Desloges immediately made an equation between his deafness, his language, and his nationality when he wrote:

> As would a Frenchman seeing his language disparaged by a German who knew at most a few words of French, I too felt obliged to defend my own language from the false charges leveled against it by Deschamps... (30).

The debate between oralism and sign is often seen as one that pits the hearing community against deaf standards, but I think the issue is sharpened if we think of it as a political attempt to erase an ethnic group. Like the ethnic groups who have lost their language and thus their existence as nationalities (the Cornish in the United Kingdom, the Frisians in Holland, the Sorbs and Wends of Eastern and Central

Europe), the Deaf were in danger of being wiped out as a linguistically marked community.

The Deaf were not alone in this struggle. Groups like the Romanians had to establish their own press and print a grammar in 1780 to keep from being erased by the Transylvanians, as did the Bulgarians resisting the dominance of Greek Orthodox clerics in the eighteenth century (Brass 30). Further, in dominant nation-states, foreigners and minorities, as well as the lower classes in general, were denigrated in cultural forms of symbolic production as a way of establishing national solidarity. One has only to think of hundreds of examples of French people being ridiculed in English literature of the period, particularly Captain Mirvan's excoriation of all aspects of Madame Duval's Frenchness in *Evelina* or of Cimarosa's ridicule of an English suitor's accent and, tellingly, of a deaf father in the Italian opera *The Secret Marriage*. Class accents will not do either, as a nation attempts to create a standard, printed, representation of the official language.[8]

The nexus of deafness, class, and nationality was put in its most extreme form when Jane Elizabeth Groom proposed in the 1880s that the deaf leave England and found a deaf state in Canada. Groom's reasoning was particularly related to class. She advocated founding a deaf state because the deaf in England were poor and could not compete with the hearing in a tight labor market. The answer could not be revolution, but secession. There was, in America, another movement to found a deaf state out West.

The fact that some Deaf wanted to found a separate state is a strong enough argument for seeing them as a nationality or an ethnic group. It is more than possible to consider the flexibility of the concept of nationality and to see the way that the nation-state, in its formation in the 18th and 19th centuries elided various groups not normally thought of as national minorities—women, gays and lesbian, linguistic sub-groups—in an attempt to make one nation out of many.

I have been using the Deaf as a particular example to discuss the relationship of impairment to nationhood. I hope I been able to establish that the Deaf may indeed be thought of as a nation within a nation, or as an ethnic group, or a linguistic sub-group in a dominant and dominating society. Now I would like to muddy the waters somewhat by introducing the idea of class. As Desloges' book emphasized, there is a strong connection between Deaf culture and working-class culture. Further, there is a very deep relationship between disability, in general, and class. Mike Oliver in *The Politics of*

Disablement: A Sociological Approach makes the point that "just as we know that poverty is not randomly distributed internationally or nationally... neither is impairment" (13). One expert notes that in the Third World not only does disability usually guarantee the poverty of the victim but, most importantly, poverty is itself a major cause of disability (Doyal 7).

If it is the case that disability is reciprocally related to poverty, and that poverty in turn causes disability, since poor people are more likely to get infectious diseases, more likely to lack genetic counseling, more likely to be injured in factory-related jobs, in wars, and have more dangerous work environment, then we have to see disability as intricately linked to capitalism and imperialism, or the latter-day version of imperialism that shifts factory work to Third World countries and creates poor and rich nations to facilitate a division of labor. The distinction some might want to make between disability and poverty collapses at this level. For example, David Rothman in his account of the development of the asylum in the United States notes that in the colonial period the mentally ill were primarily seen as a category of the indigent. "The lunatic came to public attention not as someone afflicted with delusions or fears, but as someone suffering from poverty" (4). Later the first almshouses sheltered not so much the poor as the disabled poor. In the first such institution built in New York City, about half the population was composed of people with physical or mental disabilities, including those with age-related impairments (Rothman 39).

Class is not absent even in the broad classification of disability. For example, in the case of people who use wheelchairs, the paraplegic or quadriplegic, we need to consider that among the approximately one million Americans, class and race figure largely. Injury to the spinal cord through accident is one of the most common causes of paralysis, and this type of injury occurs disproportionately among young, working-class men (Murphy 139). Particularly among the baby-boom generation, those wounded veterans who returned from Vietnam make up a large number of wheelchair users, and they were largely drawn from the working class. The chief cause of traumatic paraplegia and quadriplegia in American cities now are injuries sustained from gunshot wounds—and most of the people so injured are drawn from the lower classes, particularly from people of color. Contact sports, job injuries, and automobile accidents still tend to draw largely from young, working-class males (Murphy 139). So even "chance" and "accidents" fit a pattern involving class and race.

Industrialization recreated the category of work, and in so doing recreated the category of worker. The very idea of citizenship came to be ideologically associated with this kind of work. Various kinds of inclusions and exclusions in the category of nation were thus associated with work and work-related issues. Thus we see women initially bracketed out of the work force and into the domestic sphere in middle-class life, while proletarian families were redistributed into the factory orbit. In effect, the imperatives of industrialism and capitalism redefined the body. "Able-bodied workers" were those who could operate machines. The human body came to be seen as an extension of the factory machinery. Ironically, this reciprocity between human and machine led to a conception of the mechanical perfection of the human body. A strange paradox arises between theories such as the 18th-century notion that the human body was a divinely crafted machine on the one hand, and the increase of destructive acts against the human body in the form of factory-related mutilations. Thus the machine, like a latter-day Moloch, demanded human bodies and transformed them into disabled instruments of the factory process.

Friederich Engels, in *The Condition of the Working Class in England* described this necessary chain of transformation. "A number of cripples gave evidence before the Commission, and it was obvious that their physical condition was due to their long hours of work. Deformity of this type generally affects the spine and legs" (171). He cites a report by a Leeds physician, one Francis Sharp who wrote,

> During my practice at the hospital, where I have seen about 35,000 patients, I have observed the peculiar twisting of the ends of the lower part of the thigh bone. This affection I had never seen before I came to Leeds, and I have remarked that it principally afflicted children from 8 to 14 years of age. At first I considered it might be rickets, but from the numbers which presented themselves particularly at an age beyond the time when rickets attack children, and finding that they were of a recent date, and had commenced since they began work at the factory I soon began to change my opinion. I now... can most decidedly state they were the result of too much labor. So far as I know they all belong to factories, and acquired this knock-kneed appearance from the very long hours the children worked in the mills (171).

The report mentions varicose veins, spinal distortions, and deformities of the limbs. Engels himself corroborates these observations. "It is easy to identify such cripples at a glance, because their deformities are all exactly the same. They are knock-kneed and deformed and the spinal column is bent either forwards or sideways" (173). Miners are described as "either bandy-legged or knock-kneed and suffer from splayed feet, spinal deformities and other physical defects. This is due to the fact that their constitutions have been weakened and they are nearly always forced to work in a cramped position" (280). Factory accidents contributed to this 19th-century version of negative body sculpting. As Engels writes, "In Manchester, one sees not only numerous cripples, but also plenty of workers who have lost the whole or part of an arm, leg, or foot" (185). Engels records that there were 962 machine-related injuries in Manchester in 1842 alone.

If Engels' work gives us an insight into the way the body was perceived in the 19th century, it becomes clear that industrialization was seen as a palpable force in the reshaping quite literally the body of the members of the body politic. Even the mind was seen as subject to the ills of a capitalist society. In 1854 Edward Jarvis attempted to explain to a Massachusetts medical society how the tensions of the free market led to mental illness.

> In this country, where no son is necessarily confined to the work or employment of his father, but all the fields of labor... are open to whomsoever will put on the harness.... their mental powers are strained to their utmost tension; they labor in agitation... their minds stagger under the disproportionate burden (Rothman 115).

Jarvis notes that in pre-capitalist countries, "these causes of insanity cannot operate" (Rothman 115).

Repeated references to diminished physical size, lack of robustness, delayed puberty, mental illness, endemic disease, and physical deformity lead to a collective realization that the nation was in peril as a result of industrial practice. The symbol of this problem was the deformed worker. Likewise, the technical solution to this problem was the breeding of a better, more robust national stock. The eugenics movement came into existence as a way of repairing the declining stock of England and America, the result, so the eugenicists saw it, of a rapidly multiplying lower class and an influx of "foreign" peoples with lower intelligence, less physical strength, and greater licentiousness than the natives.[9]

The relationship between disability and industrialization is a complex one. The argument has been made that in a pre-industrialized society, people with impairments might more easily be part of the social fabric. Martha L. Edwards argues that disability in ancient Greece did not limit the ability of men to fight or engage in wars. While no utopia for the disabled, ancient Greek society provided "an acknowledgment of human physical variety. There was a wide variety of physical variation, and one did what one could given one's ability."

In a similar vein, J. Gwaltney describes the way that blindness was not perceived as a disability in a Mexican village. Other works describe how deaf people were fully included in societies on Martha's Vineyard and in the Amazon in which most hearing members of the community could also sign (Groce; Farb). Thus the communal life and pace of rural society may not have constructed the disabled body in the way that industrialized societies did.

The blind and the deaf growing up in slowly changing scattered rural communities had more easily been absorbed into the work and life of those societies without the need for special provision. Deafness, for a person working alone at agricultural tasks that all children learned by observation with little formal schooling, did not limit the capacity for employment too severely. Blindness was less of a hazard in uncongested familiar rural surroundings, and routine tasks involving repetitive tactile skills could be learned and practiced by many of the blind without special training. The environment of an industrial society was however different (Topliss 11).

The demands of a factory system require another version of the body and another version of time. "The speed of factory work, the enforced discipline, the time-keeping and production norms—all these were a highly unfavourable change from the slower, more self-determined and flexible methods of work into which many handicapped people had been integrated" (Ryan 101).

Another seemingly unlikely area in which we may connect disability with national identity and class was in the freak shows that began in the middle of the 19th century. Robert Bogdan in his book *Freak Show: Presenting Human Oddities for Amusement and Profit* makes the rather interesting connection between physical disability and race when he discovers that not only were the obviously disabled—the mentally retarded, the physically different—exhibited at freak shows, but physically normal native peoples of colonized countries were grouped under the heading of "freaks." As one press agent for the amusement world noted "The Borneo aborigines, the head-hunters, the Ubangis, and the Somalis were all classified as freaks. From the point of the showman the fact that they were different put them in the category of human oddities" (177). These people came from Oceania, Asia, Africa, Australia, South America and the Arctic, and the notion of a racial difference put them in the same category as the disabled. As Bogdan says, "showmen took people who were culturally and ancestrally non-Western and made them freaks by casting them as bizarre and exotic: cannibals, savages, barbarians" (177).

Some of those put on display were actual residents of the countries they were said to be from,[10] but more often than not they were Americans whose relatives had earlier come from those foreign locations. For example, in 1872, P. T. Barnum announced the appearance of four Fiji natives who were cannibals, including a princess. As it turned out, the three men were brought up since childhood as Christians and lived in California, and the woman was African-American, a native of Virginia (Bogdan 183). In this strange arrangement, people of color, disabled by society in so many ways, were transformed into non-western natives who would then be seen as "freaks" and commodified as such.

The equation between people with disabilities and the non-western worked both ways. Bogdan points out that beginning in 1850 and continuing through the 1940's, a "pattern" can be discerned in which "showmen constructed exhibits using people we would now call mentally retarded by casting them in an extreme form of the exotic mode" (Bogdan 119). Such people were made to seem as if they were representative of other races or "missing links" in evolution. Two severely mentally impaired, microcephalic siblings from Circleville, Ohio were exhibited as "Wild Australian Children" and said to be "neither idiots, lusus naturae, nor any other abortion of humanity, but belonged to a distinct race hitherto unknown to civilization" (Bogdan 120). Hiram and Barney Davis, each approximately three-feet tall and mentally impaired were billed as "The Astonishing Wild Men, From the Island of Borneo." Maximo and Bartola, two microcephalic children bought from their parents in Central America were hawked as "The Last of the Ancient Aztecs of Mexico." Other microcephalics tended to be exhibited as Aztecs because of their small heads and facial features. Or, in the case of William Henry Johnson, a fairly high-functioning, African-American microcephalic, the publicity projected this mentally retarded man as the "missing link" found in Gambia. Johnson, described as "What is It? or The Man-Monkey," was said to have been found in Africa "'in a perfectly nude state' roving through the trees like the monkey and the orangutan." His "keeper" is quoted as saying that "the formation of the head and face combines both that of the native African and the Orang Outang... he has been examined by some of the most scientific men we have, and pronounced by them to be a CONNECTING LINK BETWEEN THE WILD NATIVE AFRICAN AND THE BRUTE CREATION" (Bogdan 137).

What is most interesting about this strange phenomenon is that the category of disability defines itself through an appeal to nationalism. The disabled person is not of this nation, is not a citizen, in the same sense as the able-bodied. That the freak show begins in the same period as we have seen statistics and eugenics begin indicates a change in the way one thought about the physically different. In addition, discussions of disability always slide into discussions of race. The connection we have seen here between non-western and disabled—both in the sense of the simple fact of non-western culture being seen as "freakish" and in the glib elisions made between microcephalics, non-humans, and colonized world, show dramatically how close race, nation, and physical identity are defined. We might also add that the people who tended to make up the freaks, hoaxes or not, were drawn exclusively from the lower classes.

I want to end this discussion of nationality by looking at another disabled person, perhaps a kind of freak in this sense, who became a national symbol of identity. I am speaking of Franklin Delano Roosevelt.

The President of the United States has become more than a simple physical entity; he has become an icon of the power and vigor of the country. Much public-relations time and effort is spent on making the man in office seem physically perfect and devoid of illness or disability. Countless photographs of the President golfing, jogging, romping on the beach emphasize his robustness and joi de vivre. Yet moments slip through the veil of well-being surrounding the President, and these moments are memorable in a disconcerting way. Who does not recall Carter's collapsing during a running race or Bush's vomiting into the lap of the Japanese Prime Minister? Johnson's revealing his surgical scar was an unwanted reminder of his mortality. More profoundly, Eisenhower's heart attack and a series of assassinations and assassination attempts are reminders of the physical debility of the person in office.[11] When Reagan survived an assassination attempt, the White House publicists covered up the extent of the President's injuries and the pain of his quite lengthy recovery. The unwillingness to show the public the autopsy photographs of Kennedy stems from, among other possibly conspiratorial reasons, an impulse to prevent the nation from visualizing the President as having a wounded, mutilated body or being physically damaged.

In fact, Kennedy had what we could certainly call a disability—Addison's disease. This debilitating and possibly life-threatening dysfunction of the adrenal glands was consistently managed by those who controlled public relations around Kennedy. The back pain was romanticized as stemming from war wounds when Kennedy was the captain of P.T. 109. The President's rocking chair, used to alleviate the pain of his illness, was transformed into a rather evocative symbol associated with New England, the presidency, and the battle story. The fact that Kennedy was constantly medicated with painkillers and cortisone was erased, and even the tell-tale puffiness of Kennedy's face, a side-effect of long-term cortisone use, was forgotten.

But none of these attempts at management come close to the efforts surrounding Roosevelt's disability. Roosevelt himself was made into a symbol of the triumph over a physical disability, and his own story was seen as paralleling America's recovery and triumph from the Depression. Roosevelt's erect posture, with upturned face and jauntily held cigarette holder was a symbol for America of hope, possibility, and recovery. Roosevelt's case is so interesting because he was the first President to be truly "mechanically reproduced," to use Walter Benjamin's term. His was truly the first media presidency, with his time in office spanning the period of photography, photojournalism, radio, and television. Although radio was in a sense the primary medium, Roosevelt had to control the medium of photography and film as no President before needed to. In this sense, Roosevelt forged the visual icon and aural identity of the presidency for the modern media.

Of the hundreds of thousands of photographs and films of Roosevelt, spanning the period from 1928, when he became governor of New York, until 1945, when he died in office, there are only two photos extant showing Roosevelt using a wheelchair. This archival evidence confirms the popular notion of Roosevelt—that he had contracted polio, went to Warm Springs to recover, and then went on to become President. As Hugh Gallagher notes,

> ...Roosevelt's biographers have tended to treat his paralysis as an episode—with a beginning, a middle, and an end. By their accounts,

> Roosevelt gets polio, struggles through his rehabilitation, and then overcomes his adversity. End of chapter. The handicap is not mentioned again. It is viewed only as one of the stages through which FDR passes in preparation for the presidency (210).

Because of a need to see the President's body as an extension of our own and of the body politic, rather than being a product of a well-coordinated public relations effort, America never had the facts about Roosevelt's polio. These, according to Gallagher's meticulously documented study *FDR's Splendid Deception*, were that Roosevelt became, as a result of polio, a paraplegic who never was able to move his legs or stand without assistance after his illness. This fact was well known to Roosevelt's family and friends. One visitor to Hyde Park wrote of Roosevelt in 1921: "He's had a brilliant career as Assistant of the Navy under Wilson, and then a few brief weeks of crowded glory and excitement when nominated by the Democrats for the Vice Presidency. Now he is a cripple—will he ever be anything else?" (28) The writer of this letter expresses a common assumption—that the disability will become the person.

Roosevelt was determined that people should not define him in this stigmatized role, and so he managed the reception of his image. According to Gallagher, "from the very first, Roosevelt was determined not to be seen in a wheelchair unless absolutely necessary, and not to be lifted up stairs in view of the public." This desire not to be seen as visibly disabled, connects us to the realm of the senses—the visual sense in particular. We might link up this notion of the visibility of disability with the notion of the invisibility of nationalism. As Balibar points out there is an assumption that true nationalism is invisible, a degree zero of existence, but that false nationalism can be seen: Thus we have "the alleged, quasi-hallucinatory visibility of the 'false nationals': the Jews, 'wogs', immigrants, Blacks... racism thus inevitably becomes involved in the obsessional quest for a 'core' of authenticity that cannot be found, shrinks the category of nationality and de-stabilizes the historical nation" (60). So in this way, the visibility of the President's disability goes to the "core" of his national identity. Roosevelt saw that to be visibly disabled was to lose one's full nationality, which should be an invisibility, a neutrality, a degree-zero of citizenly existence.

When Roosevelt addressed the Democratic Convention to place Al Smith's name on the ballot in 1924, he formulated a plan later used consistently. He and [his son] James arrived early each day in order to get to their seats before the arrival of the other delegates. James would take his father by the wheelchair to the hall entrance closest to the seats of the New York delegation. At the door, Roosevelt's [leg] braces would be locked, and he would be pulled to a standing position. With James on one arm and a crutch under the other, he would slowly make his way down the aisle. At times he gripped James's arm so tightly that James had to concentrate to keep from crying out in pain.... He [Roosevelt] did not leave the hall until the session had ended and the hall had cleared (60).

Four years later at Houston, Roosevelt determined not to be seen with crutches. Eleanor wrote to him, "I'm telling everyone you are going to Houston without crutches, so mind you stick to it" (63). Roosevelt solved the crutch problem by developing a new technique that he practiced for a month with his 18-year-old son Elliot.

Elliot would stand, holding his right arm flexed at a ninety-degree angle, his forearm rigid as a parallel bar. Roosevelt would stand beside Elliot, tightly gripping his son's arm. In his right hand Roosevelt held a cane. His right arm was straight and held rigid with his index finger pressed firmly straight down along the line of the cane. In this posture he could "walk," although in a curious toddling manner, hitching up first one leg with the aid of the muscles along the side of his trunk, then placing his weight upon that leg, then using the muscles along his other side, and hitching the other leg forward.... He was able to do this because his arms served him in precisely the same manner as crutches (65).

Roosevelt's system for walking was, according to Gallagher, "treacherous, slow, and awkward." Indeed, crutches would have been more sensible and safer. But Roosevelt wanted above all to be seen as a "cured cripple." In a rare reference to his own condition, Roosevelt mentioned his paralysis in a campaign speech in the 1928 governor's race, "Seven years ago... I came down with infantile paralysis.... By personal good fortune I was able to get the best kind of care and the result of having the best kind of care is that today I am on my feet" (66). But he was on his feet only in the sense that he wore metal braces that could be locked into an upright position.

Roosevelt succeeded in convincing the world that he had beaten his disability. Will Durant's description of Roosevelt at the Democratic convention in 1928, written for *The New York World*, makes us see an upright Roosevelt. "On the stage is Franklin Roosevelt, beyond comparison the finest man that has appeared at either convention.... A figure tall and proud even in suffering" (Gallagher 67).

Rumors that Roosevelt was actually paraplegic did surface in the press. During his run for President, a *Time* magazine article quoted an observer as saying "This candidate, while mentally qualified for the presidency, is utterly unfit physically" (84). An "objective" writer was hired by Roosevelt to say that Roosevelt's health was superb, and then thousands of reprints of the piece were sent to each Democratic party county chairperson in the country as well as prominent Democrats everywhere. Georgia's governor Gene Talmadge brought the subject up again in 1935, saying: "The greatest calamity to this country is that the president can't walk around and hunt up people to talk to.... The only voice to reach his wheelchair were [sic] cries of the 'gimme crowd.'" (Gallagher 96). Despite the rare mention of Roosevelt's disability, the President's image was so thoroughly controlled that the image remained the cigarette holder and not the wheelchair.

As President, Roosevelt used his wheelchair a good deal of the day. But he did not want the public to know this, and he lied to direct questions, as he did to one reporter who charged that Roosevelt was still "wheelchair bound."As a matter of fact, I don't use a wheelchair at all except a little kitchen chair on wheels to get about my room while dressing...and solely for the purpose of saving time" (92).

That little kitchen chair was in fact Roosevelt's own design for a wheelchair that would be streamlined, small, and unobtrusive, as opposed to the rather large sanitorium wicker chairs then currently in use. In addition, the Secret Service now became the agency that concealed Roosevelt's disability, and Washington became a ramped city. As Gallagher writes:

> The White House imposed certain rules, which were always obeyed. For example, the president was never lifted in public. If it was necessary to lift him in or out of the car, this was done in the privacy of a garage or behind a temporary plywood screen constructed for the purpose. He was never seen in public seated in a wheelchair. Either he appeared standing, leaning on the arm of an aide, or he was seated in an ordinary chair (93).

The rule was that lecterns had to be bolted to the floor. At least once this was forgotten, and Roosevelt crashed to the floor. Although reporters were present, no one filmed the event or took pictures. There was a clear wish on the part of the President not to be photographed looking crippled or helpless. Once, during the race for governor, when Roosevelt was being lifted out of a car, some newsreel cameramen were

Nationality, Disability, and Deafness

filming the event and Roosevelt said "No movies of me getting out of the machine, boys" (94). The Secret Service would intervene if any photographers attempted to take such photos, and they would seize the camera and expose the film. This was an official governmental action to erase any visual trace of the President's disability.

Roosevelt's car went everywhere up ramps constructed by the Secret Service. When he had to get into or out of his car, he was carried by two strong men. This carrying was the most disconcerting scene for many. John Gunther recalled: "The shock was greatest of all when he was carried; he seemed, for one thing, very small" (94).

I have taken a bit of time to detail the extraordinary steps that Roosevelt and governmental agencies took to have the President seen as ambulatory. This deception was a two-way street, since neither Roosevelt nor the public wanted to see him as a "cripple." And the film industry, deeply implicated in the national sense of the body, even made a post-war film entitled Till the End of Time in which a mother encourages her disabled veteran son to identify with FDR. The identification works so well that the son renounces his wheelchair and hides his prosthesis under his pants legs, just like FDR (Norden 320).

The sense of national identity associated with the President, with the almost sacred nature of his body and physical presence, was paramount. If in the post-Depression America every citizen had to get to work and build a better future, if the model of the able-bodied citizen was to be writ large on every WPA mural, then the President had to embody normality, even if the efforts taken were Herculean to create this illusion. Since, as I have been asserting, the disabled are a kind of minority group within the nation, it would hardly do to have the President be a representative of that minority group. In the perverse logic that marks the political imagination of the United States, only an aristocratic WASP could embody the aspirations of the working-classes; only a physically intact man could represent those who were crippled by the ravages of an economic disaster.

This contested battle of Roosevelt's disabled body continues. In 1995 a controversy arose over the construction of a memorial to FDR (*New York Times* 10 April 1995: A10). Disability-rights activists were appalled that none of the memorial's three sculptures and bas-reliefs would show the former President with the wheelchair, crutches, braces, or canes that he used. The members of the memorial commission, headed by Senator Mark Hatfield and Senator Daniel Inouye, and including members of Roosevelt's family, opposed any such representation, arguing that Roosevelt's elaborate avoidance of public representations of his disability indicate his wish to be seen as intact and normal. While subsequent negotiations have succeeded in including a visual representation of FDR's chair, the controversy still goes on, most recently over texts used in the memorial. What resounds through this argument is the tenacity with which national images and identities are tied to notions of the body. More than half a century after Roosevelt's death, the specter of his "abnormal" body still needs to be exorcized so it will not haunt the nation's sense of its own wholeness and integrity.

Notes
[1] I am following common usage among Deaf academics of capitalizing "Deaf" when I am speaking of the culturally, socially, and liguistically Deaf, and I am using a lowercase "deaf" to indicate the simple audiological fact of hearing impairment.
[2] See Said's *Beginnings: Intention and Method* (pp. 152–156) for a sense of how he approached this material.
[3] Ironically, it was also Mussolini who said, "National pride has no need of the delirium of race" (cited in Stille 22).
[4] Harlan Lane makes a telling comparison between the colonization of Africans and the treatment of the Deaf (*Mask of Benevolence*. New York: Knopf, 1992: 35–66). He particularly examines descriptions of both groups and shows how the deaf and the native are constructed in similar ways.
[5] Ironically, a recent study shows that approximately 50 percent of Americans are virtually illiterate in that they lack the skills necessary to write a simple letter or read a bus schedule (*New York Times* 10 September 1993: A1). That would mean that the concept of a linguistic community exists in some kind of ideal form—at least at the level of writing and reading. One might better speculate on the degrees by which individuals are included or excluded from the ideal community of language users, rather than assume that all normal members of the community are users of language and all deaf are not.
[6] It is worth remembering that nationalism is a two-edged sword. It cuts a broad cloth out of divergent peoples and creates the groundwork for imperialism and colonialism. However, nationalism in the Third World has been an important means of resisting domination by imperialist countries. (See Simon During, "Literature—Nationalism's other? The case for revision" in Homi Bhaba's *Nation and Narration*. New York: Routledge, 1990: 138–153.)
[7] Ironically, all three of these steps have taken place. Deaf education in the 19th century was taken away from Deaf educators. Oralism was made official in the 1880 Congress of Milan. And more recently, American educational policy has emphasized mainstreaming of deaf children in hearing schools. This pattern coincides with an effort to nationalize other "non-national" populations by removing their own ideological apparati.

Nationality, Disability, and Deafness

[8] See Chapter Five of my *Resisting Novels: Fiction and Ideology* (New York: Methuen, 1987).

[9] This argument is being made today again as if it were new thinking in three books: *The Bell Curve: Intelligence and Class Structure in American Life* (New York: The Free Press, 1994) by Richard J. Herrnstein and Charles Murray; *Race, Evolution, and Behavior* (New Brunswick, N.J.: Transaction Publishers, 1994) by J. Philippe Rushton, and *The Decline of Intelligence in America: A Strategy for National Renewal* (Westport, Connecticut: Praeger, 1994) by Seymour W. Itzkoff. All of these works maintain that intelligence levels are declining since the underclass, poor and disproportionately of color, are dragging the "norm" down with their rapid reproduction of low intelligence and social dysfunctionality. The wonder is that anyone thinks these arguments are any more than the old eugenicist saws brought out, with very little resharpening.

[10] The extent of the colonizing of these non-western peoples included giving them names so that their "disabilities" might be identified. Thus the famous "Ubangi" women with artificially enlarged lips, a tribal practice to beautify women by inserting increasingly large disks into their lips, turn out to be not "Ubangi" at all. These women were from the Congo, but the press agent for Ringling Brothers Circus, Roland Butler, was looking at maps of Africa and found an obscure district named Ubangi, several hundred miles from the tribe's actual location. The name sounded properly exotic, and so, in Butler's words, "I resettled them." This act of renomination also represented their own beauty practices as "freakish" disabilities. They were presented as "Monster-mouthed Ubangi savages" and as "Crocodile Lipped Women From the Congo" (Bogdan 193–4).

[11] Paul Tsongas' cancer became an issue that detracted from his candidacy in 1992. Although he tried to commandeer the media coverage to show him swimming everyday, he was unable to beat the perception that he was disabled by his disease. Dan Quayle's complications from phlebitis had to given some spin and could not be "blamed" in his decision not to run for President. More recently, John McCain's melanomas have come into national attention.

Works Cited

Anderson, Benedict. *Imagined Communities: Reflections on the Origin and Spread of Nationalism*. London: Verso.

Balibar, Etienne, and Immanuel Wallerstein. *Race, Nation, Class: Ambiguous Identities*. London: Verso.

Baynton, Douglas. "A Silent Exile on this Earth: The Metaphorical Construction of Deafness in the Nineteenth Century." *American Quarterly* 44:2 (June 1992): 216–243.

Bell, Alexander Graham. *Memoir upon the Formation of a Deaf Variety of the Human Race*. Washington, DC: Alexander Graham Bell Institute for the Deaf, 1969.

Bogdan, Robert. *Freak Show: Presenting Human Oddities for Amusement and Profit*. Chicago: University of Chicago Press, 1988.

Brass, Paul. *Ethnicity and Nationalism: Theory and Comparison*. London: Sage, 1991.

Burke, Edmund. *Reflections on the Revolution in France*. New York: Penguin, 1980.

Connor, Walker. "The Nation and its Myth." *International Journal of Comparative Sociology* 33 (January/April 1992): 48–57.

Desloges, Pierre. *Observations d'un sourd et muet sure 'Un Cours e'le'mentaire d'e'ducation des sourds et muets' publie' en 1779 par M. l'abbe'* Deschamps (A Pamphlet).

De Vos, George. "Ethnic Pluralism." *Ethnic Identity: Cultural Continuities and Change*. Eds. George de Vos and Lola Romanucci-Ross. Palo Alto: Mayfield Publishing, 1975.

Doyal, L. "The Crippling Effects of Underdevelopment." *A Cry for Health: Poverty and Disability in the Third World*. Ed. O. Shirley. Rome: Third World Group and ARHTAG, 1983.

Engels, Friedrich. *The Condition of the Working Class in England*. Trans. W.O. Anderson and W.H. Chaloner. Palo Alto: Stanford University Press, 1968.

Farb, P. Word Play: *What Happens When People Talk*. New York, Bantam, 1975.

Gallagher, Hugh. *FDR's Splendid Deception*. New York: Dodd, Mead, 1985.

Groce, Nora Ellen. *Everyone Hear Spoke Sign Language: Hereditary Deafness on Martha's Vineyard*. Cambridge, MA: Harvard University Press, 1985.

Lane, Harlan, ed. *The Deaf Experience: Classics in Language and Education*. Cambridge, MA: Harvard University Press, 1984.

Minh-ha, Trinh. *Women, Native, Other.* Bloomington: Indiana University Press, 1989.

Norden, Martin F. *Cinema and Isolation: A History of Physical Disability in the Movies*. New Brunswick: Rutgers University Press, 1994.

Oliver, Michael. *The Politics of Disablement: A Sociological Approach*. New York: St. Martin's Press, 1990.

Rothman, David. *The Discovery of the Asylum: Social Order and Disorder in the New Republic*. Boston: Little, Brown. 1966.

Ryan, J. and F. Thomas. *The Politics of Mental Handicap*. Harmondsworth: Penguin, 1980.

Stalin, Joseph. *Marxism and the National Question*. 1913. *Marxism and the National and Colonial Question*. Ed. A. Fineberg. New York: International Publishers, 1934.

Stille, Alexander. *Benevolence and Betrayal*. New York: Penguin, 1991.

Topliss, E. *Provision for the Disabled*. Oxford: Blackwell, 1979.

Wallerstein, Immanuel. *See* Balibar, Etienne.

Imperial Britain and the American Nation: Transatlantic Readings

Deirdre David

In a popular 1766 American political cartoon published in Philadelphia, a once Great Britain sits dismembered upon the ground, reduced to beggary, her rebellious American colonies chopped from the Britannic body. This raw image was generated shortly after the Stamp Act triggered colonial protest, and its literalness of mutilated empire graphically discloses American warnings to a greedy mother country. Restrain our trade, destroy our currency, tax our people unjustly, and you will be left penniless, is the message. Body images of empire quickly entered the transatlantic discourse of Britain and her amputated child/colony, as one hears in 1775 when Edmund Burke, arguing for Conciliation with America, describes a people "who are still, as it were, but in the gristle, and not yet hardened into the bones of manhood" (188). A century later, despite possession of an enormous empire whose revenues far exceeded anything culled from America, British culture was still trying to explain to itself what caused the dismemberment. Tennyson, for instance, in 1886 attributes it to mercantile greed, in some lines on the "Opening of the Indian and Colonial Exhibition by the Queen," declaring that political avarice "Drove from out the mother's nest/ That young eagle of the West/ To forage for herself alone" (lines 27–29). It's notable, I think, that where Burke's image for America is a male one (the nation hardening into manhood) Tennyson's is female (the eagle driven to forage for herself alone). At the end of this paper I shall return to these gendered images for America, after exploring two related issues: the first is the varied ways that British writers imagined America in the aftermath of its severance from the mother country, and the second is the question of how we, as critics interested in issues of empire, should theorize this writing.

After the Revolutionary War, British travelers and authors were faced with a nation similar in race, culture, and language, yet different in political identity. What, then, is the appropriate political discourse for description of severed colonies whose gristle had hardened into the bones of an energetic, surging nation? Engendered by Britain, America could not be dismissed with the usual provincial, Podsnappian constructions of things not British; these views were spawned and nourished by imperial governance and they ranged from continental raciness and revolution, to African darkness and savagery. But Philadelphia was not Paris, Baltimore not Barbados, and America was not full of shifty "natives"—at least not when British travelers tended to go no further south than Washington and no further west than Cincinnati. America was mostly "New England," a former colony of white, northern European settlement, with the Germans and Scandinavians grudgingly admired and the Irish predictably despised. Later, of course, immigration from southern and eastern Europe and travel to the western states and territories changed the way travelers perceived the ethnic composition of its former colony. But whether produced at the beginning or at the end of the 19th century, British writing about America remains difficult to categorize by virtue of its peculiar post-colonial nature, and this leads us to a second issue: what is an appropriate critical model for talking about this writing?

Among others, Homi Bhabha's name comes to mind when one thinks about relationships between empire and colony: British writers, after all, well into the 19th century, see America as a former possession and in a number of essays, Bhabha argues that in mimicking the rule of the master/the possessor (primarily in textual ways), the colonized/the possessed forces the colonizer, in turn, to repeat civil and military rules of governance. The result is something slippery, deformed from its first, intended meaning. One can certainly say, then, that the former colony, America, in her language and in her manners—if not in her system of government—repeats and sometimes parodies the master text of the former colonizer, Britain. And Britain, as she witnesses this repetition and parody, may be said to adopt a defensive strategy of rehearsing cultural superiority. In this rehearsal, as I shall show in a moment, she repeats the ideologies of race, class, and gender that govern her imperial and domestic rule. But one stumbles, I think, in applying Bhabha's theory of political resistance through mimicry to Britain and America, for, obviously, what's lacking is the dynamic political relationship of governor and governed. To be sure, the child-colony's repetition may be seen as disruptive, and Britain's national identity gets dislodged, in part, by the assertiveness of the growing American child, but a complex, white European affiliation of former colonial master and new post-colonial nation muddies this picture of resistance.

Gayatri Spivak has both explored and interrogated the existence of a subaltern voice in a dominant culture: if such a voice may be said to exist, she asks, what form of agency might it possess? In the peculiar political relationship of Britain and post-colonial America, however, the once subaltern voice is in full possession of the platform, as it were, and speaking far too raucously for most British ears. Agency, in other words, is hardly the issue. A large body of analysis, centered primarily in Australia and South Africa, examines post-colonial literature produced by writers such as Nadine Gordimer and J.M. Coetzee, descendants of white, European settlers. But the complex bond I'm talking about is clearly different from those existing between Britain and former colonies that became Commonwealth countries.

This has lead me to the kind of reading proposed by Edward Said in *Culture and Imperialism*. In urging that we put aside a politics of blame and confrontation, he notes that all cultures "are involved in one another; none is single and pure, all are hybrid, heterogenous, extraordinarily differentiated, and unmonolithic." I think, then, that we must read transatlantically, put writing British writing about America in active engagement with writing about domestic issues. In recent work, I explored the way Victorian women both wrote about empire and were resonant images of cultural sacrifice for civilization of the subordinated "savage." Edward Said's work was profoundly influential to me, for it enabled me to move beyond merely "blaming" these women for their participation in the construction of empire. Currently, I'm placing Victorian indictments of American slavery and distrust of native-Americans alongside contemporary writing about race in the empire. I'm aligning Victorian denigration of the American Irish with Britain's seemingly indelible contempt for Ireland and her culture. I've seen that the traveler's distaste for mercantile materialism and American working-class assertiveness derives from contemporary laments about the "cash-nexus" driving British society and fears of the mob clamoring for the franchise. I've come to understand that the British male writer's discomfort with what he sees as hard, aggressive, bossy, American women belongs with patriarchal discomfort at home about Victorian feminist agitation. For me, this writing is cross-bred, hybrid, generated from Queen Victoria's plump maternal body, and further back, from the dismembered body of the 1766 political cartoon. In writing about the rough reality of the American nation, British Victorian writers constructed a transatlantic discourse of racialism, class-bound fears of the mob, and unease about independent women. What follows, by the way, is not intended to denigrate the Victorian intellectual curiosity and fundamentally decent politics one often encounters: rather, I'm aiming at the British domestic ideologies that tend to dominate, even if only provisionally, as Edward Said's call for contrapuntal reading suggests they may. And I should add that what follows is less an elaboration of *Culture and Imperialism* than a local demonstration of some of its multiple imperatives.

First race. In terms inseparable from that deployed by British imperialism to describe its supposedly less than civilized subjugated peoples, British travelers dwell upon the surly savagery of the native American, the infantile intellect of the American slave, and the filthy sloth of the Irish. Beginning with John Smith's observation in 1608 that he was forced to trade "with that churlish and trecherous nation" (1:39)—native Americans encountered by the English voyagers to Virginia—and ending with Isabella Bird's remarks in 1879, that all Indians are "without any aptitude for even aboriginal civilization" and that the only difference between "the savage and the civilized Indian is that the latter carries firearms and gets drunk on whisky" (49), we encounter the familiar dualism of European civilization and native barbarism.

An early British explorer in America, John Josselyn tells his readers that native Americans are

> Of disposition very inconstant, crafty, timorous, quick of apprehension, and very ingenious, soon angry, and so malicious that they seldom forget an injury, and barbarously cruel, witness their direful revenges upon one another... all of them Cannibals, eaters of human flesh. And so were formerly the Heathen-Irish who used to feed upon the Buttocks of Boyes and Womens Paps; it seems it is natural to Savage people to do so (91).

In all this writing, cannibalism quickly emerges as a primary obsession. In a captivity narrative published in 1757, a time when such works had shifted from recording Puritan trials of faith and punishment for lax observance, to embroidering sensationalist tales of savage barbarism, we read about a trader who is not only scalped "but immediately roasted before he was dead; then, like cannibals, for want of other food, they ate his whole body, and of his head made, what they called, an Indian pudding" (*Held Captive* 222).

British writing about American slavery in the Victorian period is, of course, more complex, strongly influenced by abolitionist sentiments and also by commercial alliances with the South before (and during) the Civil War. As a way of elaborating this complexity, I'd like you to imagine Fanny Kemble, a British actress who toured the northeast with her father's theater company in the 1830s and then married the owner of cotton and rice plantations in Georgia. She arrived in Georgia in 1838. During her four-month stay she kept a journal, composed in the form of 31 letters addressed to an abolitionist friend. She encountered a world of black suffering and at best white indifference, yet this suffering is caused, managed, and perpetuated by people of English origin, by people who speak English, and by people who aim to live like English gentry. What is an appropriate political discourse to describe this world in which her agency and subjectivity are inexorably bound up with her position as slave-owning mistress, a world in which she is a principal actor in the political family romance of Britain and America by virtue of Englishness, her marriage, her motherhood? Her principal textual model is, of course, abolitionist literature and the *Journal* qualifies as one of the most harrowing documents to be encountered. What's also interesting is its cross-bred, transatlantic nature. Consciously or not, she affiliates her writing with the many texts evoking British social suffering that were produced in the 1820s. As an intelligent reader of poetry, novels, and newspapers, Kemble shared the indignation of a politically engaged liberal British middle class: advocates of the gospel of work, of female philanthropy, and sometimes of racial superiority. This all gets mixed in with her close observation of slave conditions in Georgia.

In documenting the physical abuse of slaves, her prose is graphic, visual, gesturing: her descriptions of slave hovels remind one of the Manchester back alleys described by Elizabeth Gaskell in her social-problem novels, of writers of the Parliamentary Blue Books taking us into the coal mines where ten-year-old children pulled cars through tunnels too small for adult maneuvering. We travel into filthy huts and in the grimy darkness see groups of small children delegated as "minders" for the babies whose mothers are in the fields. Throughout all this, Kemble records her limited female power to stop violence and abuse, and thus participates in transatlantic fashion in a British feminist interrogation of a female moral agency only achievable within the patriarchal subordination of women. She recounts many entreaties to her husband, pleading for slave women to be allowed more time after childbirth before returning to the fields, and I'm reminded of the many women characters in 19th-century British novels whose identity in the public sphere is derived from their sympathetic encounter with human suffering and whose power to alter the political conditions that create such suffering rests not with them. Kemble finally realizes that in marriage to a slave owner she has given up, as she puts it, "the great means of good, to myself and others" in exchange "for a maintenance by the unpaid labor of slaves"(139). She sees a dark, true meaning of slavery: that labor exacted without payment enables the existence of families like her own. Yet at the same time, she records her distaste for the "laziness... filthiness... inconceivable stupidity" of the slaves, regularly indicating her British Victorian preference for those with European features (41). Noting the tall, straight figure, oval face, and high forehead of one "Morris," she adds that he comes from a certain tribe from which the West Indian slave market is recruited; he is unlike "the ignoble and ugly Negro type, so much more commonly seen here" (120–21). The *Journal*, with its amalgam of feminist predicament, abolitionist politics, a racialism constituted by empire, is, for me, a complex piece of writing, its ambiguities and contradictions less frequently encountered in the writing of more well known literary types traveling in America.

Charles Dickens in 1842 is powerfully and graphically opposed to slavery, sees America as born from a struggle for individual liberty yet enslaving its Negroes and wiping out its indigenous people: for him, it is a place, as he puts it, where "cowards notch the ear of men and women, cut pleasant posies in the shrinking flesh, learn to write with pens of red-hot iron on the human face" (242). William Thackeray, though, laconically declares in 1853 that the Negroes do not excite his "compassionate feelings at all; they are so grotesque and happy that I can't cry over them. The little black imps are trotting and grinning about the streets, women, workmen, waiters, all well fed and happy" (3 March 1853).

Anthony Trollope observes entirely without embarrassment that slaves are like children, mentally unfit to cope with white men, although he does allow that the Civil War is punishment for the continuance of slavery after the Revolutionary War: "But such punishments come generally upon nations... Ireland's famine was the punishment of her imprudence and idleness" (2:355). Such statements bring us to Ireland, and the Irish, immigrants to America who, in the eyes of virtually all British observers, corrupt the political system with their "Romanist" sympathies and ruin the economic system with their inherent disinclination for work. Fanny Kemble, so sensitive to the misery of slaves, observes that in America the Scots turn "everything to good account" and the Irish "leave everything to ruin, to disorder, and neglect." On the one hand, she says, we have "careful economy and prudent management" and on the other "reckless profusion and careless extravagance" (283). And Dickens, indignant at the living conditions of slaves, describes some Irish immigrants in the Catskills as living in the following way: "Hideously ugly old women and very buxom young ones, pigs, dogs, men, children, babies, pots, kettles, dunghills, vile refuse, rank straw and standing water, all wallowing together in an inseparable heap" (214). British contempt for the Irish crosses the Atlantic, ready to mix with the race and class prejudices already at work.

More appealingly (at least for us, I suspect), America was also a haven for disaffected British radicals. For a political idealist such as William Cobbett, America is the new Eden, the new Jerusalem, utopian hope for a world free of British political corruption and hypocrisy. Cobbett celebrates a place without "boroughmongers" and "fat parsons." And Anna Barbauld's long poem, *1811*, as it participates in a radical critique of Britain's "Midas dream," imagines a New World "beyond the Appalachian hills" where "Thy stores of knowledge the new states shall know,/ And think thy thoughts, and with they fancy glow:/ ...And Milton's tones the raptured ear enthrall,/ Mixed with the roar of Niagara's fall" (lines 82–96). The cross-fertilization here will unite Britain's cultural history (not her mercantile interests) with American nature.

The sentimentalism and righteous indignation of *Oliver Twist* and *Nicholas Nickleby* under his belt, Dickens in 1842 finds America to be mostly a political sewer, plumbed in *American Notes* (1842) and in *Martin Chuzzlewit* (1843), the site of "despicable trickery at elections," "scurrilous newspapers," and "shameful trucklings to mercenary knaves" (120). For Frances Trollope (Anthony's mother), America is a rowdy wilderness where food is "seized and devoured" and "strange uncouth phrases" uttered in alternation with "loathsome spitting" (18). For these writers, and for countless others, we're in a paradoxical place of innocence falling into rank decay—think of Dickens's descriptions in *American Notes* of the junction of the Ohio and Mississippi rivers as a site of stunted trees, rotting houses, slimy vegetation. America is also awesomely beautiful, yet cramped, nasty, full of noisy boarding-houses, filthy manners, and frightening buildings like the huge slaughterhouse in Cincinnati that makes the Ohio run with blood.

By way of concluding this transatlantic journey, let me take things back to Britannia's body and the gendering of her sawn-off colony. In the familiar metaphor of Britain as the mother country and America as the child colony, the gender of the child varies according to the historical moment. On the eve of the Revolutionary War, for instance, America is peopled by Britain's vigorous sons, some behaving themselves, some not: a Scottish woman named Janet Schaw traveling with her brother in North Carolina witnessed the drilling of revolutionary regiments and cried out to the mother country: "Oh Britannia, what are you doing, while your true obedient sons are thus insulted by their unlawful brethren; are they also forgot by their natural parent?" (191). Here, Britain is reminded of her maternal responsibility to maintain family-political discipline. In the middle of the civil war, Anthony Trollope appeals for British support for the northern cause, for the mother country to aid that part of the former colony that remains faithful to her teachings. He sentimentally observes,

> There is, I think, no more beautiful sight than that of a mother, still in all the glory of womanhood, preparing the wedding trousseau for her daughter... She is to go forth... under the teaching which her old home has given her... So it is that England should send forth her daughters.

He goes on to say that America is "our eldest child," her people thewed and muscled by British blood in their veins...

> These people speak our language, use our prayers, read our books, are ruled by our laws, dress themselves in our images, are warm with our blood... They are our sons and daughters, the source of our greatest pride, and as we grow old they should be the staff of our age (2:293).

What one sees, I think, is the becoming female of America in the British imagination. Paradoxically, as the nation becomes stronger, the gristle not only hardened into manhood but became muscle fueled and fed by America's own imperial conquests of indigenous peoples, appropriation of their land—she becomes for Britain something to boast about: an obedient daughter like herself who has so dutifully absorbed the teachings of the mother country that she threatens to surpass her in global domination. No longer a severed limb, she has become a separate nation. Her adolescent male vigor having acquired land, people, wealth, she can attend to the tempering mystification of that crude aggression into civilization, just as Britain herself in the 19th century was busy transforming imperial greed into imperial civilization. Severed limbs, after all, are said still to be felt somewhere in the brain as a twitch. Perhaps the varied British Victorian writing about America may be seen as a twitch in her imperial consciousness of a former colony/limb grown mighty through dutiful repetition of the teachings of imperial expansion. Edward Said's insistence that we not isolate cultures as monolithic enables us to disentangle some of the related threads in this writing.

Works Cited
Barbauld, Anna Laetitia Aikin. *Eighteen Hundred and Eleven. A Poem.* London: J. Johnson and Co., 1812.
Bird, Isabella, *A Lady's Life in the Rocky Mountains.* 1879. Intro. Daniel J. Boorstin. Norman: University of Oklahoma Press, 1960.
Burke, Edmund. *Two Speeches on Conciliation with America and Two Letters on Irish Questions.* Intro. Henry Morley. London: George Routledge and Sons, 1886.
Cobbett, William. *A Year's Residence in the United States of America.* 1819. Carbondale: Southern Illinois University Press, 1964.
David, Deirdre. *Rule Britannia: Women, Empire, and Victorian Writing.* Ithaca: Cornell University Press, 1995.
Dickens, Charles. *American Notes and Pictures from Italy.* 1846; 1850; 1862–68. London: Oxford University Press, 1957.
Held Captive by Indians: Selected Narratives 1642–1836. Ed. Richard, Van Der Beets. Knoxville: University of Tennessee Press, 1973.
Josselyn, John. *An Account of Two Voyages to New England:* made during the years 1638, 1663. Boston: William Veazie, 1865.
Kemble, Frances Anne. *Journal of a Residence on a Georgian Plantation in 1838–1839.* Ed. with Intro. John A. Scott. Athens: University of Georgia Press, 1984. Reprint Alfred A. Knopf, Inc., 1961.
Schaw, Janet. *Journal of a Lady of Quality; Being the Narrative of a Journey from Scotland to the West Indies, North Carolina, and Portugal, in the years 1774 to 1776.* Ed. Evangeline Walker Andrews. New Haven: Yale University Press, 1921.
Smith, John. *The Complete Works of John Smith (1580–1631).* Ed. Philip L. Barbour. 3 vols. Chapel Hill: University of North Carolina Press, 1986.
Tennyson, Alfred. *The Poems of Tennyson.* Ed. Christopher Ricks. London: Longmans, Green, 1969.
Thackeray, William Makepeace. *The Letters and Private Papers of William Makepeace Thackeray.* Ed. Edgar F. Harden. New York: Garland Publishing, 1994.
Trollope, Frances. *Domestic Manners of the Americans.* 1832. Ed., with a History of Mrs. Trollope's Adventures in America, by Donald Smalley. New York: Alfred A. Knopf, 1949.
Trollope, Anthony. *North America.* 1862. London: Dawsons of Pall Mall, 1868. 2 vols.

Edward Said and the Future of the Jewish People

Marc H. Ellis

Since the founding of Christianity, Jews and Judaism have had many interlocutors, most of them negative and operating from the vantage point of an ideological superiority enforced by material and military power. This is certainly the case in the West and elsewhere over the last two thousand years, as the dominance of Christianity and Christian culture rendered Jews and Judaism both essential and peripheral, visible and invisible, a combination that led to false polemics, exile, and massacre. As is well documented by historians, Jewish history in the West is hardly linear in relation to European Christian culture, with eras of peace and prosperity followed by eras of persecution and degradation. At the same time, the movement from arguments about the superiority of Christianity vis-a-vis Judaism to the racialist movements against Jews, regardless of their religious expression, has accelerated over time, and the mixture of anti-Judaism and anti-Semitism in the middle of our century provided the worst manifestation of violence against Jews in history, a mass slaughter commonly known as the Holocaust.

In some ways the Holocaust awakened the world, especially Europe and the Western Christian world, to the horror of asserting theological, cultural, and racial superiority. The ecumenical dialogue between Christians and Jews after the conclusion of World War II, with the epoch-making importance of the Roman Catholic Vatican Council II and its statements on Jews and Judaism in relation to its own self-understanding, is the fruit of the Christian discovery of its own culpability in the attempted annihilation of the Jewish people. Though the dialogue and subsequent confession of mainstream Protestant Christian denominations with regard to Jews and Judaism seems altruistic, its main thrust has been one of self-examination and renewal. The horror of the death camps raised the question of Christian authenticity and commitment, in essence the future of Christian faith and institutional presence in the world. In many ways, the attempt to jettison the anti-Jewish and anti-Judaic elements of

Christianity provides a new way of looking at the world beyond Jews and Judaism and beyond the West and those state structures that have traditionally supported the churches. Coming to grips with those who created the pre-history to Christianity, and who traveled with them throughout their history, allowed an ecumenical religiosity that culminated in the emergence of liberation theologies around the world.

At the same time that Europe and Western Christianity came to understand Jews and Judaism in a new light, Jews themselves found a voice and affluence in the West far in excess of anything previously known to them. Though the non-linear aspect of Jewish ascendancy and descent remains within Jewish consciousness, the situation clearly changes in the post-war period. As the devastation of the Holocaust became known, Jewish ascendancy advanced both in the United States and in the formation and expansion of Israel. Barriers to Jewish empowerment in the United States fell quickly because of a new sensitivity of the wider non-Jewish culture and because of financial success and a burgeoning intellectual class. At the same time, and for the first time in two thousand years, Jews successfully created a state where a majority of its citizens were Jewish and the power of the state was exclusively in Jewish hands. This dual empowerment and the narrative that emerges from this experience is crucial to Jewish ascendancy and more: it represents the reversal of dialogue about Jews and Judaism and actions taken against them and their religion. From this point onward Jews are central to the drama of the West and Western Christianity in a narrative provided and fashioned by the Jewish community itself. Those who once were spoken to and lectured are now to speak and lecture; those who once were seen as failing and sinful now present themselves as prevailing and innocent.[1]

The emergence of the Jewish post-Holocaust narrative in the West and its connection with the state of Israel is illustrated most vividly by Elie Wiesel. Born in Eastern Europe and a survivor of Buchenwald and Auschwitz, Wiesel assumes a prominent place in Holocaust literature and ethical discussions in the post-war world, so much so that he was awarded the Nobel Peace Prize in 1986. His books and essays, as well as his many commentaries on current events, emphasize the need to speak out against injustice and how silence in the face of injustice becomes complicity. Wiesel's reference point is the displacement and destruction of the Holocaust, and because of his own suffering and loss, his speech takes on the gravity of a moral witness in our time. As a refugee from Europe, his understanding of America is one of welcome and gratitude; as a diaspora Jew, his support of Israel is unwavering, even to the point of refusing to criticize individual policies of the state. In Wiesel's view, a view that is held by a broad segment of American Jewry, America and Israel are places of refuge for Jews in a hostile world and their fundamental character is one of compassion and goodness. The policies of both nations are shadowed by the Holocaust, with America as the bastion of democracy able to confront injustice around the world and Israel as the place of refuge and renewal for the Jewish people, whose policies exist only to insure both. Those who oppose either America or Israel or critically confront the policies of either are therefore engaged in opposition to an essential goodness rather than an informed and political opposition. By grounding the Jewish narrative in the suffering of the Holocaust and the survival and revival of the Jewish people in the twinning of America and Israel, the policies of both states are shrouded in a morality few commentators ascribe to any nation-state.

If the extension of American or Israeli power is presumed to be innocent, Jewish spokespersons and actions are still farther removed from criticism. Contemporary Jewish life springs from untold suffering, the suffering of the innocent, which informs the speech and actions of Jews who are heirs to the Holocaust. In Wiesel's understanding, Jews who have every right to hate because of what they have been through are incapable of hate; even Israeli soldiers are witness to this inability, characterized as reluctant warriors who embrace violence only as a necessity thrust upon them. At the same time, they are affected by the suffering imposed on others because of this very necessity. The 1967 War exemplifies this understanding for Wiesel as a war forced upon Israel and whose soldiers fought without cruelty. "During the Six-Day War the Jewish fighters did not become cruel," Wiesel writes, "They became sad. They acquired a certain maturity, a very moving maturity, which I simply cannot forget. And if I feel something toward them, the child-soldier in Israel, it is profound respect." Wiesel concludes that Israel itself represents a moral victory and that its military victories are only secondary to the character that produced them. His pride in Israel reflects this sensibility: "My pride is that Israel has remained human because it has remained so deeply Jewish."[2]

Wiesel's analysis of the 1967 War is crucial to the evolving Jewish narrative in the West, as it establishes a moral sensibility and religious tone that outweigh the policies of Israel or grounds them in a way unavailable to serious political criticism. The "moral" victory of Israel in the 1967 War is extended to its founding and to its future beyond the war, as it represents a drama, almost cosmic in scope, of a disinherited people being reborn. The drama includes all of Jewish history and penetrates to the very question of God and God's presence in history. "Suddenly all Jews had become children of the Holocaust," Wiesel writes, and the "great mystery in which we are encloaked, as if by the command of the Almighty." Because of this, the Arab armies are defeated: "millions of the martyrs of the Holocaust were enlisted" in the ranks of the Israeli military and they shielded their "spiritual heirs" like the Biblical pillars of fire. With such support as this, how could Israel ever be defeated?

Wiesel is hardly alone in this understanding of Israel. Emil Fackenheim, a European Jewish refugee, post-war citizen of Canada and now of Israel, sees the survival of Israel as a religious commandment, the 614th commandment which completes the Orthodox understanding of 613 commandments to fulfill Jewish practice. For Fackenheim, post-Holocaust Jewish belief in God is uncertain, and secular and religious Jews must come together in the task which defines contemporary Jewry, that is the rebuilding of Jewish life exemplified by the founding and defense of Israel. Thus Israeli soldiers who fought in the 1967 War were warriors with a religious mandate, hearing the commanding voice of Auschwitz. They responded in the only way an authentic Jew could respond after the Holocaust—they gave their lives for the survival of Israel and, in this sense, for the survival of all Jews and Jewish history. Many Christians outside Israel also heard the commanding voice of Auschwitz in uniting for Israel and against the Arab enemy. By doing this, Jews denied Hitler a "posthumous victory" and refused those who, at least in Fackenheim's mind, wanted to carry out Hitler's mandate.

What lurks behind both Wiesel's and Fackenheim's "religiosity," defined by Jewish history and the Holocaust, is the threat of another holocaust, this one signaling the end of the Jewish people. Israel is the guardian of Jewish history and America, with its power and moral purpose, its guarantor. Anything that threatens Jewish unity around the question of Israel or undermines America's power and purpose in the world is thus defined as enemy and more; conscious or not, these enemies invite another holocaust. This warning applies to Jews and non-Jews alike, the first accused of self-hate, the second accused of anti-Semitism. If the mission and policies of Israel, even its expansion and wars, are defined in terms of morality and religiosity, then its critics are accused on the same terrain. The circle is complete and Israel and America are brought together in the realm of innocence and redemption, the latter being proposed as the future of a secure and prosperous Israel with the backing of America. Cloaked in the Holocaust, Israel and America are agents of the ultimate reconciliation between God and the Jewish people, between God and humanity at large. The Jewish drama continues this time on the other side of anti-Jewish and anti-Judaic understandings. Yet this drama is continually threatened by a reversal often experienced in Jewish history, shadowed by another holocaust, which would bring this history to an end.[3]

Hence the "new anti-Semitism" widely heralded in the 1970s and 1980s by these Holocaust theologians and by other Jewish commentators. The list is long and includes such notables as Norman Podhoertz, editor of the conservative journal *Commentary*, but it also includes liberals such as Nathan Perlmutter who wrote *The Real Antisemitism in America*. What is evident in Perlmutter's book is a neo-conservatism emerging among Jews in response to shifting currents regarding Israel's and America's domestic and foreign policy. The specifics and tone of the message are clearly demarcated, naming friends and enemies and suggesting shifting alliances. Liberal commentators and institutions, including those traditionally seen as friends of the Jewish people such as the mainline churches and the United Nations, have become captive to anti-Israeli and anti-American sentiment, while those traditionally seen to be anti-Jewish, such as conservative politicians and Christian fundamentalist denominations, have embraced Israel and American power that supports it. Perlmutter suggests that a sea-change has occurred within Jewish history, one that Jews have been late in understanding. Indeed, the struggle against anti-Semitism has shifted from those groups on the margins of Western society who espouse traditional Jewish hate propaganda to liberal and revolutionary ideologies and institutions that seek the reversal of an American-centered global economic and military world-view, and with that the decentering of Israel's hegemony in the Middle East. Those toward whom Jews naturally gravitate and who in the past joined them in their quest for dignity and inclusion in the societies in which they live are now seen as endangering Jewish interests and defense. In an age of empowerment, political alliances need to be flexible and capable of change. Started in the 1970s, this neo-conservative movement within the Jewish world continues today with the publication of Elliott Abrams' *Faith or Fear: How Jews Can Survive in a Christian America*.

Challenging Jewish Innocence

Those who are critical of understandings and policies supported and/or carried out by Jews in America or Israel are forewarned. Though the terrain seems to be the engagement of ideas in the clash and compromise of public debate, the reality, at least as seen by many Jewish commentators, thinkers and political actors, is quite different. The terrain is historical, ideological, and theological in a specifically Jewish modality and the stakes are thereby heightened, skewed, in fact, in a direction unknown to most who enter the fray. Jewish discourse is less modern, 20th-century, Western, or even within the context of the nation-state, though these forms are used in a sophisticated manner; it is rather defined by paradigms of thought developed over a 5,000-year history. This Jewish sensibility, heightened in our time by immense suffering *and* unparalleled empowerment, is on the world stage in a way that harkens back to Jewish origins and projects itself into the future as the central drama of human history. Other interests and concerns, even if they appear to others to be central to their life and survival, are judged to be secondary and peripheral, allowed only if they do not appear to impinge on the more important Jewish drama. Therefore what seems to others to be a natural assertion of their own interests and rights of critical analysis may be seen by Jews as an assault on Jewish sensibility and well-being. In the drama of suffering and redemption so evident and articulated with the force, though often unannounced, of a history seen by Jews as central to the divine and human journey of humanity, the resistance to critique and the accusation of another threatened event of mass suffering is enough to reduce most critics to silence.

Yet silence on the issue of Jews and Judaism is more than demanded; it is enforced with psychological and material penalties. The charges of Jewish self-hatred, the new anti-Semitism, and the encouragement of another holocaust are complimented by the highly organized and well-financed Jewish political apparatus and institutional structure. Examples abound, and one only need mention AIPAC (American Israel Public Affairs Committee) and the ADL (Anti-Defamation League) to strike fear in the hearts of many who want to question contemporary Jewish understandings in relation to America and Israel. Perlmutter's book itself carries this warning, as his ideological analysis is buttressed by his leadership role in the ADL. The power to pursue political ends as illustrated in aid packages to Israel, with over twenty percent of America's foreign aid going to Israel, a country with less than one-thousandth of the world's population, is striking, but the ability to punish opponents of such support is equally impressive. Witness Senator Charles Percy and Representative Paul Findley, both defeated in reelection bids by organized and targeted Jewish pressure. Furthermore, this power has had a chilling effect on public discussion regarding Israel, especially in the academic and media arenas. The ADL's infamous anti-Israel list has targeted those who seek to break the silence on issues central to Jewish life. Here, too, examples abound, with the attempt to dishonor and render unemployable those critical of the use and abuse of Jewish power. While Percy and Findley are non-Jews, the attempt to silence in the academic arena often focuses specifically on Jewish dissidents, the most prominent being Noam Chomsky, but extending to younger Jewish scholars like Norman Finkelstein and Jonathan Boyarin. In a very tangible sense, the attempt is to eliminate criticism from without and within the Jewish community.[4]

The attempt to marginalize thought and action by the organized Jewish community has been in large part successful. Since the founding of Israel, the Western narrative and policy implementation have been overwhelmingly pro-Israel, and even more so in the years since the 1967 War. Despite the setbacks in the moral sense of Israel in the last years, including the invasion of Lebanon and the bombing of Beirut in the 1980s and the attempt to crush the Palestinian intifada in the 1980s and 1990s, and despite the more vocal and expanded debate evidenced because of these events, it remains that those who question the innocent and redemptive features of contemporary Jewish life are on the defensive, liable to accusations and character assassination. For these reasons, Jews and Judaism have lacked voices that can call to account abuses of power, or rather have refused a hearing to those who see the possibility of Jewish life in an alternative way. At the same time, the voices of the suffering, especially Palestinians, have been relegated to a peripheral position, heard only as a reference point for contemporary hatred of Jews. In essence, Jewish leadership has acted to protect its moral standing in a way that all groups with power do: claim the high ground by characterizing dissent as unpatriotic and even demonic and at the same time make the material conditions for dissent difficult, if not impossible.

Within this context two immediate questions arise: How are people who are affected by Jewish power, especially Palestinians, to redress their suffering and concerns? And how is the Jewish community itself to be called to account and an alternative way of life proposed? The first question deals with injustice against another people, the second with foundational issues of what it means to be Jewish and what the Jewish future will be. In an immediate sense, these questions may seem unrelated, to be addressed independently and often this is the case. Palestinians are interested quite properly in their future, which is significantly impacted by policies of Israel with the support of American foreign policy. Their interest in Jews and Judaism ends in the formation and implementation of policies that impact them. In another time, and even today, the policies of others, say Jordan and Egypt, are dealt with on their own terms and with the same goal in mind: an independent nation that allows the survival and flourishing of Palestinian life and culture. In the long view, Jews and Judaism remain important to Palestinians because Jews and Palestinians live side by side, share a history and a future, and will in many ways, as enemies or friends, interact on the economic and political front. Aside from intrinsic merit, the future of Jews and Palestinians are unassailably tied together. For Jews the question is more complicated; aside from the fact that Jews and Palestinians are and will live side by side, and therefore interact economically and politically, the internal question of dispossessing another people and organizing the community to be silent and complicit in that dispossession has profound ramifications for the internal life of the Jewish people. What is at stake is the claims of Jewish history and the future path Jews will embrace. The capacity of Jews to do to others what has been done to them profoundly alters the *raison d'etre* of Jewish existence, that is the embrace by a majority of the Jewish community of Jewish state power in Israel, and the related embrace of the American state, represents a situational shift in Jewish history to rival or even surpass the momentous effect of the Holocaust. Creating a Jewish-state culture fundamentally alters the trajectory of Jewish history.[5]

Of those who have commented on Jews and Judaism within the context of empowerment as interlocutors from outside the Jewish community, two are preeminent. The first is John Murray Cuddihy, an American scholar, who approached the subject, at least initially, in terms of modernity. In his ground breaking work, *The Ordeal of Civility: Freud, Marx, and Levi-Strauss and the Jewish Struggle with Modernity,* Cuddihy explores the interaction of Jews with the modern West as a series of intellectual maneuvers designed to subvert Christian religious and cultural hegemony and its transmutation into secularized modernity, thus establishing a beachhead for Jewish participation in modernity. As latecomers to modernity, and with a history of suffering and exclusion in Europe, intellectual giants such as Sigmund Freud, Karl Marx, and Claude Levi-Strauss establish ideological arguments and fields of study that have their own revolutionary scientific merit *and* an unannounced agenda of reversing the established Gentile order to provide a path for Jews to transition from a ghettoized and—at least as compared to the refinement of Western civilization—a backward culture. The challenge of these intellectuals is daunting, as they outline this path of assimilation in the West by analyzing European civilization from the perspective of the outsider with modern tools. In doing so, Jews become the interpreters of the West and enter this more powerful, established and often hostile culture on Jewish terms. By advising the West that in psyche, politics, and anthropology, an underground, subversive and reorienting process is underway, these Jewish thinkers turn the ordinary world on its head and allow Jews to undergo the "hurricane" of modernization with dignity and perhaps even with the advantage of insight. Nonetheless, modernity remains an ordeal, as the Jewish community—with its particular patterns of thought and culture—is left behind to enter this foreign culture. In analyzing these figures, Cuddihy shows the inner turmoil of prominent Jews, and of Jews in general, that accompanies such a transition. Freud, Marx, and Levi-Strauss are great and in some ways tragic figures who parallel the path of Western Jews seeking admission to a modernity that promises and exacts so much. Clouding all, of course, is one distinct destination—the Holocaust—a price that none of these thinkers foresaw and which Freud experienced in the most intimate way.

If the ticket to enter modernity is a civility that breaks apart traditional cultures, Jews are forced, willing or not to pay the price. Yet the survival of Jewish understandings, the ability to bring aspects of Jewish culture into modernity, even and especially in disguised forms, is established and celebrated in Cuddihy's analysis. Cuddihy marvels at the ability of Jews to in a sense "beat" Protestant modernity at its own game, and in a very short time move from a conversation piece in the West—the Jewish question—to become intellectual giants to whom the West comes for insight. From Cuddihy's perspective these seemingly assimilated Jews carry the burden of a peoples' journey as previous Jewish leaders did in times of crisis. Cuddihy's respect is clear and his attempt to show the subversive aspect of Freud, Marx, and Levi-Strauss reverses the anti-Semitic stereotype of the insidious Jew so prominent in the West into a positive sense of Jewish commitment and

Edward Said and the Future of the Jewish People

exploration that exposes the hypocrisy at the heart of a civility seeking to disguise injustice and barbarism. The tragic aspect of leaving behind the old is, in Cuddihy's analysis, complimented by a sense of a heroic struggle that is a gift to Jewish and universal history. The centrality and uniqueness of the Jews, often self-ascribed, is demonstrated and affirmed by Cuddihy in the crucible of the 20th century. As a Catholic of Irish ancestry, Cuddihy delights in the bravado and courage of Jewish intellectuals and the larger Jewish community that enters a foreign culture as the despised outsider and creates a home for itself with its own distinctive flavor.

Cuddihy's later work, published in essay form, traces the continuing Jewish journey into modernity after the Holocaust. Cuddihy analyzes contemporary Jewish intellectuals within their present preoccupation of reflecting on the Holocaust and the state of Israel, and finds a continuation of bold thought *and* a new defensiveness. The latter has to do with another shift of Jewish life in the 20th century, the movement from pariahs seeking survival in Western modernity to an empowered community seeking to fend off commentary about Jewish use of the Holocaust to enhance its status in the West and protect Israel against an accelerating and potentially explosive critique. Asserting the uniqueness of the Holocaust, Jewish thinkers are doing more than remembering the dead; at least in Cuddihy's mind, Jews are using this memory to complete their ascendancy in the West. Though Cuddihy sees this as understandable, claiming the Holocaust as only Jewish, without comparison or comparability to the tragedies of other victims, is a form of trivializing the claims of the latter. Moreover, the memory of the dead in the present discussion is a claim to superiority in disguise, which has consequences for contemporary intellectual life, denoting entire categories of reflection off limits. Cuddihy reflects on the meaning of Holocaust remembrance as grief work but also as a claim by "cultural status-seekers" who are "engaged in an inner-ethnic and intra-societal *kulturkampf*"("Latent Issue" 73). Cuddihy realizes the force of the argument and terrain which he is entering, in essence the shift he himself is analyzing and undergoing with reference to contemporary Jewish life, and begins his essay with a statement to his readers explaining that his disputation with the Holocaust is not its historical occurrence, but its use in intellectual discourse. His statement differentiating the history and historiography of the Holocaust made, he emphasizes his own struggle in even raising the issue. As part of his introduction, Cuddihy writes of reading Chaim

Kaplan's *Warsaw Diary*, "I cried,—from sadness, from joy that the Diary and its testimony had survived in triumph, that a Pole had been its custodian, and that Kaplan had had the last word, for here was I, now, reading those very words, and crying"(63). Cuddihy understands that some of his ideas may indeed offend.

In an earlier essay, subtitled "The Incivil Irritatingness of Jewish Theodicy," Cuddihy had already acknowledged that some of his ideas will offend Jews. Cuddihy wonders how anti-Semitism can only be a one-way street, as if Jews are only victims of others rather than agents of their own history. In this sense Jews see themselves as "morally blameless," escaping the give-and-take of history. This is the contemporary theodicy of the Jewish people according to Cuddihy: the presumption of total innocence in historical and contemporary matters. "Yet, when Jews' own historical actions, in the Middle East for example, create a stateless people who, in turn, blame the Jews and Israelis, what does Jewish theodicy do?" Cuddihy asks. "It blames the victims, the Palestinians, and sees nothing irrational in this" ("The Elephant" 24–25). For Cuddihy, blamelessness in terms of weakness (anti-Semitism) and strength (Israel) is "irritating" because it violates reciprocity. What results is "Wieselian bolus," a combination of claiming to be an eternal victim even within empowerment. In this way "public *kvelling* and sanctimonious moralizing" come to be seen by non-Jews as a strategy of avoiding accountability. With great insight, Cuddihy sees this theodicy as emanating from the historic position of powerlessness in the Diaspora and so a sense of moral superiority is understandable, even necessary, to survive the dominant culture. However, the "luxury of powerlessness ended with the founding of Israel" when Jews "dirtied their hands" (28). What continues today is a conflict between two rhetorics, one historical, the other contemporary, "between the Diaspora Reform rhetoric of the Jew as ethical, moralistic, and pacifistic and the Israeli rhetoric of Sabra victory and pride, between if you will, the *New York Times* editorial talk and the talk of Menachem Begin and General Ariel Sharon." Cuddihy concludes that Jews come honorably by their paranoia but when it comes to their own behavior "they go on a moral holiday, legitimated by their secular, post-emancipation ideology" (35).

The second scholar who has commented on Jews and Judaism in their time of empowerment is Edward Said. Unlike Cuddihy, who experiences the onslaught of modernity as a person of Irish Catholic ancestry and thus was born and struggles within the Western tradition,

Edward Said and the Future of the Jewish People

Said, a Palestinian Arab by birth and identification, has lived a life of exile in America. While Cuddihy can identify with the struggle of Jews to assimilate to and survive modernity, and at the same time be outraged by Jewish attempts to have both innocence and power, Said at an early age experienced the loss of his homeland because of Jewish power. As part of a refugee community in America, Said also encounters the West, and Jews within the West, as culpable in his dispossession, and experiences the invisibility of his natural identification. Whereas Cuddihy traces the coming of Jewish intellectual power as a model for his own people's empowerment, the exercise of Jewish intellectual and material power promises Said and millions of other Palestinians a diaspora community without a name, one often identified with weakness and shame. In fact Jewish ascendancy in America and Israel represents a hurricane for Palestinians, in some ways, similar to the hurricane Jews experienced in the wake of modernity. In this hurricane Jews have survived and prospered in the reverse proportion to Palestinians who have experienced the winds and storms of Jewish power as their demise.

In one sense Said, as an intellectual living his adult life in the West and making important contributions to the fields of literary, cultural, and political criticism, is the logical extension of the Jewish journey in the 20th century traced by Cuddihy. Said raises the next question within this journey, one of arrival, just as Cuddihy addressed the point of embarkation. In his later work Cuddihy begins to analyze that arrival, writing about the confusion of Jewish empowerment in its attempt to maintain the rhetoric of subversion and inclusion even as Jews mobilize to displace Palestinians and others who challenge that empowerment. Cuddihy searches for an intellectual current that can confront Jews in their new stage of empowerment and does so as an outsider whose central insights come from the previous stage. Cuddihy finds the attempt of Jews to have it both ways—innocence and empowerment—to be irritating, but surely something more important has occurred. The reversal of intellectual Jewish currents from one of creative subversion to aggressive defense represents the joining of powers that once derided, displaced, and sought to annihilate the Jewish people. What Cuddihy glimpses but is unable to articulate is the end of the Jewish tradition of critical thought, and with that end a final assimilation and assent to that which Jewish intellectuals fought against. In many ways, what Cuddihy glimpses is the *end of Jewish history as we know it*.

Where for Cuddihy the question is intellectual and deeply felt—if not why the anger, the disappointment, the almost desperate cry to Jews to look again at what is occurring?—for Said this shift in Jewish life is palpable, embodied as a disorienting and formative experience in his own life, the life of his family, friends, and people. Said and the Palestinian people are victims of the victims, and the claim of innocence is not to be struggled against because for Palestinians it has not existed, and the claim of exclusion does not have to be reckoned with because it is Palestinians who have been excluded. Said does not have to struggle with the reversal that Cuddihy begins to analyze, but its opposite, the pretense to innocence assumed in the West. Cuddihy struggles to name the sea-change in Jewish life as Said, with other Palestinians, struggles to name what they have lost because of that change. Whereas Cuddihy catalogues the journey of Jews as they enter the West and become intimate partners in it, Said experiences the West and Jews as partners in an assault that has rendered him and his people refugees without an established identity or country. In this context the interlocutor of the Jewish world has shifted from Cuddihy to Said, symbolically and concretely from Jewish intellectualism to Jewish power.

It is Said's search to understand his own displacement and that of his people that informs his two classic works, *Orientalism* and *The Question of Palestine*. Published within a year of each other in 1978 and 1979 respectively, these books identify the mechanism by which the West has denigrated and dominated the East and the possibility of surviving and reestablishing the identity of the East, with particular reference to Palestine and Palestinians. Using the literature, academic disciplines, and politics of the West, Said demonstrates that Western domination over the last centuries is the result of a careful and strategic expansion of European and American power. Colonialism has many forms, but it is at its surest and most devastating when it can define other areas of the globe, including entire peoples and civilizations, within its own symbolic and narrative system. Orientalism is a discourse in which a position of authority is assumed by the West in the context of economic and political hegemony. Intellectuals provide the legitimation for this hegemony by creating a dominant narrative. A circulation of ideas, symbols and physical power is established whereby the Orient is defined as "other" to be studied, invaded, in the broadest sense captured for the use and edification of the West. Thus the "disappearance" of Palestine takes place within the broader context of an Orientalism that reverses the question of the West, often

Edward Said and the Future of the Jewish People

articulated as the Jewish question, to the question of Palestine. Said writes of this reversal:

> We were on the land called Palestine; were our dispossession and our effacement, by which almost a million of us were made to leave Palestine and our society made non-existent, justified even to save the remnant of European Jews that had survived Nazism? By what moral or political standard are we expected to lay aside our claims to our national existence, our land, our human rights? In what world is there no argument when an entire people is told that it is juridically absent, even as armies are led against it, campaigns conducted against even its name, history changed so as to "prove" its nonexistence? (*Question*, xvii)

At the same time Said recognizes the larger scope of such a negation, the "entrenched cultural attitude" toward Palestine and Palestinians that derive from Western prejudices about Islam, the Arabs, and the Orient. It is this attitude that Zionism drew upon in relating to Palestinians and in doing so "dehumanized us, reduced us to the barely tolerated status of a nuisance" (xiv).

Said's primary interest in Jews and Judaism is in the context of Zionism and Israel but in placing the emphasis on the latter he also focuses on their connection with the West. Though much of this journey is traced with the founding and expansion of Israel—hence the reference to the Palestinian catastrophe—his discussion of Jews and Zionism prior to the founding of the state is illuminating and provides another perspective to that of Cuddihy. For while Jewish intellectuals in the West were forging a future for the Jewish people in the West, other Jews were preparing the ground for a state in the Middle East. Said cites Chaim Weizmann, a leading advocate of Zionism, negotiating with Arthur Balfour, then British Foreign Secretary and in certain ways an anti-Semite, and establishing a common understanding of Arabs and the Orient that spoke to British superiority and Jewish concerns. With Balfour, Weizmann plays upon the myth of Semitic backwardness while changing places with the Arab. Weizmann's burden as a Semite is to demonstrate that Jews, under the beneficence of the West, have altered their nature while the Arabs in Palestine remain the same. In fact, from this moment on Jews are considered to have a special insight into the Semites of the Arab world, identifying with the West over against East. As Said so aptly writes: "By a concatenation of events and circumstances the Semitic myth bifurcated in the Zionist movement; one Semite went the way of Orientalism, the other, the Arab, was forced to go the way of the Oriental" (*Orientalism* 307). This division of Semites into Orientalist and Orientals is fundamental to the creation of Israel, to the creation of a network of realities—language, colonies and organizations—that lead to the conversion of Palestine into a Jewish state. Jews acquired a legitimacy for this effort by giving it an "archeology and a teleology that completely surrounded and, in a sense, outdated the native culture that was still firmly planted in Palestine" (*Question* 86). Zionists Jews proceeded in two directions: by appealing to the West to restore Jews to their "native land," to which they feel themselves entitled as Semites *and* by degrading the Semitic inhabitants of Palestine as backward and interlopers. Both depend on the Jewish position within the Christian West arguing from a premodern perspective within the context of a modern, or at least modernizing people.

What Cuddihy identifies as a Jewish schizophrenia, the rhetoric of Diaspora innocence and Sabra power, Said identifies as narrative that inserts Jews into a sympathetic solidarity with the West as a cover to policies that systematically displace his own people. The narrative gains adherents because of Jewish suffering in the West and because of the superiority the West feels with regard to the East. Yet this same narrative is inherently unstable, as the assertion of Arab backwardness as well as the essential absence of Palestinians needs to be continually proven to others and to Jews themselves. Argument is constructed in which Palestinians are visible in order to be degraded and invisible so that no hue and cry can be raised with Jewish settlement. Jews thus pose as civilizers of the backward and return to their ancient land which is "unsettled." Palestinians are continuously derided *and* removed from Western and Jewish consciousness because their mere presence and humanity challenge Jewish claims and power.

Because Palestinians do in fact exist, and in great numbers, and because Palestinians are native to Palestine and the Arab world, a competition over "native" status ensues. This Zionist claim to be native demands a physical and ideological apartheid system, which aims to create and sustain a vision of righteousness and apartness. Any challenge to the Jew as native—such as the very presence of Palestinians is or discussion of Palestinian nationhood and culture—must be debased or erased. Furthermore, the native presence of Palestinians can only be seen as a threat to the entire Israeli, and later Jewish, narrative in the Middle East and the West, thus transposing resistance to displacement into a threat of annihilation. An explosive

Edward Said and the Future of the Jewish People

contradiction enters Jewish life precisely at this moment, as the apartheid vision is disastrous for Jews as it is for Palestinians. Because Arabs are seen as synonymous with everything degraded and irrational, Jewish institutions which are humanistic and progressive for Jews—and here Said cites the kibbutz, the desire to take in immigrants, and the Law of Return—are "precisely, determinedly inhuman" for Palestinians (*Question* 88). By Judaizing territory, even with a European and progressive sensibility, Said contends that the Jews at the same time de-Arabize the same territory and produce a contradiction of massive proportions between the assertion of innocence and the practice of politics

What follows is Said's charge that those who refuse to face these contradictions have become, in the terminology of Antonio Gramsci, "experts in legitimation," that is "dishonest and irrational despite their protestations on behalf of wisdom and humanity." Describing this shift in Jewish sensibilities—and those non-Jews who are equally uncritical of Israel—as "one of the most frightening cultural episodes of the century," Said names some of those who function as experts in legitimation, including Senator Daniel Patrick Moynihan and the novelist Saul Bellow, but most startling is the name of the Jewish philosopher and binationalist Martin Buber. Said cites Buber as approving, or at least not protesting, the story told to him of Israeli soldiers who in the 1956 war with Egypt were ordered to kill any Egyptian soldiers who became prisoners. When Buber was told of the difficulty that Israeli soldiers had in carrying out the order—a difficulty with reference only to the Jewish soldier's internal sensibility rather than the agony and humanity of the Egyptian soldiers who were executed—Buber spoke of the greatness of the story rather than the horror of the executions. Said, who characterizes Buber somewhat sarcastically as "moral philosopher, humane thinker, former binationalist," makes clear the transposition of Jewish thought in the context of empowerment: Jewish vision is clouded by an internal reference point and dramatic narrative that leaves others outside, diminished, peripheral actors in a drama that Jews narrate. There is a blindness in the experts of legitimation, a necessary blindness that once afflicted those who consigned Jews to the status of victim. Buber exemplifies this transition, for the discussion of these executions occurred in 1962 less than twenty-five years after Buber was expelled from Nazi Germany (*Question* 113).

Said addresses the fact that Zionism and Israel have as their primary victims the Palestinians and the Arab world, but other victims are also to be found, including Jews who dull their intellectual ability to legitimate actions that once adversely impacted their own community. Or perhaps better stated, Jews now hone their intellectual ability to conceal rather than expose, to cover-up rather than enlighten, to participate in an intellectual game that such thinkers as Marx, Freud, and Levi-Strauss once subverted. Those thinkers and activists who speak out against injustice around the world—for example, in the 1970s, human rights abuses in Argentina, Chile, and South Africa—are silent about preventive detention, torture, population transfer, and deportations of Palestinians. This silence is a complicity, to be sure, but it also amounts to an act of aggression within the Middle East and in areas of the world, especially the West, where the Palestinian cause and narrative is diminished and demonized.

Jews and the Ideology of Difference

Said understands that the discourse and power that displaces his people and seeks their disappearance is not solely sponsored by reactionary or even conservative elements, but often is a liberal undertaking. In one sense the conservative elements are easier to confront and expose because of their jingoistic Americanism or overt racism. The liberal speaks in more sophisticated terms, travels in circles where jingoism and racism are frowned upon and condemned, and typically leans toward internationalism and empowerment of oppressed peoples. In fact, the peculiar aspect of the question of Palestine is that it is seen differently than other struggles and has difficulty claiming its rightful place in the solidarity network often frequented by progressive thinkers and activists, among whom are many Jews. Not only has this had a deleterious effect on the actual struggle of Palestinians to reestablish Palestine, it has also had an almost catastrophic effect on the formation of Palestinian identity, at least in the West.

This is the reason for Said's strong and ironic description of Buber, but closer to his new home in the West there are other contemporary Jews who figure prominently in his later, more polemical interventions. Among those whom Said singles out for special approbation are the Orientalist Bernard Lewis and the ethicist Michael Walzer. With regard to Lewis, who attempts to sum up the Arab world for his Western readers as never-changing and mired in mythology, Said writes that he is a "perfect exemplification of the academic whose work purports to be liberal objective scholarship but is in reality very close to being propaganda *against* his subject material" (*Orientalism* 316). In an exchange with Walzer, whose book-length analysis of the Exodus is triumphal toward others who the Israelites ultimately vanquished and is profoundly Western in orientation, claiming, among other things, that the Exodus legend is Western, liberating, this-worldly and linear over against other ideologies that have the opposite origins, values, and results, Said writes as one on the other side of the Exodus tradition—if you will, as a Canaanite. Noting Walzer's reading of Exodus as a contemporary one whose purpose is to place contemporary Jewry and especially Israel as a flowering of this tradition, Said responds in the context of the Exodus story with contemporary import. "But the one thing I want Walzer to remember," Said writes,

> ...is that the more one shores up the sphere of Exodus politics the more likely it is that the Canaanites on the outside will resist and try to penetrate the walls banning them from the goods of what is, after all, partly their world too. The strength of the Canaanite, that is the exile position, is that being defeated and "outside," you can perhaps more easily feel compassion, more easily call injustice, more easily speak directly and plainly of all oppression, and with less difficulty try to understand (rather than mystify or occlude) history and equality" ("Michael Walzer" 105).

Said outlines the underlying sensibility to this liberal discourse in his essay "An Ideology of Difference," written in the wake of Israel's invasion of Lebanon. In some ways, the question Said raises—how Jews can hold fast to a notion of Israel's innocence and mission when its behavior contradicts these notions—is the same question found in his earlier writing, but now more sharply honed. It is almost as if the sheer blatant quality of Israel's behavior engages Said's sensibility, or perhaps the contradictions, known by Palestinians since the founding of Israel, are now more identifiable in the public discourse of the West. If Jews were justified in their need for a state, thus framing the 1948 War as an example of a struggle defying the odds of history and geography, and the 1967 War could be celebrated as a miraculous response to the Holocaust and final return to the Jerusalem, what could be said about the invasion of Lebanon and the bombing of Beirut? Could Lebanon be seen as a defensive war, one fought against great odds and only with the most basic necessity? How could this war be justified within the Western and Jewish narrative? How would the experts in legitimation place the war in its proper context? Or would the truth finally be told and if so how would it be told? Would the invasion of Lebanon become a place of denial, or be admitted as a transgression to keep the larger denial in place, or would the invasion become a place of reckoning, and if so, what might that place look like for the West, for Jews, for Israel, and for Palestinians ("Ideology")?

Cuddihy's shift in sensibility, his labeling of the "Wieselian bolus," comes in the wake of the invasion of Lebanon as well. Cuddihy's understanding of Jewish intellectuals as a subversive force and their movement to one of defensive maneuvering is accompanied by his sense that the Jewish use of chosenness, already secularized in the 20th century and used as a wedge to enter modernity while retaining a particularity unrecognized by non-Jews, is now attached to the Holocaust and Israel. Therefore the argument for the Holocaust as unique and Israel as innocent has a latent, unannounced quality and the assertion of Jewish chosenness, though framed in fine and logical arguments, is unavailable for rational critique. In essence a religious assertion is promulgated with professional and academic learning behind it, as Said points out, with the power of the university, the social sciences, and the state behind it.

Said focuses on this point of chosenness in the theological realm as the positing of "difference." The translation of this theological concept to the actualities of Israel is impossible for Said to understand through reason because it proposes a unique bond to the land of Palestine/Israel, "distinguishing Jews from all other peoples." Jews are somehow different from others in an essentialist manner, always and everywhere, and thus those who are not Jewish are posited as "radically *other*, fundamentally and constitutively different." Policies in Israel are based on that understanding as fact established beyond argument. Thus land is reserved for Jews only and held in trust for the Jewish people; even the kibbutz, the herald of European socialist liberation, is only for Jews. Within this understanding separation is not racism—hence the outcry against the United Nation's resolution that asserts Zionism as a type of racism—and the policy of separation is rarely argued and more often assumed. Even the peace movement in Israel assumes elements of this ideology of difference, and thus in Said's view helps perpetuate the political and state forces which, despite their protest, carry out this ideology. So, for example, Peace Now, an Israeli peace movement formed in the wake of the invasion of Lebanon, actually prevents a "true critique" of Israel from taking place, at least one that touches the essence of the dispute between Israelis and Palestinians and its possible resolution. The ideological premises that Zionism acts out toward the Palestinians—the origins of Palestinian displacement, the colonization of Palestine, the creation of Israeli identity in the negation of Palestinian identity—all remain untouched in the narrative of the peace movement.

In some ways, the articulation of the need for peace and the belated recognition of Palestinian nationality and rights preserves the ideology of difference and thus allows the essential division of Jews and Palestinians in thought and practice to continue. A false symmetry is asserted by those who ostensibly argue for peace: "In the first place, the conflict between Palestinian non-Jew and Israeli Jew were never discussed in the theoretical or philosophic terms that might have elucidated its core as ideology imposed upon a 'different' (i.e., non-Jewish) population" ("Ideology" 88). Alternating between discussing Palestinians in pragmatic terms (let us forget history and just solve the contemporary problem) and essentialist terms (the division between Jew and Palestinian is to be taken for granted, otherwise a threat of displacing Jews is evident), Said feels that both understandings conclude with

> Zionists berating Palestinians for not being forthcoming enough, for not recognizing Israel, for not renouncing violence, for not being like Peace Now, as if all of these things were equal in magnitude to the destruction of Palestinian society and the continued ethnocide waged by the Israeli government, in possession of all the land and all the weapons, against the Palestinian people (99).

False symmetry denies the damage done to Palestinians and other Arabs, in this case Lebanese civilians, but it is also denies the very rights Jewish liberals and progressives are now ready to recognize. The recognition itself is predicated on Jewish assumptions and needs, and Said illustrates this by the insistence of many Jews, including Michael Walzer, on denigrating the leadership that Palestinians recognize as their own. Palestinians are thus recognized *and* dismissed at the same time, both defined within a Jewish framework. Analyzing the war in Lebanon as an aberration from the pristine history of Israel, hence articulating a desire to jettison the present war and return to an innocent Israel, is itself part of the denial of Palestinian history and aspiration *and* part of the conundrum unto which Jews have fallen. For Said it is only by recognizing that Israel has always been and continues to be a disaster for the Palestinian people that the hypocrisy of Jewish thought can be exposed and the possibility of Jewish practice can undergo a radical change. By understanding this thought and action as the ideology of difference, no way out is allowed. Instead a sophisticated and circular level of argumentation jettisons insight for a moral posture that reality cannot justify.

"Difference, in short, can become an ideological infection and a generalized *trahison des clercs*," Said writes, especially when it becomes a cover to prevent the understanding of massive socio-economic and political problems (105). Fraud, deceit and utter contempt for the truth are the results of difference when reified in commentary on questions that are diverse and interconnected. Zionism is not the only ideology to suffer such truncation, to be sure, and, according to Said, Palestinians must be wary of the same trap, that is "essentializing" Israel, Zionists and Jews, and thus imputing to them unchangeable characteristics. Israel and Zionism are not stable and essentialized objects anymore than Palestine and Palestinians are, and the appearance of draft resistance, an incipient civil rights movement, public debate and ongoing historical revision, are all real efforts by Jews to come to grips with this history. There are Jewish figures who honestly grapple with Israel, Noam Chomsky and Israel Shahak preeminent among them, and Said feels that the common humanity of Jews and Palestinians will always assert itself, at least on the margins of personal and public discourse. The task is to continue to hammer away at the ideologues who mask their chosenness argument in political speech that legitimates injustice. In fact, the challenge is less to dispute difference, though on close examination any detailed definition of difference is difficult, if not impossible, to define, but to deny difference a political meaning and especially political power. One can be for difference and at the same time be against "rigidly enforced and political separation" of population groups (93). As Said writes with regard to the Palestinian argument: "Not only is it manifestly the case that different national, ethnic, and religious groups exist, but no one has the inherent right to use 'difference' as an instrument to relegate the rights of others to an inferior or lesser status" (87). Palestinians have learned this prohibition not only in the face of Israel, but also in their experience with Arab states that similarly essentialize Palestinians through ideology and practical politics. The reality of life is different and this is what must be emphasized in the coming years: that far from separation and purity, life actually involves "mixing or crossing-over, of stepping beyond boundaries, which are more creative human activities than staying inside rigidly policed borders" (89–90). To raise these questions is existentially important to Palestinians in their struggle to overcome their defeat and to Jews who ultimately must overcome their victory, which on the moral level is also a defeat. Indeed a new logic is needed if Jews and Palestinians are to live together with respect, justice, and peace. Said defines this logic as one where "'difference' does not entail 'domination'" (106).[6]

In 1988, three years after Said's essay on difference, Daniel and Jonathan Boyarin responded with an essay seeking a new level of dialogue. The Boyarins are Jewish scholars active in Jewish affairs, the former, at that time, living in Israel, the latter in the United States; both are affiliated with progressive Jewish politics and have substantive questions about Israeli policies. Further, both realize that Said's challenge to Jews and Israel is important to engage, to affirm at some points and dispute at others. Their argument is sophisticated and nuanced: on the question of racism for example, Said's discussion of Israeli apartheid is challenged with the following statement: "Apartheid is a racist ideology *tout court*; Zionism is an ideology that has racist aspects and effects, and also is a response to racism" (629). Though apartheid and Zionism share some common roots, the difference with Zionism is that it is a flawed response to oppression in Europe and, unlike apartheid in South Africa, it is possible for Zionism to be purified of its racist aspects. To see Zionism as unable to be cleansed of racism, as the brothers Boyarin claim Said is in danger of positing, is to become part of a "totalizing thrust toward the utter delegitimization of Zionism" (631). In their view Said stops short in his analysis and simplifies the difficult position of Jews vis-a-vis the West and Israel itself. Though for the Boyarins Israel is deeply problematic as the post-genocide embodiment of Jewish identity, Israel remains important because "Jews have been victimized in ways analogous (though obviously not identical, and the difference once again must be specified) to the victimization of Palestinians" (632). As Jewish nationalists, who believe that Zionism is a national liberation movement for Jews and who respect other national movements of liberation, including the Palestinian national movement, the Boyarins believe that Said shortchanges the desire of Jews for a homeland where Jewish renewal and cultural development can take place alongside Palestinian renewal and cultural development in their homeland. Thus difference can be respected and projected in its own spheres, Jewish and Palestinian, without denigrating the other. Therefore it is possible while critiquing Zionism to see the possibility of a commitment to Zionism entailing a commitment to Palestine: for the Boyarins such a commitment is "a direct consequence of Zionism properly understood" (627).

Said's response is written against the backdrop of the Palestinian intifada and the brutal repression of this movement of national liberation by the Israelis. For Said, the "Wieselian bolus" identified by Cuddihy had already issued into a Walzerian jumble where the history of the victor is claimed as a passport for the victim to oppress another people, and here, in the midst of this continuing and escalating oppression, the Boyarins, brothers whose intellect and active life are committed to the left, are engaged in a further act of symmetry. Beginning with the bold statement that they are "fully committed to national liberation for the Palestinian people" as part of their commitment to Zionism, and ending with the three interrelated issues that fuel their argument—Israeli repression of the Palestinians, the historical predicament of the Jewish people, and the Jewish struggle for self-determination—Said is almost overcome with the self-referential aspect of their argument. In five pages of closely reasoned and carefully worded text, the Boyarins manage to traverse the entirety of the struggle that has been waged for almost a century, explaining and committing themselves to both Jews and Palestinians in the process. To the point that historically the Zionist movement was one of liberation because there were no other historically feasible alternatives at the time, Said asks if this is "somehow to mitigate the suffering imposed by Jews on non-Jews and obligates us always to recall and write extensively about the travails of Europe" ("Response" 635). To the Boyarins sense that Said does not deal sufficiently with anti-Semitism, seeing it as a subordinate term in the formulation of his argument, Said responds that this sensibility is "staggering in its impropriety," especially at this moment:

> Can they not get it into their heads that as Palestinians, whose total dispossession and daily—I repeat, daily—torture, murder, and mass oppression by "the state of the Jewish people" occurs even as the Boyarins speak, we are not always compelled to think of the former suffering of the Jewish people. Can you imagine the brothers Boyarin standing next to the residents of Beita as their houses were being blown up by the Israeli army, and saying to them, "It would help you to know and remember that the Jews who are now killing you were once cruelly and unfairly killed too"? Or consoling the parents of a Palestinian child just shot by an Israeli soldier by saying that the soldier may have had relatives who were exterminated by the Nazis (635–636).

Said concludes strongly by asking how the Boyarins can write these things, as if "dialogue with the Palestinians was completely separable from the outrages taking place in the Occupied Territories." Said's criticism of Jewish intellectuals remains in place: "What they cannot accept is that the Palestinian and Israeli positions are not symmetrical today, and that whatever the horror of Jewish suffering in the past it does not excuse, abrogate, or exonerate the practices of the *Jewish* state against the Palestinian people" (636).

The Jewish Assimilation to Power

With the essay on difference and the response to the Boyarins, Said's discussion of Zionism and Israel and the role of Jewish intellectuals with regard to both comes full circle. His two important insights—that Jewish intellectuals have, in the main, become experts in legitimation, and that the ideology of difference, no matter how carefully disguised and argued, is ultimately an assertion of chosenness reinforced with the apparatus of the state of Israel—are clearly and forcefully enunciated. For the most part, and in light of his experience and that of the Palestinian people, Said's tone is analytical, remarkably restrained, even. Said's anger as seen in his response to Walzer and the Boyarins is born of commitment to his own people; at only one other point does Said demonstrate such anger, and that is in response to Palestinian leadership signing and implementing the Oslo accords. What Cuddihy chides the Jewish community for—a lack of reciprocity, Said fulfills in the Oslo era. In light of his essays and editorials since 1993, Said's honesty in addressing the Jewish people becomes even clearer: power and the abuse of power, the necessity of intellectuals to honestly evaluate that power regardless of where it emanates from, is Said's hallmark. When he feels that his own people are being neglected or abused by their own leadership, he is forthright, rigorous, and vigilant in the same tone and manner as when he criticizes the abuse of Jewish power. Even in the most tenuous of situations, where Israel clearly has the upper-hand, there is a responsibility to refuse to be experts in legitimation and to refuse the ideology of difference that blinds one from the follies, shortsightedness, and corruption of power. By refusing to essentialize the Palestinian cause, by airing his critique of the Palestinian leadership in exactly the same way he has encouraged Jews to do, and, in doing so, jeopardizing his standing among Palestinians and Palestinian leadership, Said embodies his ideas in a way that removes them from any hint of suspicion of ulterior motives or special interests.[7]

In the entire body of Said's work there is never a hint of overt or covert anti-Semitism, nor even the construction of an argument that cleverly conceals such a view. From the beginning of Said's writing on the subject of Orientalism and Palestine, his sensitivity to Jews and Judaism is evident, along with a willingness to take both seriously in the forms that impact the Western perception of the East and the Israeli perception of Palestinians. While the dominant practitioners of Orientalism, at least historically, are not Jewish, those who are Jewish are analyzed like the others and without rancor. Zionism and its adherents are criticized for their practical policies and the ideas which legitimate them; mystification, whether in charges of Jewish aggressiveness or conspiracy, are, in Said's work, completely absent. Rather than being absent for strategic purposes, however—for example to avoid aligning oneself with a fringe anti-Semitism in America or to gain a better hearing in a context which is openly pro-Israel and, at least to some extent, though not without ambivalence, pro-Jewish—Said's critique of paternalism and injustice is highly principled and biased only in the most natural of ways. Perhaps because of his disposition, upbringing, context, and character, Said seems to identify with those on the other side of power and clearly would, were the situation different, identify with Jewish suffering.

Because Said deals with Jews, Zionism, and Israel in a principled manner and in a broader framework of ethics and justice, he addresses the Jewish people and Jewish history in a variety of ways. First and foremost, Said decenters Jews and Jewish experience by looking at Orientalism from the perspective of the East and the West and by looking at Palestine and Palestinians from the perspective of their history and aspirations. The question of Palestine arises in history for Palestinians because every people in each generation must search for their identity, and the recent experience of dispossession and diaspora demands a new commitment to that search. That the dispossession has occurred at the hands of Jews with the support of the West is a detail of absolute importance because it frames a concrete context for the Palestinian struggle, not because of any intrinsic Jewish sensibility or blame. No doubt, if another people had dispossessed the Palestinians, the particulars would be different but the challenge would be similar: the reconstruction of Palestine and Palestinian identity in the wake of catastrophe.

Decentering Jewish experience and history is important for Palestinians in that they recognize their struggle as against invaders and occupiers rather than against a mythicized community, thereby refusing to essentialize Jews as Palestinians have been essentialized.

Edward Said and the Future of the Jewish People

At the same time, decentering Jews is an important contribution to the Jewish community because it reverses the blindness that the ideology of difference demands. For Said, though Zionism and Israel are *the* problematic for the question of Palestine, it is simply because of the power of the West and Israel at this time in history. Though Jews do indeed have a particular and special history in Said's eyes, this lies outside his interest. In fact, that Jews hold this view of their history, that Jewish history is central and unique, is contradicted by the very normality of their abuse of power and the attempt to hide that abuse. If there are to be any claims about Jewish history, they will now have to proceed through the filter of this aggression. Said neither affirms nor denies Jewish self-understanding. Rather he challenges it by refusing abstraction and by paying attention to the details of Jewish history vis-a-vis his own people. That there is no other agenda in Said's analysis is problematic for Jewish intellectuals because it does not allow a retreat into a specialness via negation of Jewishness or exaggeration through the myth of the Jew. Jews in the guise of Zionism and Israel insofar as they operate as experts in legitimation must be opposed just as any others who dispossess and legitimate dispossession must be opposed. If, for Cuddihy, the attempt on the part of Jews to have both power and innocence is irritating, the opposition to dispossession that is caused and furthered by Jews without any other motive or agenda is confusing, even disorienting, as it undermines the very concepts which Jews, often unconsciously, employ. It cuts to the very heart of Jewish identity.

Whereas Cuddihy uncovers the foundations of Jewish identity as Jews move in and through modernity, Said probes the reality of Jewish practice in the context of communal empowerment. For the most part, Cuddihy analyzes the movement of Jews into the twentieth century; Said traces their trajectory into the twenty-first century. In some sense Jews are in both of these contexts at the same time, and here is a difficulty that has two aspects: an unconscious and unintended suspension between differing and to some extent overlapping situations—emancipation and empowerment—and a conscious desire to maintain innocence within empowerment as a strategy of self-interest and lack of concern for others. Whatever the instances, and in some cases there is a mixture of the unconscious and intended, Said calls Jewish intellectuals and public actors to account, to realize the change in Jewish status, influence and power and to respond accordingly. In lieu of this, Jewish intellectuals at least have the responsibility to end the moralizing from and emphasis on their suffering and to begin to simply state the facts of Jewish empowerment boldly. It is almost as if Said is challenging Jews who believe in the dispossession of Palestinians as a right to say so boldly: say that Israel is right in humiliating, torturing, and murdering Palestinians, and that anyone who criticizes those policies should be fought to the end. Is this not the policy of Israel and the Jewish establishment from 1948 to the present?

For Jews to admit this power and its use, and for Jewish intellectuals to admit their role as experts in legitimation, is perforce to surrender on the question of difference. Jewish soldiers are like any other soldiers, even in the 1967 War, and in a larger sense a Jewish state is like any other state. The military and the state, especially one marked by colonialism and expansion, needs intellectuals and theologians to legitimate its policies. Thus Jewish thinkers like Bernard Lewis and Michael Walzer are intellectuals in service to the state as were many intellectuals who supported governments that displaced and murdered Jews. Said does not articulate this connection as Noam Chomsky does, but the implications of his analysis are clear. As a Palestinian, the aggression of Israel and those who justify its policies—even, as Said points out, by maintaining the overall thrust of the state through selective criticism and false symmetry—are agents of doom that must be confronted and struggled against. The agony of Jewish intellectuals and their often twisted arguments are, as Said suggests in his response to the Boyarins, ultimately irrelevant and absurd.

If the entry point of Jews into modernity is an intellectual and ethical probity, thereby allowing the claim of distinctiveness in secular terms, what is left of that distinctiveness when Jewish intellectuals are found, like many non-Jewish intellectuals, to be in service to the state, and when Jews who wield power are found, like non-Jews who wield power, to be unjust, coercive and self-aggrandizing? If there is no difference, is there any content to Jewishness in the contemporary world? Said's challenge is deepened because, though born outside of the West, he, like Jewish intellectuals before him, has penetrated the West and made a home for himself at the center of Western intellectual life. Said thus is an outsider/insider who has experienced Jewish power in its raw and objective rather than distant and mythical reality. Contrary to the assertion of anti-Semitic propagandists in Europe, Jews did not control European life or participate in a global conspiracy to control the world's wealth, but Jews *did* (and *do*) displace Palestinians and destroy Palestine. Jews are in control of a state that sponsors, among other things, a systematic policy of settlement, expropriation of land, torture and creation of refugees. In Said's generation, a Palestinian diaspora has been created by Jews in Israel with the support of Jews around the world. Though Jews have continually and with great difficulty fought the myth of anti-Semitism, Said presents, indeed embodies, a nightmare of epic proportions, because his criticism is of a Jewish power that is abusive *and* real.

Thus Said presents Jews with the other side of Jewish life in our time. The consequences of that presentation are intended to unmask oppressive power, and unintended to challenge chosenness, uniqueness, and ethical character articulated in a secular and modern form. Once that critique is accepted, the consequences are immediate and long-range. As Said remarks in his exchange with Walzer, instead of demanding their place in the West as if nothing has happened in Jewish history since the Holocaust except the lamentable need to defend Jews against new enemies, Jews should express compassion and atonement for what they have done and what has been done in the name of the Jewish people. This compassion and atonement means, among other things, an honest confession that goes beyond what is normally found in intellectual discourse and a desire to rectify as much as possible the dispossession of the Palestinian people. To do so is to highlight the truth of what has occurred, a rarity to be sure, but a truth that has been articulated by those Jewish intellectuals and activists who have broken through the acceptable discourse and suffered at the hands of the very thinkers who are now called to confession. Confessing is an opening to the Palestinians *and* to the Jewish tradition in pursuit of justice and to a renewed sense of dignity and honest discourse. It entails the end of privileged testimony; the ideology of difference would be disconnected from the state and the power it wields. Instead of defending Jews from the vicissitudes of history, understandable in the wake of Jewish suffering, Jews reenter the risk of history—of "mixing"—beginning in the reconfiguration of Israel/Palestine (Said, "Exchange: Exodus" 259).

Without specifying this trajectory, and always in a completely secular manner, Said asks for a decentering of Jewish experience and the re-embrace of an authentic diaspora sensibility in the West and in Israel/Palestine. By pulling back the "curtain of sentimentality and casuistic argument drawn around Israeli-Zionist brutality and inhumanity," the "only hope," a community of Palestinians, Zionist and non-Zionist Jews, can take root on the land of historical Palestine. The choice of prolonging the now mutual antipathy between Jews and

Palestinians inherent in Israel's exercise of power is challenged by a vision that refuses to "privilege the experience or the contemporary situation" of either peoples (Said, "Response" 637; "Ideology of Difference" 106). Difference is acknowledged as a bridge to sharing insight; the rigid enforcement of separation, so necessary for a state that claims to embody the essence of Jewish history, can be relaxed. Stepping beyond the boundaries of the known where the more creative human activities are found is then a challenge rather than a danger. One wonders, and again Said does not address this directly, whether this crossing-over is the way out of the isolation that many Jews feel and Jewish intellectuals often operate from. The shadow of the Holocaust, used as a protection but also deeply felt, may then become more distant in time and feeling. To realize and admit the capabilities of Jews to suffer *and* to cause suffering and as intellectuals to subvert *and* legitimate injustice, to experience the Jewish claim on the world to be just *and* unjust, all depending on the historical era and context, is to realize that being a victim or a victor is not pre-ordained. Whether underneath or riding the wave of history there are situations that can be fought and refused in light of the possibility of an interdependent journey with others. Seeing power as univocal, either being without it or having it, is the way of legitimation and difference as a survival of power or use of power over against the "other." Seeing power as an avenue to interdependence, to mutuality in politics and thought, is a way of using difference to heighten and deepen a joint enterprise where no one is alone and where the infringement of one is the infringement of all.

Where does this humility and confession lead? What if the Jewish state became a joint homeland of Jews and Palestinians? Would the Holocaust as a central aspect of Jewish identity then recede? Would Jews in the West care about a homeland that increasingly oriented itself to its actual geography and history? If Jews saw Zionism from the perspective of Jewish history and its victims, would the Jewish claim of uniqueness and ethical character suffer a death blow? After the mobilization of the Jewish community around the world in terms of Holocaust and Israel, what would become the center of Jewish identity in their stead? Are the Holocaust and Israel, the secular equivalent of Jewish religiosity, the only religiosity that can be embraced by the majority of Jews in contact with modernity? Would the head-long flight to rescue Jewish history from the prospects of annihilation in the Nazi era then fail in an era of peace and normality where Jews have no reason to embrace the Jewishness they may have left anyway, except for the Nazis and the founding of Israel? Could the fear of giving up the Holocaust and Israel as the center, twinned and invoked together, be a fear that there is nothing compelling left of Jewish life and that without this center the final assimilation is at hand?

One wonders if Said's statement to Walzer—that from the position of exile ideologies of difference are a "great deal less satisfactory than impure genres, people, activities; that separation and discrimination are often not as estimable as connecting and crossing over"—can be received as a truth about life in general and still remain within the formative identity of Jewish history as carried forward in the modern world. Or do Walzer and the brothers Boyarin fear this sensibility, struggle against it, and in different ways attempt to argue their way out or around it? That is why in the end Said needs to shout out the reality of Jewish life in its empowerment, distinguish its intellectual argument from the reality of its power to displace, and expose it in its sometimes ludicrous sensibility. When Said confronts the Boyarins with the imagined statement of Jews explaining to Palestinians who have just had their house blown up by the Israeli army—"It would help you to know and remember that the Jews who are now killing you were once cruelly and unfairly killed too"—the absolute absurd reality of such a statement in the face of that suffering nonetheless rings true ("A Canaanite Reading" 106).

As much as Said's sophisticated analysis, this statement of creative license resounds in the history of the Jewish people. It is a final caution, indeed statement of fact, that Jews are not pure or innocent or even different, and that the assimilation which Jewish thinkers as diverse as Walzer and the Boyarins fight has already occurred. That assimilation is to power and the injustice that results from its abuse.

The Future of the Jewish People

Those who seek to chart a future for the Jewish people must start with this startling fact that Said confronts us with: Jewish assimilation to the state and its culture has already occurred. The trajectory analyzed by Cuddihy has come full circle, and the intellectual power of subversion has become the intellectual power of legitimation. In an era when Jews are called upon to build and defend the state, Jewish participation and dependence on state culture is expected as the norm. In this sense, and in the span of less than a century, Jews have moved from a pariah people to a people commemorated, celebrated, and empowered in the West and in Israel. The normalization of the Jewish people, a goal of

Zionism and even some Holocaust theologians, has taken place. In a symbolic and literal sense, Jews are now among the nations.

Who could fault Jews for such a desire, especially after the travails of their history? Has there ever been empowerment without bloodshed? Should Jews be denied empowerment or called to a purity that no one else can claim? Does the need to survive override the ethical idea, religious or secular? Now among the nations, what is the responsibility of a Jewish state to others? Is it any greater than other nation-states? Does one expect a Jewish state to listen to the cries of its victims or even its own dissenters more than other nation-states? On the practical level, is the struggle within Israel now, especially after the post-1967 expansion of the state, a civil rights struggle seeking equal rights for Palestinians within the borders of what was once historic Palestine? Has the battle shifted from one of justice and accountability, and thus the ethical imperative to do what is right and redress the grievances of those who have been wronged, to acknowledging that the struggle has been lost and the new entity is here to be reckoned with in a completely different manner? The language of innocence and redemption is lost to be sure, but is the language of identity and struggle already dated as well? Said is quite right in demonstrating that Jewish discourse in its assimilation to power has lost its foundation and substance, but has the language of resistance, in light of the continuing inability to stop the expansion of Israel, also lost its bearings? Do the two questions, the Jewish question and the question of Palestine, remain in force, or have they been transformed in ways that are as yet without articulation? If this is so, if the Jewish and Palestinian questions within an expanded Israeli state have become one question, what will become of the Jewish and Palestinian diaspora communities? How will they form their questions, to what foundations will they look, and how will their identities maintain a substantive focus?

Said's disdain for the "pure" and his option for "mixing" is important here, as is his understanding that the future of Jews and Palestinians in the land will be shared. His distinction between secular and religious criticism, articulated in *The World, the Text, and the Critic*, is also important. For Said secular criticism is the continual opening to reality, especially the opening provided by distance to origins, contemporary claims, and power. By introducing circumstance and distinction where conformity and belonging reign, a distance is projected from whence criticism is born. This distance is from the ivory tower *and* from movements demanding absolute allegiance. Nonetheless there is a closeness to reality which portends and involves commitments, a state of vigilance which Said defines in this way: "To stand between culture and system is therefore to stand *close to*... a concrete reality about which political, moral, and social judgments have to be made and, if not only made, then exposed and demystified" (27). Thus secular criticism deals with "local and worldly situations" and is opposed to the "production of massive hermetic systems," a production Said identifies as religious in its orientation. Consciously or unconsciously, religious criticism reinforces these hermetic systems by indulging in "unthinkability, undecidability, and paradox together with a remarkable consistency of appeals to magic, divine ordinance, or sacred texts" (291–292). The secular deals with a "knowledge of history, a recognition of the importance of social circumstance, an analytical capacity for making distinctions," all of which trouble the religious who long for the acceptable, the known, and the comfortable (30). The secular is close to the world as it is and how it might be, while the religious create a world above reality and seek to protect it through retreat and mystification. The tension that Said sees in the world—between filiation (birth, nationality, profession) and affiliation (social and political conviction, economic and historical circumstances, voluntary effort and willed deliberation)—is one that needs to be struggled with rather than resolved. Closure is a form of mystification just as the pretense to be without roots and context is. Connection *and* distance, a sense of identity *and* openness, fosters criticism that is intelligent *and* compassionate. Because of this, secular criticism is life-enhancing and opposed to all forms of tyranny and injustice: such criticism acts to develop space where alternative acts and intentions can flourish. In Said's view, this is the path of advancing human freedom as a fundamental human obligation.

How can one remain close to the Jewish community, especially its normative discourse, and remain attentive to the facts as they have been and continue to unfold in Israel? Said's sense of the intellectual as oppositional—as one who refuses a patriotism which is blind and blinding, who is open to the diversity of life especially when a univocal commitment is demanded, and whose larger commitment is to humanity even when group survival is invoked as an emotional brake on intelligence—draws one to an exilic position. Could it be that Jews are called to side with the Canaanites, participate in a Canaanite reading of contemporary reality, to be among the Canaanites *as a sign of fidelity to Jewish history and contemporary reality?* It may that Jews who have opposed the experts in legitimation and use of difference as a form of domination are in fact in exile. Still, many have argued their exilic position as way of confronting the community, calling it to an alternative sensibility, and hoping that in doing this they will once again join the ranks of the community in good standing. Though understandable and in many cases laudable, this position may itself become a form of mystification whereby the ethical propensity of Jewish life can be reasserted *while the abuse of power continues*. The confrontation with state power is thus affirmed *and* jettisoned at the same time. A new comfort level can be achieved, a new innocence proclaimed, a renewal of Jewish life celebrated as the Palestinian diaspora grows and Israel reaches ever deeper into the last reservoir of Palestinian life and culture. This, too, is an assimilation to power by which celebration of renewal occurs in the protective embrace of the state even as displacement and destruction continue. Thus claiming exile is not enough. The rigors of exile must be attended to so that exile itself does not become part of the pattern of domination.

In our time, and for the foreseeable future, the exile of Jews and Palestinians will continue and perhaps even escalate. The foundations of Jewish life, already seriously undermined, will continue to erode until the exilic situation will become the norm. Of course nation-states can operate, at least for a time, on coercion and bribery, and there are intellectuals enough who will sell their thought and be honored for it. They will claim continuity with the Jewish tradition, dismissing the exiles as those who threaten to unlock the gates of power. If it is true that we have entered the terminal phase of Jewish life, if indeed we have come to the *end of Jewish history as we have known it*, this does not mean that the rhetoric of Jewishness or Judaism will grow faint. Just the opposite. The voice of Jewish life resounds as never before in history and it does not seem to matter, at least to those in power, that it returns as an empty echo. That emptiness is deafening both for those on the other side of Jewish power and for Jews who through birth and commitment seek a fidelity now shrouded in darkness. It is strange, perhaps, though on deeper reflection absolutely fitting, that a modern Canaanite, Edward Said, lights that darkness with his own intelligence and compassion. One wonders if this light will one day become a beacon of recognition and reconciliation for Jews as it has been all these years for his own people.

Notes

[1] I have addressed questions relating to the history of Jewish suffering and ascendancy in the West and empowerment in Israel in *Toward a Jewish Theology of Liberation* (Maryknoll: Orbis, 1987), *Beyond Innocence and Redemption: Confronting the Holocaust and Israeli Power* (San Francisco: HarperCollins, 1990), *Ending Auschwitz: The Future of Jewish and Christian Life* (Louisville: Westminster, 1994), and *Unholy Alliance: Religion and Atrocity in Our Time* (Minneapolis: Fortress, 1997).

[2] For an analysis of Wiesel with regard to the 1967 War, see *Beyond Innocence*, 9–12.

[3] While this shadow of another holocaust can be found in Wiesel and Fackenheim, it also features prominently in the work of the Holocaust theologian Irving Greenberg. Even as late as 1988, in a long essay responding to the Palestinian uprising, Greenberg evokes this possibility. See Irving Greenberg, "The Ethics of Jewish Power," *Perspectives* (New York: National Jewish Center for Learning and Leadership, 1988).

[4] The most recent chronicler of the scope and use of Jewish power in the United States is J. J. Goldberg, *Jewish Power: Inside the American Jewish Establishment* (New York: Addison-Wesley, 1996).

[5] This is what I consider to be the eighth Jewish culture in Jewish history, a concept I develop in my latest book *Jerusalem and the Broken Middle: Embracing the Jewish Covenant at the End of Jewish History* (forthcoming from Fortress Press). For the first seven cultures, see Efraim Shmueli, *Seven Jewish Cultures: A Reinterpretation of Jewish History and Thought* (Cambridge: Cambridge University Press, 1990).

[6] For an interesting early recognition of Chomsky's work see Said's "Chomsky and the Question of Palestine," 323–337. This essay was originally published in the *Journal of Palestine Studies* 4 (Spring 1975).

[7] See a collection of his dissents from the Oslo process in Edward Said, *Peace and Its Discontents: Essays on Palestine in the Middle East Peace Process* (New York: Vintage, 1996).

Works Cited

Abrams, Elliot. *Faith or Fear: How Jews Can Survive in a Christian America*. New York: Free Press, 1987.

Boyarin, Daniel and Jonathan. "An Exchange on Edward Said and Difference II: Toward a Dialogue with Edward Said." *Critical Inquiry* 15 (Spring 1989).

Cuddihy, John Murray. "The Elephant and the Angels; or, The Incivil Irritatingness of Jewish Theodicy," in Robert Bellah and Frederick Greenspahn, eds. *Uncivil Religion: Interreligious Hostility in America*. New York: Crossroad, 1987.

_____. "The Holocaust: The Latent Issue In The Uniqueness Debate," in Philip Gallagher, ed. *Christians, Jews and Other Worlds: Patterns of Conflict*

and Accommodation. New York: University Press of America, 1988.
——. *The Ordeal of Civility: Freud, Marx, Levi-Strauss, and the Jewish Struggle with Modernity*. New York: Dell, 1974.
Fackenheim, Emil. *God's Presence in History: Jewish Affirmations and Philosophical Reflections*. New York: New York University, 1970.
Perlmutter, Nathan and Ruth Ann. *The Real Antisemitism in America*. New York: Arbor House, 1982.
Said, Edward. "An Exchange on Edward Said and Difference III: Response." *Critical Inquiry* 15 (Spring 1989).
——. "An Ideology of Difference." *Critical Inquiry* 12 (September 1985). Rpt. in *The Politics of Dispossession: The Struggle for Palestinian Self-Determination, 1969–1994*. New York: Vintage, 1994.
——. "Michael Walzer's 'Exodus and Revolution': A Canaanite Reading." *Grand Street* 5 (Winter 1986).
——. *Orientalism*. New York: Vintage, 1978.
——. *The Question of Palestine*. New York: Vintage, 1979.
——. *The World, the Text, and the Critic*. Cambridge: Harvard University Press, 1983.
Said, Edward and Michael Walzer. "An Exchange: 'Exodus and Revolution.'" *Grand Street* 5 (Summer 1986): 247–259.

TWO

ON ORIENTALISM

Humanizing the Oriental: Edward Said & Western Scholarly Discourse

Yasmeen Abu-Laban

As someone trained in political science, rather than literary criticism, my text base tends to be items like government documents rather than what is commonly associated with the literary, even if the boundary between art and politics is murky.[1] But as a political scientist my broad interest is in the workings of power, and my aim in this discussion is to relate Edward W. Said's work to the issue of power and to Western scholarly discourse. In speaking of his work in relation to Western scholarly discourse, three distinct though not necessarily mutually exclusive features are suggested:

1) His work challenges Western scholarship regarding the East, and the assumption that the East and its people cannot speak for themselves, cannot understand themselves, and are hopelessly doomed to the base of the global pyramid. His work interrupts the dominant assumptions regarding "the East" and people from "the East";

2) His work provides a critical alternative to mainstream Western scholarship on the East. His work encourages us to listen to the voice of "the Other" and to take responsibility and action in our social and political world (speaking truth to power);

3) His work has catalytic potential for more nuanced scholarship about the West and Western culture. His work can expand our understanding regarding the nature of power by exposing the interconnections between the powerful and the less powerful, and expand our praxis by challenging monolithic and essentialist constructions of either oppressed or oppressor.

My argument then, is that Edward Said's approach can potentiate the study of power. To illustrate this argument, my discussion takes a two-fold approach. First, I highlight how Said's work is of importance across a number of different disciplines. More specifically, one major contribution made by the cross-disciplinary reverberation of his work is to humanize groups that have been dehumanized as a result of historic and contemporary asymmetric relations of power. Second, I address the continued salience of scholarship that masquerades as "knowledge" or "expert opinion" that trades in essentialist and monolithic thinking. As a paradigmatic example of this kind of essentialist scholarship, I will touch upon the recent work of political scientist Samuel Huntington dealing with the so-called "clash of civilizations," and relate that back to the promise of Said's approach for more nuanced scholarship about "the West."

Edward Said and Western Scholarly Discourse

One of the striking features of Said's work is that the pressing import of its challenge, and its weighty presence, goes beyond the discipline of comparative literature in which Professor Said received his training and teaches. As exemplified in different ways and with varying degrees of contestation in industrialized countries, the academy today remains divided by disciplinary borders. But Edward Said's work uniquely demonstrates that these borders are, at least, semi-permeable.

His work has a multidisciplinary following, and provides a common reference point across significant pockets of the humanities and social sciences. This may be related to Said's role in developing literary theory, where the implications have significance for in many fields (for example, the relationship between knowledge and power involves figures such as Nietzsche and Foucault, whose work is also relevant in many fields). As well, Said approaches a text in terms of how it links to the world, and to human and social and political life, thereby bringing out the centrally important questions of unequal power relations and resistance that animate more radical sectors of the academy. In his words:

> The realities of power and authority—as well as the resistances offered by men, women, and social movements to institutions, authorities and orthodoxies—are the realities that make texts possible, that deliver them to their readers, that solicit the attention of critics. I propose that these realities are what should be taken account of by criticism and critical consciousness (The World 5).

Not least, Said's multidisciplinary following may be related to the way in which his approach serves to illuminate the flesh and blood people who have been maligned, unrepresented, or represented in ways that are dehumanizing.

The 1978 publication of *Orientalism* captured these diverse dimensions of Said's appeal in Western scholarship. As he defines it, Orientalism roots itself in the history of the formation of "Europe," and is a manner of thinking and style of scholarship based upon an ontological and epistemological distinction between societies and peoples of "the Orient" (East) and "the Occident" (West). The distinction between "us" "rational," "Christian" Europeans and the "irrational," "Muslim" "others" in essence allowed for the assertion that a European identity is different than (and superior to) that from non-European cultures, and provided the justification for colonialism, and continued dominance by the United States over the Muslim and Arab world in the post war period. For Said, the failure of Orientalism is not only intellectual but human: "...for in having to take up a position of irreducible opposition to a region of the world it considered alien to its own, Orientalism failed to identify with human experience, failed also to see it as human experience" (*Orientalism* 328).

Without doubt, this book's rendering of Orientalist knowledge and scholarship as imperialism drew mixed responses—Orientalist thinker Bernard Lewis, for example, quibbled, to put it mildly, with the thesis in *The New York Review of Books*—but the book has had an important effect on the development of studies on the Middle East in the West. As Sullivan and Ismael observe, the 1978 appearance of *Orientalism* "constitutes an important benchmark in Middle East Studies and the study of the Arab World," precisely because much subsequent work drew from and reacted to the book (x). Hence the contribution of feminist analysts who have highlighted the ways in which Orientalism can take gendered forms. For example, Muslim women have been subjected to similar stereotypes as Muslim men, and also additional stereotypes that mark them as fundamentally different than Western women in their failure to achieve autonomy and social equality. In this sense, they are the "other other."[2]

In addition to studies about the Middle East, *Orientalism* was also to influence developments in the study of colonialism. For example, Williams and Chrisman state: "it is perhaps no exaggeration to say that Edward Said's *Orientalism*... single-handedly inaugurates a new area of academic inquiry: colonial discourse" (5). For this reason, contemporary critics of the book, such as Marxist writer Aijaz Ahmad, have approached the book *Orientalism* with an eye toward its significance as a "modern classic" in the West.

Finally, *Orientalism* is a book that has left a lasting theoretical imprint by virtue of its introduction of the term "Orientalism" with Said's meaning assigned to it, into a shared humanities and social sciences lexicon. In my own discipline of political science, even

Humanizing the Oriental: Edward Said & Western Scholarly Discourse

conservative political philosopher Roger Scruton's *Dictionary of Political Thought* contains the entry "orientalism" and defines it as the term introduced by Edward Said in the book of the same name (397). Roger Scruton's dictionary is illustrative in another way. In distilling and alphabetizing the terms that political scientists ought to know in this dictionary, ironically the entry "orientalism" comes just after the term "oriental despotism." This placement, however unintentional, nonetheless serves as a reminder of how Said's work, while a corrective to Oriental ideas that rest on stereotyped and essentialized ways of speaking about peoples of the East, which in turn rest on inequitable power relations, never obliterated these terms and ways of thinking. I shall return to this point.

To continue on the humanizing theme, Edward Said's 1979 book *The Question of Palestine* expands on the notion of Orientalism to explain the Palestinian cause to an American audience. The emphasis in this book is on humanizing the face of the Palestinian—a strategy that in itself speaks volumes about the absence of informed understanding of the Palestinian position in American political discourse—who else but the most marginalized must vouchsafe their claims by appeals to "label me human"? Taking as its starting point how Palestinians have been hidden, or misrepresented as simply "terrorists," Said underscores the connection between Orientalism and the Zionist settler-colonial project which rested on the dehumanizing erasure of an indigenous population, as contained in an early slogan for the Zionist movement: "a land without a people for a people without a land." As Said notes:

> Most of all, I think, there is the entrenched *cultural* attitude toward Palestinians deriving from age-old Western prejudices about Islam, the Arabs, and the Orient. This attitude, from which in its turn Zionism drew for its view of the Palestinians, dehumanized us, reduced us to the barely tolerated status of a nuisance (*Question* xiv).

As captured in the title of the chapter, "Zionism from the Standpoint of Its Victims," *The Question of Palestine* throws light on the colonial nature of Zionist project and its displacement of Palestinians by uncovering the justness of the Palestinian claim:

> The real strength of the Palestinian is just this insistence on the human being as a detail the detail likely to be swept away in order for a grandiose project to be realized. The Palestinian therefore stands on a small plot of land stubbornly called Palestine, or an idea of peace based neither on a project for transforming people into nonpeople

nor on a geopolitical fantasy about the balance of power, but on a vision of the future accommodating both the peoples with authentic claims to Palestine, not just the Jews (234).

This perspective continues in Edward Said's more recent work, *Peace and Its Discontents*, which although "written from start to finish with an Arab audience in mind" (xxiii), also presents Palestine as "*an idea* that for years galvanized the Arab world into thinking about and fighting for social justice, democracy, and a different kind of future than the one that has been imposed on it by force and by an absence of Arab will" (xxxiii).

While *The Question of Palestine* has the status of being a major academic reference in the study of the Palestinians (see Graham-Brown), in articulating the Palestinian cause and perspective, Said has given at times remarkably personal accounts, including the very painful and moving article in *Harper's* magazine a few years back detailing his own return to the place of his birth. In this way, Edward Said has also placed a face on a cause and people that have carried a cultural deficit in the United States, in a popular magazine that does carry cultural capital.

In *Covering Islam*, originally published in 1981, but out in an updated version in 1997, Said examines the academic and media treatment of Islam. He criticizes the tendency, which he finds escalating since the 1980s, of equating Islam with fundamentalism, and this with a (if not the) major global threat. Thus, reporting on Islam in the United States in particular involves coverage that stereotypes, and consequently covers up, Islam. Instead, Said cautions that just as serious study of Western societies will reveal their complexities, so too should study of Islamic societies:

> What we expect from the serious study of Western societies, with its complex theories, enormously variegated analyses of social structures, histories, cultural formation, and sophisticated languages of investigation, we should also expect from the study and discussion of Islamic societies in the West (*Covering Islam* xvi).

At the heart of Edward Said's call for more sensitivity is a vision based on humanizing as opposed to essentializing Islamic societies:

> By using the skills of a good critical reader to disentangle sense from nonsense, by asking the right questions and expecting pertinent answers, anyone can learn either about "Islam" or the world of Islam and about the men, women and cultures that live within it, speak its languages, breathe its air, produced its histories and societies. At this

point, humanistic knowledge begins and communal responsibility for knowledge begins to be shouldered. I wrote this book to advance that goal (lix).

If we consider such works as *Orientalism, The Question of Palestine,* and *Covering Islam* as a package, the work of Edward Said presents a major challenge to those academics (and reporters), who under the cloak of objectivity, write in stereotyped, essentialist and dehumanizing ways about "the East" (Islam, Palestine, and the Palestinians). Said's work and approach presents an alternative for Western scholarship to consider "the East" and its people and societies in ways other than those that mirror power holders in the West, especially the United States. But of course Said's interventions have not eradicated essentialist and Orientalist ways of thinking. For instance, Bernard Lewis felt compelled to respond by way of critique to the book *Orientalism* in the 1980s, and he also felt compelled to write "The Roots of Muslim Rage" in the 1990s, which Edward Said takes up in the introduction to the new edition of *Covering Islam* as:

> a crude polemic devoid of historical truth, rational argument, or human wisdom. It attempts to characterize Muslims as one terrifyingly collective person enraged at an outside world that has disturbed his primeval calm and unchallenged rule (xxxii).

And it is from Lewis' very gendered account (supposedly as the Muslim male feels he is losing control over the Muslim female, his rage becomes directed at the millennial Judeo-Christian enemy) that the term "clash of civilizations" is introduced, which, as Said also notes, is later appropriated and spun into a larger argument by Samuel Huntington. Turning to Huntington's work is useful as it represents a contemporary paradigm of essentialist thinking in the discipline of political science.

The "Clash of Civilizations" and the Anti-Essentialist Promise of Edward Said

Samuel Huntington is a political scientist at Harvard University, and in 1993 he wrote an article published in the journal *Foreign Affairs* entitled "The Clash of Civilizations" which has been quite widely taken up and discussed in the discipline, and even reprinted in other books. Most political science undergraduates entering a university in the 1990s will graduate having been exposed to this argument. (Indeed, according to Rupert Taylor, as some 75–80 percent of the world's political scientists are in the United States, American developments profoundly shape the discipline internationally (885).) In 1996, Huntington published another article in the same journal entitled, tellingly, "The West Unique, Not Universal." And, to boot, his new book, *The Clash of Civilizations and the Remaking of the World Order,* recapitulates the themes in these two articles.

What Huntington calls "the clash of civilizations," he posits as "the fundamental source of conflict" following the collapse of Communism ("Clash" 22). In Huntington's view, "civilizations" represent "the highest cultural grouping of people and the broadest level of cultural identity" and are defined primarily through religion (24). For Huntington, the clash of civilizations may be characterized as "the West versus the rest," with the rest being further differentiated by greater and lesser degrees of cultural orientation to the explicit yardstick of the Western norm. Hence:

> The obstacles to non-Western countries joining the West vary considerably. They are least for Latin American and East European countries. They are greater for Orthodox countries of the former Soviet Union. They are still greater for Muslim, Confucian, Hindu and Buddhist societies (45).

Yet, ultimately Huntington's specific portrayal rests on the problematic assumption that religious groupings (such as Islam and Christianity) are static, unchanging and all "believers" are dogmatic. There is no place for casual Christians or particularly casual Muslims in this articulation, which belies the lived experience of many people.

Moreover, Huntington's portrayal assumes that the divisions are immutable. This makes it difficult to explain the very evident and very visible uniting of the Papacy and political elites of Muslim countries over opposition to abortion and non-marital cohabitation during the United Nation's 1994 Cairo Conference on Population and Development, an alliance mirrored around similar themes in the 1995 Beijing Conference on Women.[3] Indeed the social control over women would appear a powerful inducement in the international sphere to uniting elites in the governments and the religious groupings that Huntington posits as necessarily opposed.

Huntington's "clash" thesis may be seen to be Orientalist in how it delineates between "us" "Westerners" and "them" "Easterners." It is also a thesis that speaks to the nature of international dynamics today, where, as John Esposito highlights, Islam and the problematization of

Islamic fundamentalism, have been constructed as a global threat in the post-Cold War era. But just as Huntington's work reflects his construction of "the non-West other," it also reflects, as significantly, his construction of "the West."

Subsequent elaboration of the clash argument only reveals more profoundly the deep essentialism accompanying Huntington's emphasis on the "uniqueness" (that is superiority) of the monolithic West over the monolithic rest. Thus, Huntington puts forward a list culled from his reading of history, and we find, that it is only from the particular constellation of Christianity, European languages, separation of church and state, rule of law etc. that the West has taken shape. As a consequence, "Western peoples have far more in common with each other than they have with Asian, Middle Eastern, or African peoples" ("West Unique" 44). And then it all boils down to one single essence. Relying on specifically Anglo-American mythology concerning British constitutional history, and Huntington's own investment in a branch of the discipline of political science that refracts the Anglo-American experience as defining "democracy," Huntington asserts that "The essence of Western culture is the Magna Carta" (29).

For Huntington, precious, unique Western culture must be protected, and he issues a call to arms. The North American countries (specifically excluding Mexico) and the European countries, (presumably as represented by the European Union) must band together in a re-vamped NATO whose primary purpose will be to "defend and preserve" Western civilization (45). Here Huntington captures the spirit of what Etienne Balibar calls "racist internationalism": "which idealizes "timeless or transhistorical communities... which are at the same time both closed and open, which have no frontiers or whose only frontiers are... the frontiers of an ideal humanity" (61).

And moreover, Huntington is quite explicit that in order to "defend and preserve" Western civilization, Western countries must exclude non-Western immigrants from entering their borders ("West Unique" 45). Huntington's notion of the West helps illustrate how Edward Said's approach is necessary for expanding our understanding of power and helping generate a more nuanced scholarship about the West. For in addition to reading texts in terms of how they reveal the construction of "the Other," these texts can also be inverted to be read to reveal their "author": that is, as reflecting and revealing the strategies by which those with the power of representation construct themselves (Kitzinger and Wilkinson 10).

For Huntington, the West and societies in the West are unconnected to processes of colonization and to settler-colonization, and are devoid of multicultural, multiracial, or multireligious diversity. To retain this mythical coherence, Huntington advocates barring immigrants from countries outside the West. In actuality, Huntington's constructed West ignores the much more complex reality of Western societies and the cultural intermingling that has already occurred. As Said notes in *Culture and Imperialism*, "Partly because of empire, all cultures are involved in one another, none is single and pure, all are hybrid, heterogeneous, extraordinarily differentiated, and unmonolithic" (xxv). This is a view shared by many cultural anthropologists who argue that most cultures today are "creolized" (Stasiulis 160).

For Huntington, North America has to unite with Europe to protect its civilization from the Eastern/Muslim teaming masses who might otherwise want to immigrate there. But, the displacement of colonialism has assured that Muslims are already the largest religious minority group in countries of Western Europe, comprising over seven million (Anwar 71). The largest group of foreign-born Americans is from Mexico (not the West, according to Huntington), comprising close to 22 percent, according to the 1990 Census (6). And, by the way, prior to 1848 what is today Texas, California, Colorado, New Mexico, Nevada, Utah, and most of Arizona was Mexican territory. And what about the indigenous population in all three North American countries (Mexico, Canada and the US)? Given the multicultural, multiracial, and multireligious reality across Western industrialized countries today, Huntington's call to arms in the name of "the West" is like an auto-immune reaction against the complex and hybrid populations of North America and Europe.

We are, perhaps, cursed to live in such interesting times. Currently, one of the central questions that has triggered the curiosity of analysts across the social sciences and humanities concerns the impact of globalization and its meaning in social life. Globalization is characterized by the increased movement of not only goods, services, and capital across national boundaries, but also global culture. Global cultural flows include the movement of ideas, images, and, significantly, peoples—tourists, immigrants, refugees, guest workers, exiles and so on—across national boundaries (Appadurai 295–310). As a result of global cultural flows, many major metropolitan centers in the West are connected to other world societies and thus many local identities within polyethnic and cosmopolitan cities in the West are in fact based on membership in international communities of faith (Muslim, Jewish, Hindu, Buddhist and so on) which in turn have been shaped in complex ways by various ethnic and national cultures (Stasiulis 160). At the same time, across Western industrialized countries right-wing movements and parties have galvanized around ethno-nationalist discourses of protective entitlement, which have variously targeted immigrants, minorities, and the poor ("they" are taking "our" jobs, "our" welfare benefits, destroying "our" culture etc.). Indeed, Huntington's "clash" argument reinforces these kinds of discourses (for example, the anti-immigrant discourse directed primarily at North African and especially Algerian immigrants in France by the Front National posits that it is Islam and the culture of immigrants that are antithetical to French culture (see Le Pen).

In contrast to the essentialist "clash of civilizations" the fault lines of so-called difference should be seen as historically determined in relation to power and inequality, which has included processes of slavery, colonialism, and imperialism. But they should never be essentialized. In *Culture and Imperialism* Said closes his account by reminding his readers of the complex and layered character of ethnic and cultural identity in the modern world:

> No one today is purely one thing.... Imperialism consolidated the mixture of cultures and identities on a global scale. But its worst and most paradoxical gift was to allow people to believe that they were only, mainly, exclusively, white, or Black, or Western or Oriental (336).

Conclusion

As we enter the twenty-first century, there has been a revitalization of movements, discourses, and scholarship based on essentialist constructions of East and West. Yet, Edward Said's work has influenced and will continue to influence scholars outside his discipline, and outside the country where he lives. His work challenges dehumanizing essentialized constructions of societies and peoples from the East, encouraging us to listen to the voice of "the Other," at the same time providing a basis for more nuanced study about the West, and the inter-connections between East and West, and between those with more power and those with less. Edward Said's work can attune us to how Orientalism plays out, including within Western polities (indeed the construction of a European identity and the introduction of a European citizenship in the European Union have developed along side an excluded and often vilified "Muslim, immigrant other" (Abu-Laban). Consequently, how we approach the study of the West matters as much in human terms as how we approach the study of the East.

Notes
[1] See Yasmeen Abu-Laban and Victoria Lamont, "Crossing Borders: Interdisciplinarity, Immigration and the Melting Pot in the American Cultural Imaginary," *The Canadian Review of American Studies* 27, 2 (1997): 23-43.
[2] See Helma Lutz, "The Myth of the 'Other': Western Representation and Images of Migrant Women of So Called Islamic Background," *International Review of Sociology* 2 (1991): 121–137.
[3] For more on this, see Nathan Keyfitz, "What Happened in Cairo? A View from the Internet," The Canadian Journal of Sociology 20, 1 (Winter 1995): 81-90.

Works Cited

Abu-Laban, Yasmeen. "The Nation-State in an Era of Regionalism and Globalization: A Comparative Study of the Politics of Immigration in the United States and France." Diss. Carleton University, 1995.

Abu-Laban, Yasmeen and Victoria Lamont, "Crossing Borders: Interdisciplinarity, Immigration and the Melting Pot in the American Cultural Imaginary." *The Canadian Review of American Studies* 27: 2 (1997): 23–43.

Ahmad, Aijaz. "Orientalism and After." *Colonial Discourse and Post-Colonial Theory*. Ed. Patrick Williams and Laura Chrisman. New York: Columbia University Press, 1994.

Anwar, Muhammad. "Muslims in Western Europe." *Religion and Citizenship in Europe and the Arab World*. Ed. Jørgen S. Nielsen. London: Grey Seal Books, 1992.

Appadurai, Arjun. "Disjuncture and Difference in the Global Cultural Economy." *Global Culture: Nationalism, Globalization and Modernity*. Ed. Mike Featherstone. London: Sage, 1990.

Balibar, Etienne. "Racism and Nationalism." *Race, Nation, Class: Ambiguous Identities*. Ed. Etienne Balibar and Immanuel Wallerstein. London: Verso, 1991.

Esposito, John L. *The Islamic Threat: Myth or Reality.* New York: Oxford, 1992.

Graham-Brown, Sarah. "Palestine." *The Oxford Companion to Politics of the World*. Ed. Joel Krieger. Oxford: Oxford University Press, 1993.

Huntington, Samuel. "The Clash of Civilizations?" *Foreign Affairs* 72: 3 (Summer 1992).

Huntington, Samuel. "The West Unique, Not Universal." *Foreign Affairs* 75: 6 (November/December 1996).

Keyfitz, Nathan. "What Happened in Cairo? A View from the Internet." *The Canadian Journal of Sociology* 20: 1 (Winter 1995): 81–90.

Kitzinger, Celia and Sue Wilkinson. "Theorizing Representing the Other." *Representing the Other: A Feminism and Psychology Reader.* Ed. Sue Wilkinson and Celia Kitzinger. London: Sage, 1996.

Le Pen, Jean-Marie. *Pour la Fance: Programme du Front National.* Paris: Éditions Albatros, 1985.

Lewis, Bernard. "The Question of Orientalism." *The New York Review of Books* 24 June 1982:49–56.

Lewis, Bernard and Edward Said. "Orientalism: An Exchange." *The New York Review of Books* 12 August 1982: 44–48.

Lutz, Helma. "The Myth of the 'Other': Western Representation and Images of Migrant Women of So Called Islamic Background." *International Review of Sociology* 2 (1991): 121–137.

Said, Edward W. *Covering Islam: How the Media and the Experts Determine How We See the Rest of the World.* 1981. Rev. ed. New York: Vintage Books, 1997.

_____. *Culture and Imperialism.* New York: Vintage Books, 1994.

_____. *Orientalism.* New York: Vintage Books, 1979.

_____. "Palestine: Then and Now." *Harpers* December 1992.

_____. *Peace and Its Discontents: Essays on Palestine in the Middle East Peace Process.* New York: Vintage Books, 1996.

_____. *The Question of Palestine.* New York, Vintage Books, 1979.

_____. *The World, the Text, and the Critic.* Cambridge: Harvard University Press, 1983.

Scruton, Roger. *A Dictionary of Political Thought.* 2nd ed. London: Macmillan, 1996.

Stasiulis, Daiva. "The Political Economy of Race, Ethnicity and Migration." *Understanding Canada: Building on the New Canadian Political Economy."* Ed. Wallace Clement. Montreal and Kingston: McGill-Queen's University Press, 1997.

Sullivan, Earl L. and Jacqueline S. Ismael. *The Contemporary Study of the Arab World.* Edmonton: The University of Alberta Press, 1991.

Taylor, Rupert. "Political Science Encounters 'Race' and 'Ethnicity.'" *Ethnic and Racial Studies* 19: 4 (October 1996).

U.S. Department of Commerce, Bureau of the Census, Ethnic and Hispanic Branch. 1990 Census Special Tabulations as cited in "Census Bureauc Press Release." 18 December 1992.

Williams, Patrick and Laura Chrisman, eds. *Colonial Discourse and Post-Colonial Theory: A Reader.* New York: Columbia University Press, 1994.

Angry Beauty and Literary Love: An *Orientalism* for All Time

Timothy Brennan

This is no time simply for adulation of *Orientalism*. We should follow Edward Said's own lead, by making sure we are clear about the issues that *Orientalism* inspired. There are many to choose from, of course, but let me take only one, and I will pose it in the form of a question: Did *Orientalism*—as almost everyone seems to agree—launch an entirely new scholarly field now known as "postcolonial studies"? The question may seem abstract and specialized, especially given the range of interests and knowledge represented here. But if one is to understand why Edward Said has mattered as widely as he has, we cannot forget that his authorization, if I can put it that way, was not only at the outset but also later and continually both literary and academic. His entryway into and influence on other spheres was initially launched, and later enriched, by his placement in a series of complex arguments about the scope and specificity of humanism and literary criticism. And now, at the moment of his success, the retrospective evaluation of his legacy entails his association with an embattled and insecure discipline known as "postcolonial studies," which has, we should remember, attracted the angry attention of secretaries of education, media columnists, and the president of the United States.

It is not merely an in-house question for literary scholars, but a password of sorts for a promised (or threatened) revaluation of values in society at large. At both ends of the spectrum of *Orientalism*'s reception, this question seems to have long been settled, both within specialized studies of language and literature and in that cultural critique of a more catholic variety found in middlebrow journalism. Among the book's enemies and friends—that is, in both the haunted reckonings of US academic career-making as well as in the work of *Orientalism*'s interlocutors—there is agreement on this point at least: *this* book produced *that* field. It is worthwhile, then, for me to explain why I think this is untrue.

To do so, I want to begin with an unlikely premise, which may seem

Angry Beauty and Literary Love: An Orientalism for All Time

at odds with the implied message among many of the speakers here about Edward's public personality as a Palestinian spokesperson and a spokesperson for Palestine: namely, that *Orientalism* is a profoundly American book, that it could not have been written anywhere else, and that its legacy is fused, or confused, with a national culture that remains in many ways hostile to what the book is actually saying. I have repeatedly found myself over the years comparing the Edward I knew and the Edward I read with the Edward characterized in a generation of valuable but often insufficient criticism. Since the personal relationship and the public image were not the same, I have often had to return to the texts to ask whether I had simply misremembered.

What one notices right away is that *Orientalism* is often grouped with companion texts, which typically include the poetical testimonies of Palestinian longing found in *After the Last Sky*, the interviews and conjunctural essays on Palestinian identity and Zionist politics, and the books, naturally, that complete his Orientalist trilogy—*The Question of Palestine* and *Covering Islam*. One reason for this has to do with the understandable emphasis of the scholars and public who do not come out of literature departments, or who are unmoved by the debates over language and representation that motivated Said professionally in the two books that preceded *Orientalism*. Once that earlier, and rather extensive, preparatory work is considered closely, one begins to notice that *Orientalism* in many ways more properly belongs with *The World, The Text, and the Critic* published in 1982, which as a collection of essays brings together not only the "outtakes" as it were of *Orientalism* itself (the chapters in the latter book on Ernest Renan and on Raymond Schwab, for example, were clearly written for inclusion in *Orientalism*) but also his understudied essays on American "Left" Criticism, "Secular Criticism," and "Traveling Theory"—all of them expanding upon and elaborating the mass psychology of a peculiar brand of American messianic beneficence and naiveté.

It is the American contexts of *Orientalism*'s composition, in other words, that arrest one immediately when examining the very book that addressed much of the fallout that *Orientalism* produced—the first one that expanded upon, rather than filled out or continued, the concerns of that book itself. Remember that, whatever else *Orientalism* might mean in a general, political sense; or whatever it might say about the imaginative violence of European portrayals of Middle Eastern cultures, its meanings arise by way of a sustained examination of individual philologists. In *The World, the Text, and the Critic*, the earlier themes of Schwab's "vast human portraits" and his "generous awareness" are taken directly out of *Orientalism*, only now they are placed alongside essays of striking vitriol on the scenes of American cultural theory, essays that stress, for example, the alarming religious turn in American criticism in the age of Reaganism, where the "hermetic and private" take prominence "over the public and social," and where graduate students under the banner of the "Left" sit (in Said's words) "gullibly enraptured by an uncircumstanced structural poetics." Indeed, in that sense, *The Question of Palestine* and *Covering Islam* themselves are glossed by *The World, the Text, and the Critic*, since like *Orientalism*, they appear in retrospect to be fundamentally about the latest stage of a much older crusade against the Islamic "Orient." In earlier eras that crusade appeared more literary and less specular—now it is directed by leaders in New York and Washington to the chorus of a pliant intelligentsia.

Both kinds of essay in the volume (that is, those on early 20th-century French Orientalists like Schwab and those more immediate commentaries on Criticism at the Present Time) have a common end. Therefore, when Said famously invokes the concept of "Secular Criticism," for example, it is not primarily Middle East sectoral politics that he has in mind, but the doctrinal demands of a poststructuralist "science" in its more extreme and questionable variants. This focus on humanist "science" (about which Said has been repeatedly skeptical) frankly revisits the problems of Ernest Renan's uses of Cuvier as described in *Orientalism*, uses that led eventually to the birth of what Renan tellingly, and damningly for Said, called "*la science critique.*" What Said repeatedly dubs the "slavish attitude" of American critics to their French sources had given way already (in his words) to a "secular priesthood" in the "era of scientific intelligence" (173). Said tends here toward an account he nowhere states so bluntly, but that cannot be seen other than as a declaration that the state's desire to neutralize our "technical skill as critics and intellectuals" was succeeding by our own abstention; that critics in the 1980s were conducting cultural inquiry (as he puts it) without "genuine historical research" and without the goal of "understanding, analyzing, and contending with the management of power and authority within the culture." In short, in and through the practice of theory, American critics had begun to assume the status of state functionaries. The only element of his assessment left unsaid was whether these developments were the result of class interest, or whether they were the result of a political instinct for a revolt that was really a submission.

However, this emphatic statement about *what* had happened without venturing an explanation as to *why* it had happened, is surely one of Said's more important leads, and any discussion of *Orientalism*'s legacies must give it an important place, even though that attempt is rarely made, since the more openly political treatment of Said's work tends to be arrested in what—in America at least—is a more acceptable form of dissension, an allowable protest against forms of racial discrimination or forgotten identities, for reasons I will explore below.

Enter postcolonial studies which, on the face of it, seemed to take up Said's critique in *Orientalism* for the purpose of realizing it in a comprehensive way and across an entire field of subjects and styles. What I am calling "postcolonial studies" here is surely familiar to those both within and outside of the university, even if it is not always given this ponderous name. It meant, on the one hand, giving writers and intellectuals who personally, or by family lineage, came from outside the United States and Europe a featured place on speakers' or publishers' lists, or in opinion columns; it meant a new marketability for the arts of Africa, Latin America, and the Subcontinent; it meant using concepts like "colonialism," "immigration," and "hybridity" without irony—and this all took place not only in graduate seminars but in the program notes of local theater companies, in church sermons, and on MTV. In this sense, the prima facie case for seeing postcoloniality as an extension rather than a departure from *Orientalism* is strong. The problem—as is often the case in American culture—came with the packaging. If the colloquial view of the newspapers found a place too easily in American "pluralism," the academic "other" was one whose sense of conflict in the traditional political sense had been drained out of it. The version of the "other" in academic theory was spliced onto the phenomenological "other" of philosophy, so that the world of guestworkers, Palestinians in refugee camps, or the victims of apartheid were treated, in a single breath, with the (in its own way important) problem of the formation of "subjectivity." The problem by which one only becomes a "self" by defining an "other" does, indeed, have a tangential bearing on racism and colonialism. But it became in academic practice too easy a substitute for the challenging witness of named movements and peoples in struggle.

The influence of Michel Foucault—and, again, not only within the university—is one of the vehicles through which postcoloniality took this form. In the phrasings of *Orientalism*, it is not hard not to hear in the ringing words "power" and "history" an allusion to the work of Foucault, an intellectual for whom Said had understandably high regard, both in *Beginnings* and in his testimony published in the journal *Raritan* following Foucault's death in 1984. In fact, both the opponents and supporters of Edward Said were once again united in the view that the concept "Orientalism" in the book *Orientalism* was (as Said himself concedes) a "discursive construct," and one moreover that played itself out in epochal skirmishes over Foucauldian power/knowledge.

There is very little debate, it seems, about the deeply Foucauldian structure and logic of *Orientalism*. But is *Orientalism* Foucauldian? Certainly the theoretical core of postcolonial studies is, that part at any rate, that is not Derridean or Lacanian. Among these centers Foucault would be the obvious methodological link between *Orientalism* as a text and postcolonial studies as a field. Indeed, in a simple chronological sense, the relationship appears to be causal. It was, after all, following the book's appearance in 1978, that a great outpouring of first-rate studies on imperialism and culture, race and representation began to emerge out of disciplinary settings as varied as anthropology, art history, film theory, sociology, and history. A certain constellation had gathered force, achieving critical mass by the late 1980s, and all bowing rightly to *Orientalism* as their lead, and commenting on the effective gloss on Foucault that the book provides.

Said would say often in the early 1980s that in writing *Orientalism* he had most in mind the Raymond Williams of *The Country and the City*. This would be the beginning but not the end of a skepticism toward the genealogy I am exploring. Recall, in that sense, the transitional quality, once again, of *The World, the Text, and the Critic:* its inclusion of even pre-*Beginnings* work like that on Swift and Conrad, its inclusion also of the key final chapter of *Beginnings* itself, entitled "Criticism Between Culture and System," which set out to demythify the work of Derrida and Foucault for an American audience, for precisely the reasons outlined elsewhere in the volume and to which I have alluded above. There would be some praise for Derrida and Foucault as well, their roles as liberators of language and archive for at least two generations. And yet it is astounding that over and over again, from the overviews on postcolonial studies published in the *New York Times Sunday Magazine* and *The Chronicle of Higher Education* to more

Angry Beauty and Literary Love: An Orientalism for All Time

scholarly analyses by James Clifford and Dennis Porter, Said's counter-Foucauldian demur, his balanced conclusions based on a cautious, and finally emphatic, departure from the work of that French thinker have been passed over as though they could not really have meant what they said or as if they had not existed at all.

Even before *Orientalism*—and despite the decidedly French bias of the book's framing and sympathies—Said targets Foucault's "flawed attitude to power," his "insufficiently developed attention to the problem of historical change." Foucault underestimates, says Said, "such motive forces in history as profit, ambition, ideas, the sheer love of power, and he does not seem interested in the fact that history is not a homogeneous French-speaking territory but a complex interaction between uneven economies, societies, and ideologies." "Foucault," he continues, "seems unaware of the extent to which the ideas of discourse and discipline are assertively European." Said's language becomes even more uncompromising later in "Traveling Theory": Foucault's theory of power, argues Said, has

> captivated not only Foucault himself but many of his readers who wish to go beyond Left optimism and Right pessimism so as to justify political quietism with sophisticated intellectualism, at the same time wishing to appear realistic, in touch with the world of power and reality... [W]e must not let Foucault get away with confusing [Logos with words], nor with letting us forget that history does not get made without work, intention, resistance, effort, or conflict, and that none of these things is silently absorbable into micronetworks of power.

And here I would like to bring my two themes together into one: that is, the disjunction between *Orientalism* and postcolonial studies, on the one hand, and *Orientalism* as an American book, on the other. What has appeared to many commentators as the contradictions in *Orientalism* between the real and the discursive, or between humanism and anti-humanism, can be resolved at the point of its site-specific Americanness. I don't wish to argue that the book is secretly, or allegorically, or only about the United States, but rather to remind ourselves of the New York and California media and academic sounds and arguments that formed the environment of its composition in the entrails of global capital and the new capital of the globe. *Orientalism* is most unlike the postcolonial work that enlists its name for the reason that it mounts a criticism, proleptically, of the (US) theoretical arenas in which "postcoloniality" grew up, and through which it expresses itself. What is more, it is antagonistic to postcolonial studies in a practical way, that is, as a style of performance. In the very country that professes individualism as a national creed, in the land in which multiculturalism is an imperial shibboleth, postcolonial studies has inevitably taken on the clothing of individualism in work dedicated to "identity" and in the often obtuse and willful psychoanalytic register of the "subject position." Postcoloniality hypostasizes experience and then substitutes "experience" for ethnographic representation. It is in Saidian terms "filiative" rather than affiliative, and in that sense, apart from its purported outreach and cultural sensitivities, it emphatically strengthens a culturally specific and suspect American obsession with ethnic identity as authority.

Here I would like to repeat my opening claim that Said be understood as an intellectual whose literary training is central to his political positioning and to his influence. Without grasping his role in commenting on the uses and misuses of cultural criticism, or without appreciating the elaboration of that politics *through* the study of philology, one simply cannot fully understand why he has had the effect he has. For many at this conference it will have seemed crucial that Said was precisely a Palestinian. It is an obviously central fact, and perhaps one can see that *Orientalism*'s astounding reception came in part by exploiting a contradiction—one might say a Fanonian contradiction—in Euro-American consciousness, with its emphasis on name and color. On the other hand, it would be limiting to cast *Orientalism* as primarily a text by a postcolonial intellectual "speaking back" to empire, a cross-over study as it were, now able to license work by scholars from other parts of the non-European world. I have never been able to see the book primarily this way, because given my own identity, I have been only too aware that the options for anti-imperialists who happen to be white and American are either the powerless prophetic anarchism of beat poetry and '60s counterculture, the plaintive radical liberalism of C. Wright Mills, or the reputable, but slandered, traditions of American communism, made toothless by Cold War prejudices. Part of the significance of *Orientalism*, I would argue, was that it managed what I am, perhaps strangely, calling an American critique that fell into none of these categories, and yet cut deep and long gashes in the body of Western egotism. It was a matter of its positional freshness and supple intransigence, not its geopolitical or racial "location." A good deal of postcolonial studies drew on *Orientalism* without being true to it. The book gave them a theory that did not travel well—at least for them.

Angry Beauty and Literary Love: An Orientalism for All Time

Rereading *Orientalism* in the 1990s is to be struck by the insistent themes that reinforce the lines of argument presented in *The World, The Text, and the Critic*. This is not to imply that his later writing has been a gloss on a single, repetitive idea but that *Orientalism* was the first full articulation of a series of interlocking propositions that neither he nor his generation could fully exhaust in the telling. I have mentioned some of them, but there are two others I want to explore before closing, for they bear directly on that unease that I think exists between *Orientalism* and postcolonial studies as a suspect field of specialization. Both as an invocation in his essays, and as an off-handed comment to his students, Said has repeatedly supported the idea (a methodological idea that is also a philosophical one) of reading generally, widely, and by appetite: the directive not to "read up" on a subject but to choose one's line of research by what one had come upon in an act of impure interest. Not *making* connections, but capitalizing on those that arrive—a lesson he took most directly from Erich Auerbach, but which is the peculiar provenance of the literary intellectual as Said understood it, as distinct from the sociologist or the political thinker *tout court*.

Secondly—and it is of particular interest in assessing post-coloniality—that one should not stand for a politics of culture in the sense of the always yearning but ill-fated quest for making things happen at the level of the image, and of metaphoric struggle; one must not claim for language a radical overturning of existence by way of a redefining of the categories, or of finding *in culture* an arena for revolutionary action. On the contrary—and I think *Orientalism* brilliantly achieves this—one should embrace a radical modesty. His idea is that the literary intellectual in the analysis of literary texts most matters by remaining, as it were, in literature, speaking to an aesthetic need that is also a social need. To speak always to what attracts one intellectually and aesthetically, to dwell in the love granted to humanists by their public. It is *there* that a literary intellectual can with the proper choices develop a vocabulary, and define anew a series of conceptual categories capable of nudging thought itself into a gradual change of emphasis. Compounded over time, by altering the questions asked, or by giving a name to what was rarely talked about before, they are then able to lead their readers to something new and valuable. There is for Said no master-discourse that rivets together the political and the literary in a single act. It is important to differentiate those modes of involvement, and to speak in two minds, with a "general" interest that takes the registering of opinion on politics out of the mouth of specialists.

At stake, I am arguing, is that "traveling theory" taken up by Said as a misapprehension, in which *Orientalism* has seemed to warrant an array of shortcuts and flat assertions in the uneven construction of a field. Certainly one of the things that makes Said's interventions so multiply resonant today is that he has sensed this, as it were, in a performance that constitutes what I would call his genius of *presentation*: what I have elsewhere called the "how" of his work.

Orientalism mattered because it allowed people spurred on by an uncomfortable awareness of contemporary empire to talk about such things in an acceptably humanist language. That side of things represented by the reader of newspapers, the enraged witness of the Washington talk shows, is everywhere beneath the lines of this erudite text, especially in the concluding chapters. It was, moreover, among other things, about Arabs rather than more acceptable kinds of others in the context of the United States. That is, the book's conscience enfolded precisely that population for whom racism is an almost blasé outcome—the ones against whom racism has been so open, so caustic, and so unguarded that it has appeared almost second-nature to US audiences. Said cast light upon the very group associated freely with a millennium of hostile rivalry with the West.

From the perch of a Columbia University Chair, Said managed to arrive at formulations of such uncompromisingly accusatory clarity, that many of them became the staple of exposé journalists for two decades. His influence could be seen, for example, in his pointing out the conformity between the type of racist caricatures once reserved for the Jews that were now applied to Arabs. Written with a wealth of reference and a command of history and literature from a variety of traditions, *Orientalism* was also written in many passages with a palpable anger. This cannot be underestimated in accounting for its success. For that reason alone, it can neither be forgotten nor ignored. On the other hand, it was no transformation of literary criticism into a type of nuanced political warfare. By contrast, it resurrected, in an unpromising environment of instant knowledge and media specularity, the same assured command of cross-disciplinary reading evident in philology itself. What arose was something more and other—a new kind of intellectual, not of the philological model at all. For he brought the specificity of a particular people and movement in a disciplined act of scholarship, characterized neither by the dilettantism of the amateur

Angry Beauty and Literary Love: An Orientalism for All Time

nor the pinched limitations of an *a priori* program.

On the whole it is surprising that the book received the welcome it did in the academy if for no other reason than that he demolishes a certain kind of disciplinary etiquette and scholarly bluff. This violation of what is often called "collegiality" is rarely so warmly rewarded. I ignore, for the moment, its dissenters, while drawing attention to their most frequent point: that "Orientalism" as a concept is either eternal and therefore ahistorical ("for all time") or it is an entity that requires a discrete definition that Said nowhere provides. I have never understood this argument. It seems rather clear that an epochal hostility toward the Arab world could extend from Aeschylus to Conor Cruise O'Brien without that position being historically "undifferentiated." And it seems equally clear that he is not saying European philologists or contemporary Area Studies experts got the Orient wrong, only that their Orient took no account of the Orientals' ordering of themselves. He does not argue, for example, that there is no such thing as a "real" Orient, or that it has only a discursive life. It is rather that he does not pretend in this book to describe that "brute reality" to which he repeatedly refers, and to which he gives a priority of place. His is rather a point about the relative indifference of Western intellectuals to that reality, about the confident building and elaboration of ideas and images that rely on the ideas and images that have preceded them within the same constellation of value.

This confidence, moreover, was not accidental—not a matter of some civilizational taint or genetic prejudice from which, say, the white race suffers, but a matter (in his words) of "positional superiority." However much he would recoil, perhaps, from the phrase, Said's position is in that sense a historically materialist one: European knowledge production vis-a-vis the Orient took the form it did because it could. Europe controlled the land, the trade, the government registers, and the means of disseminating information. The observation that no one could counter the European view gave way to the belief that no one need question it. It is essential in that sense to recognize that Said is speaking about a propaganda system at the same time as he is speaking about a self-generating system of images and values that professional intellectuals in a specific social setting create.

Orientalism, then, documents both the power of intellectuals to create terminologies of "mass density and referential power" and their function with regard to government and foreign policy. We begin to see the potency of humanist close readings, the study of foreign languages, the development of the techniques of scholarship and erudition in the network of institutions which seamlessly entail the less endearing offices of the state itself. The academic intellectual is involved in the formation and legitimation of state policy. What is so remarkable about the way he has written the book, however, is that while he makes these connections quite explicit—they are, in that sense, not just left between the lines—the overall impression of the study is not polemical. The charges of complicity are unmistakable, and yet the most vivid picture left in our minds is of the palpable details of the textual event—the specificities of canonical novelists, of philologists, and the subtleties of their inquiries, appetites, and quests. To say that he displays the same range and informed generalizations in the study itself is only to repeat that his strategy is one of emulating the enemy by taking what is most productive in its methods. As such, the book is marked by its coinages of key terms that themselves have now achieved "mass density and referential power"—the term "orientalism" itself, of course, but also the terms most important for my thesis here: namely, "strategic location" and "strategic formation." These might be seen as developing that key distinction outlined in earlier work between "filiation" (the bonds of nation, race—of physical and cultural identity) and "affiliation" (the chosen bonds of thought, value, and political position across the natural boundaries of identity). Here, as elsewhere, Said is emphatically for the latter.

Again, what if not the United States is being referenced in the "cultural politics" of the sort *Orientalism* provides? It is hardly a coincidence that *Orientalism* begins with personal reminiscence of the civil war in Beirut, nor that the reception of the book flourished in the catastrophic invasion of Lebanon by Israeli forces in 1982, only a few short years after the book first appeared. It is also striking—and, I think, surprising on a rereading—that he draws on the authority of Noam Chomsky in the introduction to explain the nature of his enterprise. The elaborate finesse, always lovingly related by Said, of verbal mastery and textual power in the traditions within which he himself developed, are grounded in the appalled witness of applied terror, an embodied rather than a disembodied "power." It is precisely here where Said leaves Foucault behind, and the *The World, the Text and the Critic,* then, can be seen perhaps as bringing to completion Chomsky's famous debates with Foucault on Dutch television.

There are still those who consider it sufficient, by way of a refutation of the book, to suggest that Said misses the fact that the Orientalist

Angry Beauty and Literary Love: An Orientalism for All Time

scholars he rebukes admired what they studied, cradled the object of their research in a loving embrace, and indeed fought difficult battles at home to make known the glories and achievements of non-Western lands. It is worth noting that Said opens his text proper with the drama of Arthur Balfour lecturing the House of Commons in 1910 on their arrogance toward the Egyptians, and the false sense of superiority adopted by Britons toward the peoples whose affairs they had recently entered. From the outset, then, his point is not the favorable or unfavorable eye cast toward the subject, but the inescapable fact of dominance in the act of amassing information on an "area" whose coherence is predicated on an internal, or domestically defined, set of attitudes. The outlook is itself inseparable from the pursuit of policies of expansion, forceable inclusion, and appropriation. The orientalist system of knowledge conceals preliminary assumptions of an unreflective sort by an immediate slippage into the sheer mass of intricate details and documentary "proof" placed in the service of the original concept. The finesse of scholarship is, as it were, made naked here; its very formidability and grandeur bears an inverse relationship to the more basic questions that prejudice makes elusive: why is one only an "Oriental" in the West, but never in the Orient itself? Why have the subjects never been given (as Said was to put it in a different context) "permission to narrate"?

This pointed—one is tempted to say, impish—invocation of the term "narrate" in the context of theoretical textualism points, I would argue, to an implicit critique of postcolonial studies before the fact. The tireless demonstration of *Orientalism*, after all, is of the mutually contributing work of academic disciplines, which acted in concert and with an astonishing unity of purpose. A homology is set up not only among disciplinary enclaves but among historical periods, forcing the reader to entertain the view that the imperial absurdities of the high 19th century—relatively easy to ridicule in retrospect—live on in the supposedly enlightened technologies of the contemporary news media and literary theory. To that extent as well, the book is contextually American, for it inserted into the British and French colonial enterprises described in the early chapters a contemporary U.S. imperial dynamic explored at length in *Orientalism*'s final chapter. What had in the French and British cases been sanctified by the lure of tradition and cleansed by their relative weakness (their "pastness") in regard to the geopolitics of the present becomes, especially in the late chapters, dangerous and immediate, when the subject is the American media intellectual scene. One is always aware that this archive is a window upon empire's current stagings, and (if we do not heed its message) to the next round of ameliorative theorizations of exoticism and civilizational superiority in the service of Western power. For, again, his branding of such giants as Flaubert, Edward Lane, Richard Burton as "orientalist"—despite his appreciation of their productive insights—is to suggest that theirs was a "willed human work," refusing to make a general case of discursive regimentation in which agency, in good Foucauldian fashion, is left to wander lost among the epistemes. To respond to such a branding with the accusation of anachronism by suggesting, in a move that looks very much like historical sensitivity, that they could not have known what we know now, is to vastly overrate our own capacities to see the imperial assumptions that underlie our own work.

By satisfying himself to concentrate on the cultural knowledge he already strongly possessed as a 19th- and 20th-century European comparatist, Said wisely engaged the very "Europe" most revered by American humanities departments. Had he emphasized China, for example, or German orientalist scholarship, the scope would have been greater but the sharpness of the accusations blunted by a technicist feel, by the distancing of specialization itself. Similarly, the force of *Orientalism* is not only what it is arguing but its careful tightrope walk over a "coarse polemic" of numbing generality and the merely specialized focus of the equipped academic. Underlying the whole success of the venture is his ability to make the rather basic, but for all that unarticulated, point in the 1970s: that it was possible to write about literature politically without being boring or offensively crude. He manages this by holding onto the philological "detail" over what he calls the "gross political verity." The balancing act is itself a mark of the creative tension he located in the philology of the very orientalist classics analyzed throughout the first long chapters—a fundamental doubleness represented, on the one hand, by Schwab, and on the other, by Renan: the admirable power of textual nomination and deliverance in the general intellectual, on the one hand, and the racial typologies of cantankerous arrogance of humanist "science," on the other. His rhetorical question is this: Doesn't the emphasis on an irreducible linguistic and ethnic subject redouble the problem of this latter position, and by inversion, repeat it?

Said's great contribution as an intellectual can be found not, for the most part, in the making of new knowledge (the theoretical disruption of a whole way of thinking) or in revelatory discoveries of lost or

Angry Beauty and Literary Love: An Orientalism for All Time

previously unknown materials (as in the astounding linguistic materials uncovered recently by Martin Bernal on the African origins of Greek civilization) as much as in elusive conceptual moves. What he found was that the important unasked questions arise only through an interdisciplinary hunger that does not rely for answers on existing academic jargon. Certainly writing itself also reflects personal experience—the culmination of a process of compiling an inventory of the "infinity of traces" left on one by history. But these traces are in the end, positional. *Orientalism* thrived because it turned out to be not only a book for knowing but a manual for doing. It was not just a book to emulate, but a book whose content addressed how to be the sort of intellectual Said himself became in the writing of it. This is why it cannot be exhausted. We pour ourselves into it, and therefore get ourselves back, but transformed.

Orientalism in the Arab Context

As'ad AbuKhalil

Edward Said has achieved a status unique among scholars. He has emerged as an international intellectual whose scholarship is widely recognized as relevant to a multiplicity of disciplines in the social sciences and the humanities. In addition to his universal role within the academy, Said is also a media personality known for his commentaries on Middle East affairs and Western politics and culture. Although Said's contributions distinguished him long before the publication of *Orientalism*, the book became a scholarly phenomenon that penetrated deep into Western academic culture.

Orientalism is an unusual book written by somebody with unusual gifts and skills. It allowed a Palestinian-American scholar, who has never been timid about asserting his Arab identity—not out of narrow chauvinism but as a response to Western denigration of Arab culture—to engage in a sophisticated critique of Western literary and scholarly production on the Orient. The book is not easy to dismiss, as much as it bothered people operating in Western academic institutions. In the words of Muhsin Mahdi, you can ignore it "at your own peril." To be sure, the critique of Orientalism preceded Said's book. Said himself refers, for example, to articles by Abdel-Malek and Tibawi. But no systematic and rigorous study of Orientalism had ever been made before Said,[1] and no subsequent study of the subject has been able to marginalize the magisterial work. It produced immediate results: anyone writing about the East had to address it one way or another.

Despite the critical acclaim and the unusual attention that the book received in academic journals and in the media of the culture industry, many Western writers expressed displeasure with the book. Said was frequently misquoted and his arguments were misconstrued to facilitate the efforts of his intellectual and political opponents. Bernard Lewis, who has done more to promote the version of theologocentric Orientalism that Said so successfully refutes, cannot get himself to respond to Said's criticisms. In *Islam and the West*, he simply dismisses the book as "absurd" (108) and belonging to "alternative universes beloved of science fiction writers" (109). Similarly, Ernest Gellner expresses dismay over the book because, he tells us, it treated unfairly Orientalists who are known for their sensitivity to Islam and the Arabs. His example of the unfairly treated Orientalist is none other than Bernard Lewis himself. Even Orientalists who were praised by Said, like Albert Hourani and Maxime Rodinson are uncomfortable. Hourani accepts some of Said's criticisms although he characterizes his method of expression as a "caricature" (*Islam* 63). Rodinson, whose radical background and original approach to Islamic studies would lead one to associate him with Said's method of analysis, is quite ambivalent. He praises Said's success in defining better "l'ideologie de l'orientalisme europeen (en fait, surtout anglo-francais) aux XIXe et au XXe siecle et son entrancinement dans les objectifs politiques et economiques europeens" (14). He then goes on to associate Said with dogmatic Third World nationalist ideologies and with "theorie jdanovienne." It is hard for Rodinson and others to admit the links between Orientalism and Western domination. Rodinson observes that he is talking about Orientalist studies while Said is talking about the Western ideology of hostility. The two are separate in Rodinson's mind, although Said succeeds in persuasively linking the two together. How could one separate the Western ideology of hostility against Islam from Western studies of Islam? Academic writing and literary production do not take place in a vacuum: they are influenced by, and they in turn influence, the general political climate.

To discredit the book, Said's ideas were deliberately distorted. Most critics paid tribute to the great contributions of classical Orientalists, criticizing Said for failing to do so. Only one critic, Sadiq Jalal Al-'Adhm, is fair to Said in this regard, pointing out that he has indeed expressed appreciation for the contributions of Orientalists in his book (Al-'Adhm 19; Said 96). Others, like Kanan Makiya, who is not an authority on either the Orient or the Occident and whose neo-conservative stand has been much applauded in the West, accuses Said of labeling every European as a racist (319). Makiya, who falsely associates Said with the vulgar school of nationalism, ignores the context and thrust of Said words. Makiya has to change Said's verb tense to make his case. What Said said was that Orientalism was a system of truth that was overwhelmingly present in the minds of those who wrote about the East. In that sense, who could dispute the assertion that "every European, in what he could say about the Orient, was consequently a racist, an imperialist, and almost totally ethnocentric?" The record of writings presented by Said provides conclusive evidence that has not been challenged, unless one equates scholarship with the emotional polemics of Makiya.

Another charge against Said faults him for picking easy targets: for focusing almost exclusively on Anglo-Saxon writers. But Said did not choose easy targets: he did not study obscure works of unknown Orientalists. He studied carefully—with the detailed textual analysis that provides the power of the work—the writings of major Orientalists who influence on Middle East and Islamic studies has been inescapable. That Said did not include many more German or Dutch Orientalists does not undermine his thesis, unless he was expected by his critics to write an encyclopedic analysis of every Orientalist utterance. What Said said about classical Orientalism applies to writers in different countries and cultures, and some German and Dutch Orientalists were as tied to colonial projects and administrations as were the authors featured in *Orientalism*. The Dutch scholar-administrator Snouck Hurgronje and Carl Heinrich Becker are two examples. Becker was an enthusiastic preacher of German colonization of Africa who believed in the "undeniable inferiority of the black races" (van Ess 49). Confirming the thesis of Said, Becker urged that "we must put up with the fact that there is an eternal difference between East and West" (van Ess 47). Hurgronje and A. J. Wensinck (another Dutch scholar) were at pains to deny any originality to Muhammad's mission. But many of Said's critics were personally offended by the implication of the book: that the Orientalist paradigm was more than a personal idiosyncrasy of one or two individuals and that it entailed more than Christian missionary zeal.

The question is now raised whether Said overstated his case, and whether the book is at all necessary or relevant at the end of the 20th century. The editor of the new *Cambridge Illustrated History of the Islamic World*, Francis Robinson, only sees a "grain of truth" (xv) in Said's charges, but cautions that those charges are far less applicable to 20th-century professors of Islamic studies. There is as much truth in this statement as there is in Alan Bloom's assertion that racism "did not play a role in the classic literature" (65). That Robinson cannot recognize the dogmatic tendencies of classic Orientalism with its theologocentric elements and the open ideology of hostility in the works of Bernard Lewis, Henri Lammens, Raphael Patai, Elie Kedourie, Daniel Pipes, Fouad Ajami, David Pryce-Jones, Sandra Mackey, Thomas Friedman, Judith Miller, Khalid Duran, Michael Rywkin, Sefei

Poliakov, Martha Olcott, P.J. Vatikiotis, Marina Tolmacheva, Anatoly Khazanov, William Harris, and many others belonging to the 20th century, is quite odd. Since this cannot be attributed to ignorance, given the academic credentials of the man, it must be a case of cultural insensitivity and methodological self-righteousness.

If anything, recent works about the Middle East make the case of *Orientalism* even more compelling. Not only is the message of the book missed by many of the notable Orientalists working today, but training in Middle East and Islamic studies has deteriorated over the years. More people are now writing and teaching about the Middle East without knowing any of the spoken languages of the Middle East. Reliance on official American translations of radio broadcasts has replaced old-fashioned language training, which was the staple of Orientalist studies. The persistence of Western identification with Zionism and the rise of Islamic fundamentalism has allowed many Western authors to feel comfortable in their hostility to Arabs and Islam. This was clearly the case during the Gulf War. The view of Muslims as eternally conservative and puritanical still prevails. For Robinson, a quotation from Mawdudi suffices to generalize a billion Muslims today (xviii). Furthermore, the notion that the freedom of women (presumably in the West) is the most objectionable facet of modernity for the Muslims is widely shared among Western writers who treat the West in abstraction, as a model of freedom and equality. The epistemological break between East and West has been revived in Samuel Huntington's discourse of the "clash of civilizations" and the expression of political antipathy to the US in the Middle East allows Western governments to retrieve the ideological and polemical arsenal of Christian medieval times. The record of colonialism and imperialism is now almost forgotten, and neo-conservative voices articulate nostalgia for colonial domination of Third World countries. Even the highly praised Albert Hourani attributes altruistic motives to Britain in its dealing with the Middle East. He tells us that

> the general line of British policy was one of support for Arab independence and a greater degree of unity, while preserving essential strategic interests by friendly agreement, and also of helping in economic development and the acquisition of technical skills..." (357).

Hourani's reference to the origins of the Arab-Israeli conflict absolves Zionism from the original and primary responsibility for the dispossession of the Palestinians.

The message of *Orientalism* is as relevant today as it was when the book first came out. The defeat of the Palestinian national movement and American military supremacy around the world have relegitimized sentiments of prejudice and hostility toward the people of the East. The defeatist mood in the Middle East has also created a hospitable climate for ideas long ingrained in classical Orientalist dogmas. The dogmas of Orientalism have been released from the confines of the academic world into the larger popular cultures of Western and Eastern countries. Paul Balta's introductory text on Islam published by *Le Monde* contains some of the clichés of old Orientalism. We are told, yet again, that Muslims split the world into *Dar Al-Harb* and *Dar Al-Islam* and that secularism is "totalement etrangere" to the lives of Muslims (67, 101). Typically, evidence from obsolete jurisprudential theories of medieval Islam is preferable to evidence derived from modern life. The Muslims, after all, resist change and their lives are shaped solely by their religious texts.

And even if one uses a criterion provided by none other than Bernard Lewis, one finds that the methodological problems that characterized Orientalism early in this century remain with us today. Bernard Lewis, in his commentary on the work of Ignaz Goldziher, states that

> Goldziher and his contemporaries had no need to take thought of a possible Muslim reader, but addressed themselves exclusively to a Western audience. Along with virtually all Western writers up to and including his time, he ascribes the authorship of the Qur'an to Muhammad (x).

Lewis then expresses his satisfaction that contemporary Orientalist scholarship avoids this insensitivity. Yet, Patricia Crone, writing in 1996, refers to the Qur'an as "Muhammad's own utterances" (Robinson 10). Modern Orientalism has not made an epistemological break with classical Orientalism despite the efforts of unconventional Islamicists. This is not to call for an uncritical and reverential treatment of Muhammad and Islam, which would clash with the need for the application of the critical standards of modern scholarship to the study of religion, any religion. But the sensitivity that is displayed in the West towards Judaism and Christianity is often suspended when dealing with Islam. In the words of Ignaz Goldziher: What would be left of the Gospels if the Qur'anic method were applied to them? Even the usually sensitive W. Montgomery Watt expresses strong displeasure and frustration with Muslims in his later works, condemning them for failing to have an open outlook toward "historical truth" (141). And Charles Issawi finds Western hostility to Islam quite understandable because the "religion and culture" gave "them so much trouble (369). By "trouble," Issawi meant Muslim opposition to colonialism.

Orientalism *in the Arab* World

Edward Said is widely known in the Arab world. His name became popularly spread when Anwar Sadat recommended him to head a Palestinian government-in-exile at a time when the Egyptian leader was looking for alternatives to the PLO. Said emerged as a media personality and the success of *Orientalism* produced favorable press coverage in the region. Said's prolific production in the field of literary criticisms is only known to a limited number of academics. He is known first and foremost as a media personality and a critic of US foreign policy. This paper will deal with Arab responses to *Orientalism*, focussing on the scholarly reactions.

Emmanuel Sivan published an article on the subject, choosing to ignore the numerous enthusiastically favorable reviews of Said's book in Arabic. He singles out, instead, two critics of Said, thereby allowing himself to express his strong denunciation of *Orientalism* through the mouths of two Arabs: Sadiq Jalal Al-'Adhm and Nadim Al-Bitar. Those two were also mentioned by Lewis in his critique of Said (194). Sivan also referres to an article by Hasan Hanafi, which incidentally appeared before the publication of *Orientalism*, and assures that readers that his "Egyptian and Palestinian friends" (133) informed him that the article was written as a response to Said. Sivan nowhere shares with the reader the strong criticisms of *Orientalism* by Al-'Adhm, Hanafi, and Bitar. Instead, Sivan conveniently mixes his own bone of contention against Said with the criticisms of the three authors. He then alleges that the book entailed "an all-embracing smear of the West and glorification of the East (or Islam) (141).

In reality, the reception of Said's book in the Arab world was overwhelmingly favorable. Many Arabs expressed pride in the accomplishment of an Arab scholar, who never expressed uneasiness about his Arab roots, despite residing in the West and teaching at a prestigious American university. The press and the scholarship covered Said and his book extensively although it cannot be said that the book was read and understood—perhaps because the Arabic translation is quite inadequate. The translator failed to carry the clarity and elegance of Said's prose and invented new terms for some academic terms in the original book regardless whether they conform to other standard translations of Western scholarship.[2] Discussions of the book in Arabic often celebrated the success of Said without comprehending his message or even reading *Orientalism* or any of his other works. And even if Arabs want to read and understand *Orientalism,* the Arabic translation will thwart their efforts. In one panel discussion of Culture and Imperialism published in the Lebanese scholarly journal *Ab`ad,* one of the panelists began his critique of the book by admitting that he had not read the book (Kabbarah 252). Said is better known as a media personality in the region: Arabs are familiar with his positions on the Palestinian question but they seem to assume what his writings are about, thereby wrongly affiliating him with the vulgar school of Arab nationalism.

There is a vast bibliography in Arabic dealing with *Orientalism* and with Orientalism in general. Many writers dealt with the subject either to achieve success in dealing with what was perceived to be a hot topic or to pursue an ideological campaign that Al-Azhar University has been fighting for decades against Orientalists and missionaries. The only notable Arab contribution to the debate remains the brilliant book of Hichem Djait, although his book is far less clear and coherent than Said's book. Arab criticisms of *Orientalism* lack the sophistication of Said, who never engaged in chauvinist dichotomies or self-righteous national glorification.

The book was misused, and Said should not be blamed for this misuse. The very word "Orientalist" has become a curse word. It is often used to dismiss, intimidate, and silence. One characterization of a work as "Orientalist" is sufficient to render a person intellectually dead. Muhammad Arkoun reports that Arab students in France now divide their bibliographies into Arab authors and non-Arab authors, as if Said intended to define the methodological fallacies of Orientalism in national or religious terms. No reading of Said can support such claims, the efforts of Makiya's distortions not withstanding.

The Arab Marxist Response
The section will cover two Arab Marxist critiques of Said: Sadiq Jalal Al-'Adhm and Mahdi 'Amil. Sadiq Al-'Adhm is a famous thinker trained in Western philosophy and one of the most successful polemicists in the Arab world. He is also identified with the courageous self-critical school of Arabic thought which emerged after the 1967 defeat. Al-'Adhm was for a long time a Marxist-Leninist, although he has drifted

in recent years toward a more neo-conservative stance. 'Amil is a lesser known figure: he is also known in Lebanese communist circles. A prolific writer, 'Amil belongs to the old school of dogmatic Marxism, or what is more commonly known as vulgar Marxism.

Al-'Adhm's criticisms of Said cover a wider number of issues, some of which have to do with *Orientalism* and others that are unfairly blamed on Said. Al-'Adhm accepts the criticisms of classical Orientalism while he disagrees with many of Said's assumptions and conclusions. Al-`Adhm rejects what he sees as the essentialist distinction between East and West in Said's work, although he notes that Said is opposed to such essentialism (22). Al-'Adhm also disagrees with Said on a more important point. He faults him for his criticisms of Gibb and others who commented on the peculiar religiosity and fatalism of the Arabs. Al-'Adhm is critical of Orientalism but he confuses his own brand of self-criticism with whatever is manifested from the Western ideology of hostility against Arabs and Islam. To make his point clear, and to support the contentions of classical Orientalists, Al-'Adhm asks in a self-righteous tone:

> Is it not generally true today that transcendence is more present and nearer to the residents of Damascus and Cairo than to the residents of Paris and London? Is it not true that religion means everything to the Moroccan, Algerian, and Iranian peasant in a way that it does not to the contemporary American farmer or the Soviet Kulkhoz member in our day? (35)

The simple answer to the two questions is a resounding negative, unless Al-`Adhm has more faith in the impressions and observations of classical Orientalism than in empirical evidence. Available studies on religiosity among Westerners and Arabs indicate that Americans are by far among the most religious people on earth—apparently 95 percent of all Americans believe in God (Carroll 29). The percentage of Americans who believe in faith healing was 79 percent in 1996. And 86 percent of all Americans consider themselves to be highly religious, while the percentage of those who consider themselves to be either religious or highly religious in Lebanon is 65 percent (Hanf 481). In Central Asia, 51 percent of people in Kazakhstan and 53 in Uzbekistan expressed belief in religion (Dobson 21). The reference to the religiosity of Muslims is a long-held assumption that Arabs and non-Arabs alike have rarely ventured to verify. A recent study of religiosity among Egyptian peasants, relied on the account of Lane to support the assertion of deep religiosity (Manufi). The authority of Orientalists had not been seriously questioned before Said's book, and many Arabs considered the assertions of Western experts on Islam and the Arabs to be definitive and true. Said wanted to open the door for the legitimate scrutiny of their works and findings.

As a Marxist, Al-'Adhm was offended by the inclusion of Marx among Western thinkers influenced by Orientalist production. Al-'Adhm was surprised that Said would assume that Orientalist ideas would have reached Marx, but why would it not? Was Orientalism not the only depository of ideas and facts about the East for any European writing and thinking about the East? Why should Marx, given the evidence of texts provided by Said, be exempted from such influence? Al-'Adhm denies the notion of Orientalist tendencies in Marx's mind and argues that Marx's analysis of British colonization of India was in fact the result of his intellectual coherence and his "sharp realism" (43).

Other criticisms by Al-'Adhm are less serious and may not warrant a treatment. He, for example, misconstrues Said's words to claim that Said preaches the subservience of the East to the US. No statements by Said, in *Orientalism* or elsewhere, would support this claim. Al-'Adhm then introduces his notion of "Orientalism in reverse," in which he refers to the tendency of the Arabs to argue for their cultural and religious superiority. But this notion of "Orientalism in reverse," with its acceptance of the essentialist and epistemological distinctions rejected by Said, does not belong to Orientalism. In fact, when Al-'Adhm was searching for evidence of this outlook he could not find it in the book, nor in any writings of Said. Instead, we are referred to the pages of the Damascus-based journal *Al-Ma`rifah*, as if Said is responsible for any utterance by any Arab anywhere.

Mahdi 'Amil's book about Edward Said received far less attention and it does not seem to have been discovered by Sivan and Lewis, both of whom seem to be searching for evidence of anti-Said polemics in Arabic. While Al-'Adhm argues and criticizes the book as a whole, 'Amil deals with four pages of the book, the ones that deal with Karl Marx. 'Amil, a former theoretician of the Lebanese communist party who was reportedly assassinated by members of the Party of God in the 1980s, does not seem to be concerned with the entire subject of Orientalism. Motivated by the need to defend the father of Marxism-Leninism, 'Amil concerns himself with unfairness to Marx. For him, the issues of Orientalism are peripheral.

First, it has to be pointed out that 'Amil relies in his response on the

Arabic translation of *Orientalism*, which raises questions about the adequacy of understanding although he later makes a few references to the French translation. The arguments of 'Amil will strike the reader as simple and unsophisticated because they are. Briefly put, 'Amil criticizes Said for treating Western thought as a monolith; he argues that Said fails to note the dialectical relationships between two elements in Western thought at the time of Marx: bourgeois thought versus proletarian thought. He finds Said unfair for attributing bourgeois thinking to the founder of proletarian thought. In other words, the Orientalist method is a facet of bourgeois thought and it does not belong to the works of Karl Marx. But 'Amil fails to explain why proletarian thought should be immune from racist or Orientalist influences. 'Amil, a trained social scientist, is clearly unaware of the various studies, like Theodor Adorno's famous *Authoritarian Personality* and many others since (see Sullivan), which contain evidence of working class prejudice. 'Amil could have at least resorted to the dogmatic explanation of "false consciousness" to dismiss its significance. 'Amil also makes it clear that he does not like subjecting Karl Marx to the same critical standards of that Said applies to Orientalists (23). But really, 'Amil's contribution to the debate is in fact quite insignificant, given his disinterest in Orientalism itself.

The Arab Neo-Conservative Response

Neo-conservatism, as a political movement of this century, has made an impact on the Arab world although the phenomenon has not been technically recognized. Not different from its counterpart in the West,[3] Arab neo-conservatism was born from the disillusionment with communism, even though many champions and leaders of Arab neo-conservatism were never members of communist or socialist organizations. Socialism and communism were never fashionable trends among Arab intellectuals as they were in some Western countries. Ba'thism and various other brands of Arab nationalism and Syrian nationalism (the latter particularly) competed effectively with socialist ideologies in winning the hearts of Arab intellectuals. Without going into the history of the movement, neo-conservatism's main features can be identified as follows:

1) A rejection of communism and socialism because they are seen as direct causes of human misery. Also, no trends within communism—or even leftism—are favored because they all lead to Stalinism.

2) Strong antipathy to the Palestinians. Neo-conservatives tend to

blame the Palestinians for the disaster that befell them. Palestinians are also frequently blamed for Arab problems outside of Palestine (like the Lebanese civil war).

3) Admiration for the US and support for American economic, military, cultural, and political roles in the region. Neo-conservatives also wish to integrate the Arab region into an alliance with the US.

4) Support for Arab gulf countries. Those oil-rich regimes are viewed as stable and reasonable. It is not coincidental, however, that neo-conservatives enjoy financial support from Saudi Arabia and Kuwait.

5) Support for normalization with Israel regardless whether minimal Palestinian demands (as expressed by Arafat and company) are satisfied. Neo-conservatives strongly identify with Shimon Perez.

6) Emphasis on the inferiority of the Arabs and rejection of any commonality of factors among them. The movement views all Arab problems as the product of internal inadequacies and shortcoming. Any blame of the West is rejected. Nostalgia for colonial times is sometimes expressed.

The movement is found around the Arab world, often supported by regimes that may not disagree with any of the aforementioned elements. The rise of neo-conservatism in the Arab world is related to the results of the Gulf War and the defeatist mood in the region. Many express the resignation that many among the masses felt due to the inability of anti-American forces to affect US plans for military and political hegemony. Neo-conservatism in the Arab world, like its counterpart in the West, was propelled by the failure of the left to offer credible alternatives. Furthermore, the left in the Arab world is associated with repressive governments and is no more judged purely on the basis of the promises of Lenin and Marx.

Neo-conservatives seem now to dominate the opinion pages of the two leading international Arabic newspapers, *Al-Hayat* and *Ash-Sharq Al-Awsat*, both of which are directly financed by the Saudi royal family. Kanan Makiya's criticisms of Said should be put in this context, as should the comments of his colleagues, Hazim Saghiyyah and Waddah Shararah. Saghiyyah is probably the harshest critic of Said and *Orientalism*. Saghiyyah was a former leftist who later was an admirer of Khomeini's revolution and model of government although he has recently settled in a firm neo-conservative position.[4] He has been an advocate of normalization with Israel and has joined the Western chorus regarding the evil of Arab terrorism.

Saghiyyah's criticisms of Said are numerous and he conforms to the position that Makiya took against Said. In Saghiyyah's criticisms of Said, it is clear that the author is not only troubled by *Orientalism* but by every political stance that Said has taken over the years. While Saghiyyah's criticisms of Said are based on gross distortion of *Orientalism*, he is clearly at pains to fight his ideological enemies through his attacks on Said. The very title of his book (The cultures of Khomeini: A stance toward Orientalism or a war against a mirage) puts Said in Khomeini's camp, although in fact it was Saghiyyah—not Said—who championed Khomeini over the years. In this book, Saghiyyah lumps Said with Islamic fundamentalists and implies that Said, who teaches at a major Western institution, desires to rid the Arab world of all traces of the West, including its educational and scientific achievements (15). Not only is Saghiyyah unfair to Said here, but he is even unfair to Islamic fundamentalists, none of whom call for boycotting Western knowledge. It is quite false—and Saghiyyah provides no evidence to support his claim—that Arab radicals want to prevent computers and fast food from reaching the region (113).

Furthermore, Saghiyyah links Said and his book to the rise of Islamic fundamentalists in the Middle East and to their violent actions: he specifically lists forced veiling, the bombing of casinos and nightclubs, and the killing campaigns in Algeria. Saghiyyah remembers Said's principled position in defense of Salman Rushdie— he remembers it in a footnote (135)—but dismisses this position as a contradiction and exception.

Saghiyyah then objects to the "politicization of knowledge": he maintains that criticisms of Orientalism—and Saghiyyah does not always make distinctions between Said and other Arab critics of Orientalism in order to facilitate his polemical endeavors—are purely motivated by ideological criteria. The Orientalist's stance towards the Arab-Israeli conflict becomes more important than the standards of critical scholarship. This, of course, does not apply to Said's work as he tackles the subject with references to writers and thinkers who lived prior to the birth of Zionism and his standards are more methodological than political. After all, Said's book upset some supporters of the Palestinians among the Orientalists. So troubled is Saghiyyah with Said's support for the Palestinians that he clearly accuses him of harboring hostility to the Jewish people. Where Said says "Zionists," Saghiyyah transforms it into "Jews" (146).

The underlying neo-conservative stance of Saghiyyah emerges more clearly with references to colonialism. Here one encounters the nostalgia for colonial rule because "it improved the status of women in the colonies" (24). American military intervention should also not be opposed, argues Saghiyyah, because it ended hunger in Somalia. The crime of Orientalism is that it stifles sentiments of admiration and support for colonialism and military domination by the West of the East.

But Saghiyyah's criticisms of Said and his championing of the colonial West is marred by his ignorance of the West (of the past and the present). Saghiyyah sees Said's book as the product of the movement for "political correctness" that he believes swept all Western countries, especially the US. Saghiyyah brings absurd examples as evidence of the prevalence of leftist ideas in the US of all places (29). He objects to Said's criticisms of Orientalism because the West of Saghiyyah is an idealized West: a humane, rational, and non-racist entity. The West and the US in particular is closer to "the human universal" and is therefor the most qualified party to judge the "others"—all others (39). Arabists in the US are all sympathetic to the Arabs, and the author's evidence is presented in a reference to Robert Kaplan's book on the subject. Even during the crusades, Saghiyyah believes that sympathy and admiration for the Arabs prevailed in Europe (81).

Finally, in the neo-conservative paradigm of Saghiyyah, the knowledge of Orientalists cannot be questioned: only their critics can be attacked and their motivations suspected. When Saghiyyah tries to discredit Said's argument he draws upon the knowledge of Bernard Lewis and Raphael Patai, because they are the ones who know, presumably because their Western experience and background grant them an epistemological advantage that Arabs cannot attain. The truth then lies with Lewis and ideology lies with Said.

The Al-Azharite Camp

The position of Al-Azhar toward Orientalism is quite simple to characterize: it calls for making the study of Islam an exclusive domain for Muslims. Even the historian A. L. Tibawi supported this position at the end of this life. While there are differences among the writers of this camp some general agreement exists regarding the aims of Orientalism. Writers of this camp attack interchangeably Orientalism, Westernization, and Christian proslytization. Unlike Said's careful study of the texts of Orientalism and its nuances and characteristics, they treat the production of Orientalism as a solid monolith inspired by deep-seated religious hatred of Islam. The levels of sophistication and knowledge vary among members of this group. Some wrote in

Orientalism in the Arab Context

opposition to Orientalism without having read any of the Orientalists' work, as has the famous Islamic fundamentalist intellectual Muhammad Al-Ghazzali. Other writers, such as Mahmud Zaqzuq, a dean at Al-Azhar, make use of available sources on the subject in foreign languages.

Al-Azhar writers tend to view Orientalist production with deep suspicion. The results are judged before examination: the very religion and nationality of the Orientalists are criticized. Orientalism is often traced in the literature of Azhar writings to the crusades (Aliyyan 10) although the accounts are often confused, mixing Zionism, communism, and Christian proselytization. There is, however, a consensus in this group that the study of Islam can only be done fairly at the hands of Muslims although mention is often made of "even-handed" Orientalists. The religious identity of the writers, however, is often related to hatred of Islam and an agenda of hostility to Muslims. Rarely do Azhar writers dissect the texts of Orientalism and rarely do they draw important methodological distinctions in their body of works.

The tone of the critique in the Azhar camp is unabashedly conspiratorial: Orientalist literature is interpreted as part of an alien Western conspiracy of "Westernization," which aims at the destruction of the Islamic Ummah, the imposition of usury in the economy, the erosion of the family unit, sedition in the nation, the introduction of atheism, the elimination of Arabic as a language, and the deliberate disregard of Arab/Islamic contribution to world civilizations (Al-Jundi 14–16). Yet, those Azhar-affiliated writers do not only object to Western writers and their hostile conspiracies, but also any Arab or Muslim who disagrees with the fundamentalist line. Thus, according to Muhammad Diya' Ar-Rayyis, the "real" author of *Al-Islam wa Usul Al-Hukm* was not 'Ali 'Abdur-Raziq but "most probably" a Jewish Orientalist who hates Islam and Muslims.

The most influential and earliest voice from Al-Azhar against Orientalism came out in the 1950s through a book by Muhammad Al-Bahiyy. In his book, the author relates Orientalism to an anti-Islam campaign that aims at the distortion of Islamic principles. He also elevates the role of Al-Azhar to that of the savior of the nation. For Bahiyy, however, Orientalists who had little in common in their approaches and agendas were all united by a common hatred of Islam (489–498). Other writers in this camp are more careful as they recognize the existence of even-handed Orientalists. In the words of one, Ali Husni Al-Kharbutli: "There is undoubtedly a category of

Western Orientalists who treated Orientalism as a separate science, and who devoted their lives to it and sacrificed for it a lot of effort, time, and money" (80). Like Said, writers in this camp are cognizant of the scientific contribution of Orientalism.

The Azharite camp uses Said's book out of its context and in total disregard of the author's own inclinations. They merely list the book to confirm that suspicion that Orientalism is merely a "new facade for crusaders' wars" (Al-Jabri 159). Other, like the famous leader of the Muslim Brotherhood in Syria, Mustafa As-Siba'i, treat Orientalists as a naive group of ignorant researchers who can be easily made to admit their errors. Siba'i's book on the subject contains tales of his encounters with Orientalists and their admission to him that they were wrong and the Muslims should be left to study Islam. It is in this camp that one finds a strong anti-Semitic influence and an attempt to treat Orientalism as the product of a Jewish conspiracy, despite decades of Azhar-inspired writings about Orientalism as a Christian prosletyzing movement. For Muhammad Diyab, a professor of Islamic doctrine at Al-Azhar University in Asyut, Orientalism has to be explained in terms of the Jewish plan to "control the affairs of the world." To substantiate his claim he cites the much-discredited *Protocols of the Elders of Zion* (78–79). Even the ostensibly more sophisticated and better-educated Mahmud Zaqzuq sees a sinister role for Jews in the Orientalist movement (48–50). With that said, it is clear that the message and conclusions of Said's book are totally ignored by members of this camp, the members of which are consumed with sectarian and religious advocacy and propaganda and with the desire to free Islamic studies from any critical standards of scholarship. This explains that inferior quality of Islamic studies in most Arab countries. Critical inquiries are strictly prohibited in those schools.

Arab Scholarly Responses

The scholarly responses to Said's book are diverse and varied. His book was avidly read and discussed in scholarly circles. Most of the academic discussions of the book prompted intense interest in the subject and led to special features and panels on the topic. Said's book was praised although some authors expressed reservations about some conclusions. Unlike previous groups, this group treated the subject of study carefully and made specific references to texts (of both Said and the Orientalists).

Hasan Hanafi, who despite claims by Sivan is a strong critic of Orientalism, produced what he thinks is the most serious response to

Orientalism. Hanafi thinks that the impact of Orientalism has been great in Arab thought and that an alternative paradigm is needed to free the Arab academe from the terms of reference of Orientalism. Toward that end, he produced his massive work on "Occidentalism." By Occidentalism, Hanafi refers to the need for the study of the West but without being influenced by the terms of reference of Western thought (54–55). Hanafi wants to produce a new science that would free Eastern thought from its inferiority complex and that would avoid the impartiality and biases of the science of Orientalism. His project aims at analyzing the products of Western thought in relations to "old heritage" and "direct reality" (55). But Hanafi, as successful as he is in rationalizing the need for his project of Occidentalist study—or science, to use his language—he fails in defining the features of his project and the entire work winds up being no more than a very informative textbook on Western philosophical thought. Hanafi does not fulfill his promises: he does not show the readers how it is possible to study critically Western thought free of Western thought. And if one expected him to at least engage in a study of non-Western influences on Western thought, he does that in passing, with the work of Martin Bernal barely mentioned. Occidentalism is then, despite denials by Hanafi, a response to Orientalism, thereby giving the West the precedence of the terms of reference.

Hanafi, however, who enjoys a unique command of the knowledge of Western thought and Arab/Islamic thought, is right in pointing out the inadequacies of intellectual borrowing. He laments the lack of originality in Arabic thought in recent years due to the supremacy of Western concepts and ideas. Arabic thought becomes an act of translation and interpretation instead of creativity. Hanafi wants an Arab scientific view of the world, which is impaired by the roles played by Arab intellectuals as "civilizational agents of the West" (66).

Notes
[1] For example, Najib 'Aqiqi's encyclopedic work, *Al-Mustashriqun* (The Orientalists) (Cairo: Dar Al-Ma'arif, 1965), collected information but did not provide a critical analysis of Orientalism.
[2] For a brief but persuasive criticism of the translation, see Khalil, Ahmad Khalil, "Al-Istishraq: Mushkilat Ma`rifah Am Mushkilat I`tiraf Bi-l-Akhar?" (*Al-Fikr Al-`Arabi* 5: 31, Jan–March 1983).
[3] For more on neo-conservatism, see Rob Kroes, ed. *Neoconservatism* (Amsterdam: Free University Press, 1984) and Irving Kristol's *Neoconservatism* (New York: Free Press, 1995).

⁴ For examples of Saghiyyah's pro-Khomeini writings, see his articles in *As-Safir* 1 January 1 and 14 February 1979.

Works Cited

Abdel-Malek, Anouar. "Orientalism in Crisis." *Diogenes* 44 (Winter 1963)

Al-'Adhm, Sadiq Jalal. *Dhihniyyat At-Tahrim* (The mentality of tabooing). Beirut: Riad El-Rayyes Books, 1992.

Adorno, T. W. et al. *The Authoritarian Personality*. New York: Harper & Brothers, 1950.

Aliyyan, Muhammad `Abdul-Fattah. *Adwa' `Ala Al-Istishraq*. (Lights on Orientalism). Kuwait: Dar Al-Buhuth Al-`Ilmiyyah, 1980.

'Amil, Mahdi. *Marks fi Istishraq Edward Said* (Mark in the Orientalism of Edward Said). Beirut: Dar Al-Farabi, 1985.

Al-Bahiyy, Muhammad. *Al-Fikr Al-Islami Al-Hadith wa Silatuhu bi-l-Isti`mar Al-Gharbi* (Modern Islamic thought and its links with Western colonialism). Cairo: 8th edition, Maktabat Wahbah, 1975.

Balta, Paul. *L'islam*. Paris: Le Monde Editions, 1995.

Bloom, Alan. *The Closing of the American Mind*. New York: Simon & Schuster, 1987.

Carroll, Jackson W. et al. *Religion in America: 1950 to the Present*. San Francisco: Harper & Row, 1979.

Diyab, Muhammad Ahmad. *Adwa' `Ala Al-Istishraq wa-l-Mustashriqin* (Lights on Orientalism and Orientalists). Cairo: Dar Al-Manar, 1989.

Djait, Hichem. *L'Europe et L'Islam*. Paris: Editions du Seuil, 1978.

Dobson, Richard B. "Islam in Central Asia: Findings from National Surveys." *Central Asian Monitor* 2 (1994).

Gellner, Ernest. *Postmodernism, Reason, and Religion*. New York: Routledge, 1992.

Al-Ghazzali, Muhammad. *Difa`an `An Al-`Aqidah Wa-sh-Shari`ah* (In defense of the doctrine and Shari`ah). Cairo: Dar Al-Kutub Al-Muhammadiyyah.

Hanafi, Hasan. *Muqaddimah fi `Alim Al-Istighrab* (An introduction in the science of occidentalism). Cairo: Ad-Dar Al-Faniyyah, 1991.

Hanf, Theodor. *Coexistence in Wartime Lebanon: Decline of a State and Rise of a Nation*. Trans. John Richardson. London: The Centre for Lebanese Studies, in association with I. B. Tauris, 1993.

Hourani, Albert. *A History of the Arab Peoples*. Cambridge: Harvard University Press, 1991.

―――. *Islam in European Thought*. New York: Cambridge University Press, 1993.

Huntington, Samuel. *The Clash of Civilizations and the Remaking of World Order*. New York: Simon & Schuster, 1996.

Issawi, Charles. *The Arab World's Legacy*. Princeton: The Darwin Press, 1981.

Al-Jabri, `Abdul-Mut`al. *Al-Istishraq: Wajh Lil Isti`mar Al-Fikri* (Orientalism: A facade for cultural colonialism). Cairo: Maktabat Wahbah, 1995.

Al-Jundi, Anwar. *Ahdaf At-Taghrib fi Al-`Alam Al-`Arabi* (The aims of Westernization in the Arab world). Cairo: Contemporary Islamic Issues, Al-Azhar's Advocacy Secretariat, 1987.

Kabbarah, Ahmad. "Comments." *Ab`ad* 2 (Nov 1994).

Kaplan, Robert. *The Arabists.* New York: The Free Press, 1993.

Al-Kharbutli, `Ali Husni. *Al-Istishraq fi-t-Tarikh Al-Islami* (Orientalism in Islamic history). Cairo: Ma`had Ad-Dirasat Al-Islamiyyah, 1976.

Lewis, Bernard. "Introduction." *Introduction to Islamic Theology and Law.* Ed. Ignaz Goldziher. Princeton: Princeton University Press, 1981.

_____. *Islam and the West.* New York: Oxford University Press, 1993.

Mahdi, Muhsin. *Journal of Islamic Studies* 1:1 (1990), Oxford.

Makiya, Kanan. *Cruelty and Silence: War, Tyranny, Uprising and the Arab World.* New York: W. W. Norton, 1993.

Manufi, Kamal. *Ath-Thaqafah As-Siyasiyyah Li-I-Fallahin Al-Misriyyih* (Political culture of Egyptian peasants). Beirut: Dar Ibn Khaldun, 1980.

Ar-Rayyis, Muhammad Diya'. *Al-Islam wa Al-Khilafah fi Al-`Asr Al-Hadith* (Islam and the caliphate in the modern era). Cairo.

Robinson, Francis. *The Cambridge Illustrated History of the Islamic World.* New York: Cambridge University Press, 1996.

Rodinson, Maxime. *La fascination de l'islam.* Paris: La Decouverte, 1989.

Saghiyyah, Hazim. *Thaqafat Al-Khumayniyyah: Mawqif Min Al-Istishraq Am Harb `Ala Tayf* (The Cultures of Khomeini: A Stance Toward Orientalism or a War against A Mirage). Beirut: Dar Al-Jadid, 1995.

Said, Edward W. *Orientalism.* New York: Random House, 1978.

_____. *Al-Istishraq.* Trans. Kamal Abu Dib. Beirut: Mu'assasat Al-Abhath Al-`Arabiyyah, 1981.

_____. *Culture and Imperialism.* New York: Knopf, 1993.

Siba`i, Mustafa. *Al-Istishraq wa-l-Mustashriqun* (Orientalism and Orientalists). Kuwait: Dar Al-Kutub, 1963.

Sivan, Emmanuel. "Edward Said and His Arab Reviewers." *Interpretations of Islam: Past and Present.* Princeton: The Darwin Press, 1985.

Sullivan, John L. et al. *Political Tolerance and American Democracy.* Chicago: University of Chicago Press, 1982.

Tibawi, A.L. "English-Speaking Orientalists: A Critique of their Approach to Islam and Arab Nationalism." *Islamic Quarterly* 8: 1–4 (1964).

van Ess, Josef. "From Wellhausen to Becker: The Emergence of Kulturgeschichte in Islamic Stuides." *Islamic Studies: A Tradition and Its Problems.* Ed. Malcolm Kerr. Malibu: Undena Publications, 1980.

Watt, W. Montgomery. *Islamic Fundamentalism and Modernity.* London: Routledge, 1988

Wensinck, A. J. "Ibrahim." *Encyclopedia of Islam*, Vol. I.

Zaqzuq, Mahmud Hamdi. *Al-Istishraq wa-l-Khalfiyyah Al-Fikriyyah li-s-Sira` Al-Hadari* (Orientalism and the Cultural Background of the Civilizational Conflict). Qatar: Kitab Al-Ummah, 1983.

THREE

TO PALESTINE

Toward a Pluralistic Existence in Palestine/Israel: The Demise of the Two-State Solution

Naseer Aruri

There is a new reality, unwittingly produced by the Oslo accords—a reality that seemed to escape the minds of many who watched the "historic" signing in person, or on television screens around the globe: the requirements for a just and durable peace are far different today from what they used to be. These accords have dealt a crippling blow to the foundations of the global consensus that defined the prerequisites for a just and durable peace during the 1970s and 80s—that peace was predicated on the right of the Palestinian people to establish their own independent state alongside Israel. Peace was to occur after Israel completed its withdrawal from occupied territories in accordance with UN Security Council Resolution 242, and after the Palestinians recognized Israel's existence and sovereignty in the largest part of their own national patrimony.

By early 2000, almost seven years after the "historic handshake," the pursuit of a negotiated settlement based on two fully sovereign states seemed to have run its course. That project was dealt a severe blow by a colossal imbalance of power between Israel and the Palestinians, by a steady and growing Israelization of American Middle East policy, by a vigorous drive of settler colonization, by Arab disarray and failure to respond to the Israeli challenge and to the exigencies of the post-cold war era. The Oslo process demonstrated that the so-called peace partners were not only far apart conceptually, but were also hopelessly divided over interpretations and what the end results of the process should be. We saw one agreement after another—from Oslo I to Oslo II, from Cairo I to Cairo II, from Early Empowerment to the disempowerment of the Hebron Agreement, to the 1998 Wye River memorandum and then the Sharm al-Shaykh agreement in which Arafat seemed to have accepted, by implication, that UN resolutions may not constitute the basis for a final settlement.

In 1999 and 2000, we witnessed how the lone superpower had to employ vigorous diplomatic resources to persuade Prime Minister

Toward a Pluralistic Existence in Palestine/Israel

Benjamin Netanyahu, and later Ehud Barak, to meet even the veneer of implementation of the agreements. They were drafted in such a way as to enable Israel to conquer territory, to oppress, to displace, and to disposses, without being accused of violating its commitments. Thousands of dunams of land were confiscated and thousands of Palestinians were dispossessed after the Oslo signing, while the built-in impasse continued unabated. It proved to be most efficacious for Israel, which determined the agendas, supplied the draft agreements and maps, and invested in deliberate ambiguity.

Oslo was a unique agreement: it lacked a framework defining the rules of negotiations and the ends of the negotiating process. There was neither an overarching principle, a vision, nor a road map. After the Palestinians embarked on the path of negotiations, they realized that they were still at the stage of determining whether they have rights, instead of trying to claim their internationally-guaranteed rights. They proceeded as if Israel's continuing military occupation did not even exist, and therefore, Israel's claim to what had become "disputed"(rather than "occupied") territories was at least as good as theirs.

The Israeli side knew exactly what it wanted; the Palestinian side dreamed about what it wanted. The Israeli side adhered to the letter—their own letter—of the agreements; the Palestinian side invoked the spirit. The letter said that the enterprise is a mere agreement to reach agreement, that real Palestinian sovereignty with jurisdiction over land and resources, and at the points of entry and exit was utterly out of the question; that Jerusalem is virtually an Israeli city; that the Palestinian struggle for emancipation—from the status of refugees and that of an occupied people—would be dependent on Israeli good will, when final status negotiations were finally held, and after the Palestine Authority complied with ever expanding requirements, which totally negated all prospects for Palestinian emancipation. The letter of Oslo rendered the goal of Palestinian statehood impractical, and obsolete; and yet the Palestinian Oslo dream continued to hang on the spirit, nothing more than a thin thread of hope devoid of any substance.

Paradoxically, the Oslo process led to an inevitable conclusion, which its own architects had neither envisaged, contemplated, nor pursued: The future struggle is toward integration, not separation, toward a pluralistic existence, not exclusion, toward parity, mutuality, common humanity, and a common destiny. This remains the new and important reality, which the Oslo process generated. Ironically, this reality might lay the foundations for a joint Palestinian-Israeli struggle, emanating from a realization that the lives of Palestinians and Israelis are inextricably intertwined. There was and remains a common interest in the economy, employment, water distribution, ecology, human rights, and foreign relations. But by 2000, readiness to translate that commonality into a structural framework that would enable both people to derive equal benefits remained out of reach.

Even if the Oslo process miraculously led to some kind of a breakthrough, the most that seemed possible for the Palestinians in 2000 was a fractured collection of bantustans, non-contiguous enclaves, on about 65 percent of the West Bank, and 65 percent of Gaza. Under optimal conditions, something called the state of Palestine would likely emerge, but would be only nominally independent. Genuine independence had already been ruled out by the agreement between Labor and Likud in January 1997. Entitled "National Agreement Regarding the Negotiations On the Permanent Settlement With The Palestinians," it rejected Palestinian sovereignty, removal of the Israeli settlements, negotiating the status of Jerusalem, repatriating the refugees, and dismantling the occupation. Ehud Barak reiterated all that since he became Prime Minister in the summer of 1999. The difference between Likud and Labor is that the latter is better able to disguise the structural flaws and asymmetrical nature of the enterprise.

As to the argument that Labor's classical Zionist doctrine, which presumably espouses separation, would grant the Palestinians their separate political existence, it must be kept in mind that the doctrine of separation had already been adapted to Likud's notion of "population mixture." The "mixture" idea, first enunciated by Begin and Shamir, and inherent in the autonomy scheme, was reborn as Labor's cantonization. Rabin's peace, which Arafat often described as the "peace of the brave," converged with Netanyahu's approach of the bantustanization of about a third of the Palestinian people, leaving the other two-thirds living in permanent exile or as second-class citizens in Israel itself. Likud supporter William Safire of the *New York Times*, alluded to this brand of apartheid as inevitable and seemingly desirable on September 10, 1997:

> The map of a workable final deal stares us all in the face: A Palestinian flag in a majority of the West Bank land and 98 percent of its people, with road tunnels and overpasses making the new state's large enclaves contiguous and independent of Israel.

The key words in Safire's statement are enclaves, tunnels, and overpasses—which together negate contiguity and independence. Since Oslo II (1995) the Palestinians in the West Bank and Gaza began to realize that they are residents of enclaves separated from each other and from Israel, but functionally indeed part of a "greater Israel." They were separated from the settlements, from Jerusalem, and from each other: cut off from other Palestinian cities and even villages, as well as from the Palestinian diaspora. By 2000, this fragmentation was becoming social, economic, physical and of course regional, despite Oslo's call for a contiguous Palestinian entity.

In view of all that, the "state of Palestine" that emerged from this process would be economically strangled by Israel, dominated by the US and the world financial institutions, and constrained by regional interests and global requirements. It would continue to be intolerant and repressive toward dissent, now re-classified as "terrorism." It would likely be pressed to seek a confederative relationship with Jordan and some kind of association with Israel, in which a Middle East version of NAFTA, with *maquiladora*-style tax-free and low-wage industry, would substitute for development. Moreover, the price of the facade could include a renewed, even permanent, deferral of the final status issues. Having already declared the final status issues, in effect, non-negotiable, the absence of any significant change in the status quo, could result in a renewed struggle by Palestinians and Israelis for equality in a joint democratic and binational society.

The Single-State Solution

A truncated, divided Palestinian state is not what the Palestinian people struggled for most of the past century. And, for all the reasons cited, the early 21st century's struggle for an independent state within the Oslo framework is not likely to succeed either. Which brings us to the new reality that could emerge out of Oslo's inherent flaws. By 2000, outside of the Oslo strictures, a new discourse was already developing about a broader social-economic struggle for equal rights, equal citizenship and equal legitimacy within a single Israeli-Palestinian polity. Different versions, either a democratic secular state or a binational state, were being viewed by a growing number of people on both sides as a viable alternative to perpetual conflict. On the Palestinian side, Edward Said emerged as one of the idea's key champions, advancing the idea in an interview in the *Christian Science Monitor* (27 May 1997):

> The whole idea of trying to produce two states is at an end. The Oslo peace process is really in tatters... The lives of Israelis and Palestinians are hopelessly intertwined. There is no way to separate them. You can have fantasy and denial, or put people in ghettos. But in reality there is a common history. So we have to find a way to live together. It may take 50 years. But... the Israeli experience will gradually turn back toward the world they really live in, the Islamic Arab world. And that can only come through Palestinians.

In an interview with David Barsamian, Said again endorsed secular binationalism, not only as a desirable outcome, but also as a necessary reality:

> Of course, on the West Bank, the settlers and Palestinians interact, through antipathy and hostility, but physically they're in the same place. This is something that can't be changed by pulling people back to separate boundaries or separate states... Then there is the demographic reality: By the year 2010, there will be demographic parity between the two, Palestinians and Israelis. The South Africans, in a country twenty times bigger than Israel, couldn't for long maintain apartheid. And it is unlikely that a place like Israel—which is surrounded on all sides by Arab states—is going to be able to maintain what, in effect, is a system of apartheid for Palestinians. So, although a binational state now seems like a totally long shot and completely utopian, not to say to many people a crazy idea, it is the one idea that will allow people to live with—and not exterminate—each other (35).

Other Palestinian intellectuals in the territories, inside Israel and in exile, including Nadim Rouhana, Adel Ghanem, Azmi Bishara, and Adel Samara and others, joined the call for a single state. Samara, for example, wrote the following:

> The only just and feasible form of binational state... will have to be a state which will dissolve the Zionist regime... cancel the Law of Return, stop importing new settlers, guarantee the Palestinian right of return, equality of land and resources.

Azmi Bishara, the outspoken member of the Knesset considers Israel to be a defacto binational state, albeit without equality for one of the two nationalities. He is presently engaged in a struggle for equal rights and citizenship inside Israel. Interviewed by MERIP's *Middle East Report*, he said

> We cannot sustain our national identity unless we demand equality in Israel. Otherwise, our national identity becomes merely a product

of negating forces, that is to say, a negative national identity, or a product of Israel's refusal to accept us. So, if your national identity is created through inequality only, it becomes shaky and negative. We must build our national identity. On the positive forces inherent in it. We do not exist only because Israel rejects us.

For Bishara, the struggle for equality and group rights was inextricably linked to the struggle for democratic binationalism:

> Individual equality in Israel cannot be achieved without having group rights. It is impossible for the Arabs in Israel to fuse with Jewish Israelis into a single nation as happened in France and the US, because this invalidates the essence of Israel's structure.

Other Palestinian intellectuals like Nadim Rouhana perceived the connection between Oslo's failure and the eventuality of a single binational state in all of historic Palestine:

> The failure of the Oslo process to yield a viable Palestinian State could lead to the convergence of interests of all segments of the Palestinian people in calling for a unitary state in Palestine. Indeed the most likely response to the fading hopes. For a Palestinian state will be not the acceptance of a bantustan system of government in the West Bank, but the development of a mainstream political program that redefines the Israeli-Palestinian Conflict from one over territory and sovereignty to a conflict over power sharing and equality of Palestinian and Jew in historic Palestine in the form of a binational or secular state—the same issue that the Palestinians in Israel are struggling for (78).

In "Seven Roads: Theoretical Options for the Status of the Arabs in Israel," Rouhana also argued that Israel itself, within the 1967 boundaries, should become a binational state.

On the Israeli side, endorsement of binationalism comes from an unusually diverse group, including liberal politicians, secular leftists and, strangely enough, from right-wing rabbis. From the Zionist left, for example, Meron Benvinisti described how:

> The reality in Eretz Israel is a bi-national one. The reality inside the green line is also bi-national... The model which is closest to my heart is that of Belguim. Two people, the Flemings and the Walloons; two regional governments, and one central government.... The direction I would prefer is cantonization, the division of Eretz Israel West of the Jordan River, into Jewish and Arab cantons; I want it to be clear that I include the Galilee and the Triangle in this proposal...

Haim Baram, a secular leftist, known to western audiences through his regular columns in the London-based *Middle East International*, also endorsed the concept of binationalism in order to avert an apartheid regime. On the religious right, a March 1997 *News From Within* article by Yair Sheleg indicated that Israeli Rabbi Menachem Fruman supported the idea of binationalism on the grounds that it would guarantee the "wholeness of the land of Israel" as well as the continuation of the settlements in the West Bank: "I prefer loyalty to the land over loyalty to the state. I see the whole Israel movement as a post-Zionist movement which represents an advance for Zionism over what it is today."

Fruman, however, expressed no apologies for advocating two separate legal standards in the single state—one for Jews and one for Arabs. His single state had no problem accommodating apartheid, the roots of which, he said, had prevailed in the hierarchy of classes during the Middle Ages: "If you want, you can write down that I want to take us back to the 'darkness' of the Middle Ages."

Obviously, it was and is difficult to propose a blue print for binationalism or to even seriously debate the democratic secular state versus the binational state; suffice it to say that the two peoples have always been interconnected, and are therefore challenged to explore the basis for a common existence, the proper modalities, the redress of grievances, and paths to a common vision.

Palestinian Strategies

For the Palestinians, the post-Oslo path of the single state was not a new form of political development, having surfaced after the 1967 occupation as their first program of liberation, the call for a democratic secular state. That program, however, which was linked to armed struggle, was summarily dismissed before it had even been debated, in order to accommodate the Arab states agenda of a diplomatic struggle. There were institutions and there was rhetoric, but the money came from the Arab states. Accordingly, the renunciation of the unitary state idea came as a quid pro quo: the PLO would scale down its national ambitions and accept a two-state approach, while the Arab states would provide diplomatic and material help for an independent Palestinian "mini" state alongside Israel. On the surface, diplomacy was declared a great success, particularly as Israel was isolated in much of the world that came to endorse Palestinian self-determination. In reality however, it was a Pyrrhic victory, as the widely endorsed

Palestinian state was never actually established.

By contrast, the South Africans, who had also declared armed struggle, continued to cling to the goal of a unitary state and to reject pressure to renounce armed struggle. A separate independent existence was not high on their diplomatic agenda. In the case of Palestine, the United Nations focused on the human rights of the people under military occupation and only formally on their right to a separate existence. But in spite of international recognition of their right to independence, they were never able to experience true emancipation. Palestinians continued to endure a status of refugees, of occupied people, and of an ethnic minority in a country in which, during the lifetime of many who remained, they had constituted a majority of the population.

When the Palestinian struggle finally shifted toward the political dimension during the intifada, the goal of a separate independent existence remained intact. It was, however, a struggle suited more toward empowerment and social and economic progress than toward co-existence in a single state. Its principal goal was to make the end of occupation not only desirable, but also manageable.

Alternative Strategies

When the pursuit of independence was impeded by the structural limitations inherent in Oslo, the Palestinians were challenged more than ever to resurrect the political struggle of the intifada: building mass organizations and alternative institutions that would enable them to serve the social, economic, and political needs of the populace. The ongoing and ever-increasing land grab would not be halted by diplomatic action, but would be slowed (if not halted altogether) only by popular mobilization and mass action. Undoubtedly, the task was daunting, for it challenged not only Israel's continuing occupation regime, but the Palestinian Authority (PA) as well. For the PA, any form of extra-Oslo struggle, even that designed to implement principles of international law, was considered seditious and hence subject to repression under the guise of fighting terrorism, guarding Israel's security and meeting the requirements of what Israel and the US called "reciprocity."

And yet, there could be no short cuts to genuine emancipation. The privations and hardships associated with refugees, an occupied population, and second class citizens, would continue to retard Palestinian political development despite all the trappings of statehood. (The PA created a president without executive power, a council without legislative powers, courts with insignificant jurisdiction, an over-blown civilian bureaucracy prone to corruption, and a pervasive military apparatus focused on suppressing dissent).

Any realistic alternative to Oslo must guarantee the removal of incapacities inflicted on the Palestinians in the three spheres (those living in the Palestinian territories of the West Bank, Gaza and East Jerusalem, those inside Israel, and those in the far-flung diaspora). No degree of independence or liberation could be meaningful without removing the legal, social, and economic disabilities that set the Palestinians apart and divide them into the three existing categories. That would require a determined systematic and protracted struggle, combining the three segments of the Palestinian people jointly with Israeli Jews who wish to be neither master of another people, nor privileged in an apartheid system, nor colonial settlers denying the existence of the indigenous natives of the land, nor wishing their disappearance.

The goal of the struggle would have to be equal protection of the law in any such unified state—as in the 14th amendment to the US Constitution: the illegality of any disparity or classification in the law, the end of group segregation, and its removal from the social, economic, and legal fabrics of society. Equality for every single human being in Palestine/Israel would be the motto of the new struggle.

That, of course, would be bound to collide with the interests of the major players—in Washington, Tel Aviv, and Ramallah. For it would signal that US domination of Middle East diplomacy had failed. It would serve as an indictment of Zionism—the classical Labor version of Rabin, Peres, and Barak, as well as the revisionist brand of Jabotinsky, Begin, and Netanyahu. It would serve as an indictment of the narrow brand of Palestinian nationalism, which seemed either unwilling or incapable of re-examining the past with all its errors, pitfalls, and misconceptions.

This kind of struggle may sound unrealistic, and the goal idealistic or utopian, but it certainly has more prospects for success than the 1993–2000 open-ended formula, whose explanation continued to exact higher energies than its application, and whose future was doomed by a grotesque disparity in power, divisions within the respective camps, and a declared reluctance by the self-styled peacemaker to devote sufficient energies to an issue no longer deemed the same kind of vital strategic US national interest.

Arafat's Dilemma

Negotiations between Israel and the PA have been encounters between an elephant and a fly. In 1999 and after, the Clinton Administration was put on notice by Ehud Barak and Israel's congressional backers to reduce the US role in the negotiations. The Palestinians, as the weaker party, were left with very little room to maneuver. Having traded its people's legitimacy for US and Israeli legitimacy, the PLO had placed itself in a no-win situation.

The ongoing stalemate was also fueled by divisions inside Israel. The debate centered not on whether Oslo would end the occupation and restore a measure of normalcy to Israelis and Palestinians, but on the most efficient and least disruptive approach to preserving the status quo under a more benign label. How to repackage the occupation is what really divided Rabin, and later Barak, from Netanyahu. This fact was not lost on a sizable sector of the Palestinian community, inside and outside Palestine. Some comprehend it analytically, others feel it instinctively, irrespective of Arafat's constant expressions of nostalgia for, and repeated devotion to, Rabin's "peacemaker" legacy.

Arafat placed himself in the untenable position of being unable to deliver—to Israel and its US patron, on the one hand, and to his own constituents, who were ready to scale down their aspirations, but not to surrender their rights or to legitimize what the South Africans and the world had renounced—bantustans and apartheid—on the other. Arafat's denunciations of terror and vows to eradicate violence, at the repeated urging of the US and Israel, are seen in the Palestinian street as an ominous attack on civil liberties and the right to dissent. Moreover, his assumption of responsibility for Israel's national and Israelis' personal security was becoming increasingly indefensible when that security assumed an accelerated dimension that negated Palestinian rights— including Israel's demands for water security, settlement security, demographic security (which negated again the rights of refugees).

All of these factors confirmed, prolonged, and expanded the *fin de siecle* stalemate. Oslo had not been designed as a normal diplomatic agreement. It quickly became a guarantor of disagreement and the legitimizer of the status quo. The Palestinians have no choice but to struggle for equal rights and equal dignity, even as Oslo deforms their society and undermines their future development. Not only does Oslo foreclose their option of a separate and sovereign existence, but it also denies them the right to struggle for that existence, inasmuch as most variants of the struggle became classified as either terrorism, violation of reciprocity, failure to abide by commitments, or acts against peace.

Oppositional politics in the West Banks and Gaza were viewed as a challenge to official Palestinian and Israeli security, law and order, despite the privileged position such politics occupy in Israeli and American political life. Thus Oslo, whether managed by Labor or Likud, would remain as part of Israel's negotiating strategy. It was calculated to put the onus on Arafat to prove his ability as an effective gendarme for Israel, while the latter is released from the pressure of finding a solution to its continuing occupation.

The Israeli-crafted Oslo framework meant that Arafat's deal with Israel was predicated on an impossible equation. What Israel wanted, Arafat could not deliver without becoming Israel's puppet and quisling.

The process that began in Oslo can reach nowhere because its path is grounded in the fundamental nature of the Israeli state, which precludes genuine coexistence with the Palestinian people on any equal basis. As long as the Zionist ideology of acquiring Palestinian land while excluding the Palestinian people prevails, a negotiated settlement based on the right of the two people to dignity and self-determination will remain elusive. Benjamin Netanyahu did not repudiate Rabin's strategy; he only rejected his tactics. It should be recalled that when Rabin diverted the negotiating venue from public talks in Washington to secret talks in Oslo in 1993, he was making an important shift away from the stalling tactics of his Likud predecessor, Yitzhak Shamir, while creating his own gridlock with the appearance of diplomatic progress. In a subtle divergence from Shamir, Rabin opted for an agreement with a built-in conflict over meaning, goals, and objectives. Because of that gridlock and built-in conflict, the Oslo process was born in a stalemate and continued to be effectively stalled, despite the continuous staging of diplomatic progress. The US president, after eight years in office, was not inclined to depart the political scene without a legacy. Having been disgraced as a womanizer and a liar, and having suffered serious congressional defeats in foreign policy, he clung tenaciously to the Middle East as his only means of photo-op salvation. And yet, he remained unable and/or unwilling to pay the price for that legacy. Israel's appetite for continuous concessions remained insatiable, and its resistance to pressure (at least the minimal level of pressure the Clinton administration was prepared to exert) remained unshakable. Arafat's concessions seemed never to bottom out. A just and lasting peace remained an elusive Clinton legacy-goal.

Moreover, for the Palestinians, segmenting the negotiations by issues, population categories, regions, towns, and villages, and stages of negotiations remained one of the biggest obstacles to peace. Had the issue of land and settlement not been deferred during Oslo's early "interim status" talks, the question of settlement security would not have become a barrier for redeployment. Had the issue of Hebron not been singled out and deferred, the question of "further" redeployment would not have arisen. Had the issues of Jerusalem and sovereignty not been delayed, the violence associated with the Israeli military's closure of Palestinian population centers, the 1996 tunnel crisis, settlement-building crises in Ras al-Amoud and Jabal Abu Ghneim (Har Homa), and similar "individual" crises, would not have replaced its root causes on the agenda of the "honest broker." Had the deferral pattern not been set, matters relating to self-governance, further redeployment, easing the closure, releasing tax funds, and even resuming negotiations would not have been treated as probationary. Could such a self-defeating process ever have been meant for real implementation?

A Reconsideration of Zionist Ideology

Any serious forward movement beyond 2000's no peace–no war situation would require a veritable debate of Zionist ideology and history, in which the difficult questions suppressed since the establishment of Israel would finally surface. At the heart of the debate would be the requirements of a true peace, and a necessary evaluation of the main Zionist narrative, its negative portrayal of Arabs and its distortion of history. Already, we are told, a post-Zionist debate is taking place inside Israel, but the question remains how extensively and seriously has it been followed by the general public. Ilan Pappe, an Israeli political scientist at Haifa University, studied this post-Zionist phenomenon, providing an academic and cultural critique of Zionism from within. Pappe delineates some of the salient manifestations of that critique in Israeli films, music, and fiction. He touches only slightly on the extent to which this critique has become available to the Israeli general public, and the degree to which it affects public attitudes toward Arabs and Palestinians.1 Pappe, however, reveals how intertwined the lives of Israelis and Palestinians have become. There is an implication in his work that Israel cannot prosper as an isolated Western outpost in the region:

> There is a need to dissolve the sharp contradiction between a Zionist and Jewish state and human rights and democracy. A democratic pluralist Israel as a part of the Mediterranean is also Israel with many historical narratives. Such an Israel has a chance at a common future.

The question of whether Zionism is a movement of national plundering or a movement of a persecuted people acting according to a humane ethic, seeking compromise and peace, is being increasingly raised by Israeli intellectuals. The historian Benny Morris queries the accuracy of the "Zionist ethos claims that we came to this land not to exploit the natives and expel them, and not to occupy them by force."

Only when this kind of critique is broadened to include the mainstream and penetrate the consciousness of the average Jewish Israeli, will the so-called peace process begin to assume truly peaceful dimensions. Only when the Palestinians decide to rediscover and reconstruct their democratic secular state framework, and transform it from a propagandistic slogan to a viable program that can be adapted to present realities, will hopes for real peace be rekindled. No matter what name we give to this phenomenon—a binational solution, a federal system, a cantonal system on the Swiss model—the common denominators are still equal rights, equal citizenship, plurality, and coexistence. It would manifest a common humanity in which the very identity of citizens would have to be reexamined, taking into consideration psychological and ideological factors, and not only ethnic, religious, and nationalistic factors.

Edward Said, providing a non-traditional explanation of identity, described a Palestinian as anyone who identifies with the sufferings of the Palestinians, who resists the limits of what the Oslo final status negotiations have to offer, who participated in the liberationist struggles throughout the 70s and 80s—and not only one who was born in Palestine and is willing to live in whatever ghetto has been chosen for him/her by the architects of Oslo. Said writes that we should

> ... stand firm on the matter of identity as something more significant and politically democratic than mere residence and subservience to what Israel offers us. What we ask for as Palestinians is the right to be citizens and not just numbers in the ultimately losing game being played by the Oslo participants. It is worth pointing out moreover that Israelis will also be the losers if they accept the narrow-minded and ungenerous definition of the Palestinians as a subject people confined to a "homeland" being manipulated by their government. In a decade, there will be demographic parity between Jews and Arabs

in historical Palestine. Better that we accomodate to each other sooner rather than later as full members of a binational secular state than to go on fighting what has been demeaningly called a shepherd's war between feuding tribes. To choose that identity is to make history. Not to choose is to disappear.

Note

[1] See Pappe's series of three articles on the subject: "Post-Zionist Critique on Israel and the Palestinians" in the *Journal of Palestine Studies* 26:2 (Winter 1997): 29–41; 26:3 (Spring 1997): 37–43; 26:4 (Summer 1997): 60–69. See also, his review essay on Israeli Television's Fiftieth Anniversary "Tekumma" Series: "A Post-Zionist View?" *Journal of Palestine Studies* 27:4 (Summer 1998): 99–105.

Works Cited

Barsamian, David. "Edward W. Said." *The Progressive* April 1999: 35.
Benvinisti, Meron. *News from Within*. April 1997.
Bishara, Azmi. "Equal Rights for Arabs in Jewish State: A Goal Unrealizable: An Interview with Azmi Bishara, Knesset Member." MERIP Press Information Note #12. 14 December 1999.
Morris, Benny. *Haaretz* 24 June 1994.
Pappe, Ilan. *Haaretz* 10 June 1994.
Rouhana. Nadim. "Seven Roads: Theoretical Options for the Status of the Arabs in Israel." *GivatHaviva*. Eds. Ozacky-Lazar, Adel Ghanem, and Ilan Pappe. The Institute for Peace Research, 1999.
Rouhana, Nadim. "The Test of Equal Citizenship." *Harvard International Review* 20 (1998): 78.
Edward Said. "By Birth or By Choice?" *Al-Ahram Weekly*. 28 October–3 November 1999.
Samara, Adel. *News From Within*. April 1997.
Sheleg, Yair. *News From Within*. March 1997.

The Arab Economy in Western Eyes: The Economics of Orientalism

Atif A. Kubursi

When the Berlin Wall came tumbling down it fell on a field strewn with the wreckage of the post-war International Economic Order. In the heap were the compromises of the Bretton Woods system, which balanced the exigencies of a liberal world market with domestic responsibilities of states, along with the ideology of development that said all nations can and should bring about economic improvement to their people. This economic order relied on Keynesian economics, which is built on a system of policies and values based on broad alliances and balances between capital and labor, the Welfare State and its entitlements to the vulnerable and disenfranchised, and also the smoke stacks of the Fordism structure of production of large assembly lines of high-wage labor. A power bipolarity afforded the Third World a narrow but real political space for maneuvering and protection of its interests and choices, including several United Nations development institutions that provided the Third World with department stores of technical skills and intellectual forums and platforms for airing their grievances against western domination, exploitation, and intervention. This existed along with an active and vibrant economic tri-polarity that gave the European and Japanese wide margins of independent and competitive actions. And all along, labor moved with relative fluidity across international borders.

Coming on the heels of the fall of the wall and the subsequent dismantling of the Soviet Union, the Gulf War provided a glimpse of the New World Order that has been erected on the ruins of the old one. An order—or a disorder—premised on an unipolar military hegemon unhesistant to project its power thousands of miles away to protect perceived or contrived vital interests and to use military power or services to extract, if not extort, economic advantages. This huge Western technological military industrial superiority can and will be used collectively to suppress any challenge to the increasingly iniquitous world distribution system of wealth and income from the Third World, which was becoming even more marginalized, with very

The Arab Economy in Western Eyes: The Economics of Orientalism

narrow political and economic options. At the same time, the West was more Americanized, with fewer economic and political options for Europe and Japan. The labor movement was emasculated, no longer capable of sustaining the welfare state, as the polarization, domestically and internationally, of wealth increased alongside the decoupling of production from natural resources, finance, and consumption.

Though the New World Order had of course been in the making for few years, the tumbling of the Berlin Wall and the Gulf War finally launched it with a powerful bang. The New Order defines a very specific configuration of the economic and political parameters and perimeters for the Third World. To the extent that the Third World encloses the entire Arab World, the fate and opportunities of the Arab World are inseparable from that of Third World in general. All that is necessary for understanding and evaluating the West's (America's) view of the Arab economy and society would be to look at its perception of and designs for the Third World.

While this view is true to some extent, it fails to recognize that part and parcel of the emerging New World Order is a selective and dissociative American view of the Third World. The Old Order may have viewed and treated most of the Third World areas as part of an amorphous and basically indistinguishable whole. But then the Third World was a large contested market for products and ideology and the domain where most foreign investment was directed. The New World Order has a sharper and narrowly focused view of the Third World. Only those areas that are of direct vital significance and interest to Western industrial, military, and financial interests count. These are the areas that are defined to be of *intrinsic* value and significance to Western security irrespective of any superpower equation (see Ayoob). The rest of the Third World has almost vanished from the west's consciousness, and conscience, as foreign investment is now primarily made in the West or in Eastern Europe, with the ex-Soviet Republics now the new market frontiers. This is a stark change. During the four-and-a-half decades of the post-war era, the working of the international system in general, and the policies adopted by the superpowers in particular, tended to see Third World countries as pawns and proxies played against one another as part of the "Great Game," in which the superpowers tested one another's political will and power in areas of the globe peripheral to their vital concerns and marginal to the maintenance of the central balance of power.

Viewed from within this new context, the Arab World is significantly different from the rest of the Third World because much of it is defined to be of intrinsic and vital significance to Western security. The imbalances in world oil consumption, production and reserves, the huge oil rents collected by dependent and vulnerable governments with little absorptive capacities, and the excessive dependence of Japan and Germany on imported Arab oil are at the heart of this significance, but two other aspects are equally fundamental.

Some US strategists have gone as far as to argue that in the changed strategic context of the New Order, the Third World should replace the Soviet Union as America's leading security concern (see David). Islam has now replaced communism as the major threat to western interests, culture, and values. From this perspective, the Arab World as the heart of Islam is the primary focus of the US strategic posture (see Fukuyama). The real, perceived or contrived inseparability of Israel from the West, and the escalating strong Israeli hold on the domestic articulation of international politics in the US, adds yet another dimension to the western view of the Arab economy and society. Oil, petrodollars, Islam, and Israel combine to fashion a special and specific Western view of the Arab economy and society that is distinct and different from that of the Third World.

In the next section, I will discuss the implications and consequences of the New World Order, or the New American Century, on the Third World economies and societies to the extent that the Arab economy and society partakes in and shares the same fate as that of their Third World brethren. Then I will outline the implications that are unique and specific to the Arab World.

The Third and Arab Worlds in the New Economy

The new global economy is the outcome of globalized production and finance. Its structure and dictates fashion a new and distinct context and role for the Third World within it.

Global production came in the wake of flexible, split, and high-tech manufacturing replacing old Fordist economies of scale and smokestack integrated production. Global production takes advantage of split production runs and computer-aided control to locate in many different locations playing one location against the other so as to maximize cost reductions, savings in taxes, avoidance of anti-pollution regulation, control over labor, and guarantees of political favors. The transnationalization of production necessitates the homogenization of markets and uniformity of tastes. The media is tightly controlled, monopolized in few secure hands and used to enforce a world culture of consumerism and emulation of the West. The mythology of free markets—that they self-regulate, ensuring efficiency and rationality of allocation of scarce resources—is now well entrenched. This mythology is central to the transnationalization of production and finance as it de-constructs any ideological barrier to the free flow of goods, investment, and finance. Technology and labor are locked in place, with the former exclusively in the hands of the dominant and the latter immobilized in the poorer regions of the world.

Global finance is decoupled from production, is virtually unregulated and maintains a multi-country around-the-clock electronic network that transfers on a weekly basis multiples of the international volumes of trade over a whole year (Drucker 783). The network is centered in cities, rather than nations, and has developed a supranational power of its own, in which governments are more accountable to external bond markets than to the public. Their options in exchange rate policy, fiscal/monetary policy, industrial and trade policy have all become constrained by financial interests linked to the global economy. Transnational corporations are more autonomous than the governments themselves. Finance, decoupled from production, rules over the real economy. The interest of finance is short term, basically fluid, and ultimately speculative, changing positions overnight. The supremacy of short-term finance over long-term production and investment has given rise to a new capitalism that Susan Strange calls "Casino Capitalism."

In the absence of political authority with jurisdiction coterminous with transnational markets, global transactions take place under precarious conditions. From the perspective of hegemonic stability, the main problem is that transactions are vulnerable to restrictions by states pursuing domestic interests. States may try to insulate and protect their domestic markets from foreign competition or international instability. The international economy is inconceivable in the context of this "anarchy." It can only work if one state becomes much more powerful than the others, and can bring order to the international economy by using its economic and military power to underwrite and sustain the international order, or better yet, by enforcing a deregulatory regime that surrenders domestic sovereignty and choices to the hegemon or his hegemonic institutions (e.g., the IMF and the WTO). As Karl Polyani has long demonstrated, a market does not regulate itself: it requires military or police power to enforce market rules. Globalization needs an enforcer. The counterpart today to Britain's 19th-century control of the seas is the ability of the United States to project military power world wide, and for the IMF and similar institutions to dictate economic and social policies and practices world wide that are consistent with the vital interests of the US hegemon.

The role of enforcer was increasingly, however, beset with a contradiction. The US projection of military power on a world scale has become more monopolistic, unilateral, and salient while her relative economic strength has declined. The US has increasingly resorted to extortion. The Gulf War netted the US upward of $65 billion and the cash register has not stopped ticking. It also moved quickly to depressurize its domestic labor markets. With a weakened domestic labor movement, the US government moved quickly to dismantle the old broad social alliances between capital and labor and forged new and expanding free trade arrangements with neighboring countries with lower wage rates. The US poor paid quickly for these rearrangements. Through extortion, weakening of the domestic high wage economy, broadening of its market, cajoling of competitors, the establishment of the World Trade Organization to protect its burgeoning intellectual property market (the US produces three-quarters of the world's software), the US has successfully rebalanced its military reach with an expanded and reinvigorated economic base.

The old Westphalian concept of a system of sovereign states is no longer an adequate way of conceptualizing world politics. Sovereignty is now a much looser concept. Having lost any meaningful control of the domestic economy, sovereignty is now restricted to an affirmation of cultural identity. Parallel to this affirmation of sovereignties, three macro-regions have emerged: An American region centered on the United States, an Asian region centered on Japan, and European region centered on the EC. There is little prospect that these regions can operate as autarkic regions. The facts that the same multinational firms are located in the three regions, that the US has a hold on the Gulf, Europe and Japan's main source of oil, and that the US military dominates around the world all preclude this possibility. The implosion of many Asian economies and the recent American rescue of the Japanese economy suggest that these are ultimately political-economic frameworks for organizing, within American-defined constraints and tolerance, inter-regional competition for investment and world market shares.

The Arab Economy in Western Eyes: The Economics of Orientalism

The full implications of all these developments for the Third World in general and the Arab world in particular are clear and ominous. The following is a brief summary of some of the most salient features and trends:

(A) The continued and increased subordination of UN institutions to the World Bank, IMF and the newly formed WTO. Structural adjustment institutions will play a dominant role in managing the economies of the Third World. There will be little or no reprieve for debtor countries. Net capital transfers from the relatively poor (the recent Korean catastrophe transferred huge savings from Korea to US speculators, whose interests were guaranteed by IMF loans) to the rich will continue and will escalate in the future. The margin for Third World and even Japanese independent action will further narrow. The UN will increasingly assume police functions in managing crises in Third World countries and will cumulatively shed technical assistance and developmental functions.

B) Pre-empting south-south cooperation and coordination by pulling successful segments of the Third World into the three macro trading blocs (e.g., Mexico and Chile into NAFTA, Malaysia, Indonesia, Thailand etc. into APEX in southeast Asia and east European countries into the European Union) away from their natural and traditional domains. The new major trading blocs will impinge on the Third World in many respects (see my study on the impact of the EU for the Economic and Social Commission for Western Asia for more).

C) Massive reductions in western foreign aid budgets and the reallocation of the limited funds to Eastern Europe and countries with distinct strategic value to the new US security interests. The weakening of the social groups that had in the past some sensitivity to the plight of the Third World will smooth and unfetter the dismantling of foreign aid and technical assistance. With the end of the Cold War, the full impact of the past US–Soviet rivalry, both negative and positive on development awaits assessment. What will become of the assistance that flowed to the Third World, even if it was based on the strategic calculations of the superpowers as they played the Great Game? With the collapse of the Soviet Union, the source of development assistance has been cut in half (estimates of Soviet aid to Third World countries are difficult to assess, but it is widely believed it amounted to $50 billion, primarily in kind). Moreover, the independent states of the former Soviet empire are now, in a reversal of roles, as much in competition with the Third World, seeking development assistance from the West—as once the Soviet Union was in competition with the West in *providing* assistance to some of the developing countries of the Third World. In Clinton's State of the Union Address to Congress January 1994, the most glaring change from the past was America's withdrawal from foreign aid. The international affairs budget, which covers development aid, security assistance, funding for the World Bank and the IMF programs, and special aid for the countries of the former Soviet Union, was cut from more than $32 billion in 1993/94 to $17 billion in 1994/1995 and thereafter. The US AID (Agency for International Development closed 21 of its foreign posts, mostly in sub-Saharan African Foreign Aid, which was viewed only as a soft tool of cold war strategy. As the budget states, it must change to "fit post-cold war needs." Meanwhile the US will continue to provide the largest portion of its AID money, $5.5 billion, for the regional peace and security program, mainly for Israel and Egypt, and for the arms purchases of Turkey and Greece.

D) Increased marginalization of the Third World. Now that the East/West divide is over, the North/South divide is getting deeper and wider. The Third World is no longer a contested market for products or ideology and no longer a major destination for foreign investment. The new frontier is Eastern Europe. Successful Third World countries are pulled into regional orbits and away from the Third World. Investment is now primarily directed to the three major blocs and again away from the Third World. For example, according to Abe Lowenthal, the director of USC's Center for International Studies, in the mid 1980s, the United States invested more in Denmark than in the whole of Central America (7). Globalization of production did not engulf most of the Third World. Globalization of finance is draining it from its savings. The empowerment of the structural adjustment institutions is exacting higher debt servicing transfers that are making Africa and many Third World countries capital donors to the North. The new World Trading Organization (WTO) that came to existence recently is another institution designed to disenfranchise the Third World. By protecting intellectual property, the first world is making it more difficult for the Third World to share in the information and computer technology revolution. With no new production activities, negative net transfers of capital, higher costs for soft technology and stricter controls of immigration, the Third World is left with increasing populations without the means to cope with their problems. Increasingly the West is blaming the Third World for its population plight, disregarding a fundamental dictum distilled from their own historical experience: the best contraceptive is development itself. Income and wealth disparities between rich and poor countries are widening at unprecedented rates. Per capita income disparities are now 1:150 between the poorest and richest nations. These disparities are not restricted to industrialized versus developing countries. Among developing countries there exists a wide divide between resource-rich and resource-poor countries. In the foreseeable decades ahead the challenge for these resource-rich countries of Asia, Africa, and Latin America will come from the inevitable collision (some say it is already happening) of the decline of resource-based income and the increasing demands of a restive and growing population. In political environments that have proven so far incapable of democratic restructuring, the constricting economic pressures will make it more difficult for governments to continue to support development and to confront imaginatively the task of restructuring the state to provide for a "sustainable" democratic political order. The basic truth remains: the human rights of the poor begin with breakfast, and development cannot be achieved without respect for human dignity. It is worth investigating the connectivity and separability of economic and political rights.

The Arab Dimension: The Oil Factor

If an epoch is to be identified by its most essential material, ours will have to be called the Oil Age. Oil has become the major fuel and probably the most critical and indispensable raw material of the contemporary industrial civilization. Now the largest single component of international trade, with $250 billion in exports (about 10 percent of global international trade), it supplies 40 percent of the world's primary consumption of commercial energy and is the mainstay of industry, the lifeblood of transport, and the sinews of war. Oil has perhaps become the major determinant of today's global military-political-economic balance.

While oil is versatile and its uses are pervasive, its consumption and production are concentrated in few areas and hands. On the demand side, we have the large industrial economies of the West, particularly in Western Europe and more recently the United States, together with Japan, as primarily oil-consuming nations who must depend heavily on imports to meet their needs. Alternatively, on the supply side we have a small group of developing countries, predominately Arab, that produce and export almost all their production primarily to Western Europe, Japan, and the United States.

Production, exploration and particularly refining and distribution are dominated, even in the oil exporting countries, by a handful of large fully integrated multinational corporations flying the flags of countries that only too recently colonized the oil producing countries.

As abundant as oil is in the Arab World, it is also cheap and supplied irregularly with a wide margin of fluctuation usually brought about by political instability crises that involve either the threat or actual disruption of supply. The list of these crises is long but familiar: Mossadegh in 1951, Suez in 1956, the Arab–Israeli war of 1967, the October war of 1973, the Iranian revolution in 1979, the Iran–Iraq war of 1980–88, the Iraqi invasion of Kuwait in 1990.

Oil production, distribution, pricing, and exploration all involve complex economics issues. But they are by no means purely economic questions and to view them in terms only of theoretical and practical economics is to adopt a distorting and misleading perspective. Natural resources mainly belong to governments. Decisions concerning the pace of exploration and development and rates of extraction are now assumed by governments in the producing states. Pricing policies, regulation, and taxation—all are politically motivated. Of course economic theory can shed valuable light on the possible consequences of alternate policies, but the subject as a whole is not the economics of oil. Rather and more accurately it is about the political economy of oil.

How Important is Arab Oil?

Arab oil is, in the end, just an inventory—exhaustible and non-renewable. It is nonetheless a huge inventory (the largest in the world) and is produced at very low costs (the lowest in the world).

The roots of the oil industry in the Arab Middle East go back to the beginning of the century. The earliest discoveries were made in Iran in 1908 and in Iraq in 1927. The huge oil deposits of the Arabian Peninsula were gradually discovered during the 1930s. But the region did not flourish as the world's major depository and exporter of oil until the 1950s, which it has remained ever since, and will continue to be as other regions wind down their supplies. In fact, other regions, such as Mexico and the North Sea, have only been able to be significant oil exporters for a short interval of time. In the early 1950s, the Middle East held almost 50 percent of the world's proven reserves and almost 16 percent of global output. Since then both the percentage of reserves

The Arab Economy in Western Eyes: The Economics of Orientalism

and output have expanded rapidly. In 1990, Middle Eastern oil accounted for almost two-thirds of world reserves (see Table 1). Oil production, which was as low as 6 percent in 1938, climbed rapidly to 16 percent in 1950 and kept its steady increase until 1975 when it reached 36 percent. Between 1975 and 1985 Middle East oil production as a percentage of world production declined measurably. In 1985, it stood at just 19 percent. After 1985 and throughout the late 1980s, the region recovered rapidly its share (Table 2). By 1990, the region's share had climbed back to 27 percent. All predictions suggest an ever-increasing share for the Arab Middle East as other non-Arab producers limit their production and exports in the 1990s and beyond.

Table 1: Proven Oil Reserves in the Arab Middle East

Year	Billion Barrels	Share of World Total (%)
1951	48	48.8
1970	340	54.8
1975	368	55.5
1980	362	55.3
1985	390	54.2
1990	660	65.2

Sources: Resources for Freedom (1952); BP Statistical Review (1975, 85, 91).

Table 2: Arab Middle East and World Production of Oil
(Million Barrels / Day)

Year	Arab	World	Middle East Share of World (%)
1938	0.3	5.5	6
1950	1.7	10.4	16
1955	3.2	15.5	21
1960	5.2	21.1	25
1965	8.3	31.3	27
1970	13.8	47.3	29
1975	19.5	54.7	36
1980	18.5	61.6	30
1985	10.7	56.1	19
1990	17.9	66.7	27

Sources: Darmstadter et. al (1971); BP Statistical Review (1975, 85, 91).

It is now recognized that these figures represent gross underestimates of the true magnitude of Middle Eastern oil and of the relative importance of the region in world oil supply. A number of factors substantiate this claim.

First, the huge jump in proven reserves between 1985 and 1990 reported in Table 1 is the result of a one-time upward revision of existing reserves in Abu Dhabi, Iraq, and Saudi Arabia by a total of 245 billion barrels, which represents more than 80 percent of the previously reported totals. This in itself suggests that the figures in Table 1 are tentative and do not likely represent the full or true picture of what is available in the region. In a way, the figures in Table 1 are supposed to reflect, in principle at least, the volumes of well defined oil in the ground that can be technically and economically exploited at prevailing oil prices. Economists are unhappy about physical measures that show no response to price changes.

Second, the cost of producing oil from the Middle East is still a small fraction of what it costs others to produce oil elsewhere (Adelman; Blair). It is to be expected that unexploited oil reserves also have lower production costs than reserves of oil in other areas. At prevailing prices there is no incentive to spend money on proving or developing these reserves when the rate of return on these expenditures cannot match that of the existing reserves. Though Radetzki claims that even the least economical proved reserves in the Middle East have estimated exploitation costs that are substantially below even the prices that have prevailed since the early 1970s (3).

Third, the region has shown a demonstrable lack of responsiveness of its reserves to price changes. It is expected that marginal wells will be shut down as prices fall. But in fact, the Middle East reserves were unchanged, if anything revised upward, during the period of oil price declines after 1985. At the moment no serious exploration is happening in the region at all. With an ample reserves/production ratio that exceeds 100 years (see Table 3), it is economically pointless to expand reserves any further. Actually, out of 2,346 active exploration rigs in the world outside the Soviet Bloc in 1987, only 4 were active in Saudi Arabia. The whole region had no more than 55 rigs, or 2.2 percent, of the total number of active rigs around the world (OPEC).

Table 3. Reserve Production Ratios 1989

Area	Proven Reserves (in Billion Barrels)	Reserves/Production (in Years)
North America	42.5	10.4
Latin America	99.2	40.3
Venezuela	32.5	47.0
Mexico	46.4	44.2
Western Europe	18.4	12.6
Norway	11.6	20.2
UK	3.8	5.5
USSR & East Europe	58.4	13.1
Arab East	660.3	109.0
Africa	58.8	27.5
Asia & Australia	46.8	20.2
World	1011.8	44.4

Source: Oil and Gas Journal

The facts above suggest that the dominant position of the Middle East in the world oil market is unquestioned. The dependence of the consuming world on its oil is heavy and increasing. Of special significance is the recent increase in United States oil imports from the region. The implications of this increased dependence are many and serious and may usher in some very serious changes in the oil pricing and production profiles. Middle Eastern, particularly Saudi, reserves are vital to the wellbeing of the US economy. Between 1970 and 1973, US oil imports rose from 3.2 to 6 million barrels/day, nearly a 100 percent increase amounting to 35 percent of all domestic consumption (Yergin). US dependence on oil imports has since increased. These imports in 1990 accounted for about half of the American oil consumption, compared to 35 percent as late as 1985. Virtually all the additional imports came from the Gulf; by 1990 oil from the Gulf accounted for 25 percent of total US oil imports. In 1985, this share had been less than 8 percent of the total oil imports (Al-Chalabi). According to a recent study by the Center for Global Energy Studies, US dependence on Middle East (Gulf) oil is expected to increase to 43 percent of total oil imports by the end of the century, if US production remains unchanged. If, however, US oil production continues to decline at the rates observed during the period 1985–90 (five percent annual reduction), the dependence on this oil could reach as high as 57 percent.

The United States has maintained a special Middle Eastern connection particularly to Saudi Arabia, the major OPEC producer, who by 1973 had become the decisive swing producer for the entire world. With the capacity, both technically and economically, to significantly raise or cut oil (as low as 2 million barrels/day and as high as 11 million barrels/day), Saudi Arabia could dictate the spot price in the international oil market. As Yergin indicates, Saudi Arabia's "share of world exports had risen rapidly, from 13 percent in 1970 to 21 percent in 1973, and was continuing to rise" (*Prize* 594). The trend before the price quadrupling was clear: Saudi Arabia, with a sparse population of under eight million people and possessing over a quarter of the world's known supply of oil, could singly determine the future supply-price relations of this most vital resource for the industrialized countries of the West and Japan, and earn revenue far beyond her capacity to spend (in 1981 Saudi oil revenues topped $113 billion, her imports stood at $35 billion) (Kubursi, *Oil* 32–33).

In the period after the death of Faisal in March of 1975 the American-Saudi relationship forged by oil was a given a new strategic dimension. The two partners worked out that the excess revenue earned by Saudi Arabia would be recycled through American financial institutions and military industry. In 1971 Nixon had taken America out of the Gold Standard, bringing about rapid devaluation of the dollar as inflation induced by the Vietnam war further eroded the value of the American currency. In this context the new relationship between the two countries (which was subsequently emulated by other major Middle East producers, principally Kuwait and the U.A.E.), becomes significant in explaining American Middle East policy as part of the larger strategic policy of maintaining American economic primacy over her industrial rivals. In the period 1975–1979 Saudi Arabia purchased about $20 billion worth of military equipment from the United States (Safran 296), most of this income derived from the export of oil to Europe and Japan and then "invested" most of its surplus funds, estimated at over $350 billion, primarily in American Treasury Bills and Bonds or American banks.

The Israeli Factor
The New World Order has presented Israel with new opportunities but changed her role in the global strategic context. Israel appears to be very cognizant of the new implications of the New Order; its recent moves are attempts to reposition itself in the region, ready to take

The Arab Economy in Western Eyes: The Economics of Orientalism

advantage of the new opportunities as well as to forestall any negative fall out. In a nutshell, Israel is trying to emulate the world role of the US in the Middle East. Three specific actions point in this direction. First, it is striving to act as the regional hegemon "enforcer" that can enforce the dictates of the primary hegemon. Second, Israel wants to translate military superiority in the region into economic advantage. Third, it is trying to pull part of the Arab World into its orbit and away from their natural economic environment. In sum, Israel is redefining its position in the Middle East in the image of the US in the world.

It is well recognized that the Israeli economy lives far beyond its means. It has made up for the resource gap by attracting generous foreign aid, restitution payments from Germany and Austria, and the generosity of rich Jews all over the world. The presence of the US in the region with its hands on the oil levers, the dismantling of the Soviet threat and large balance of payment and budget deficits have combined to put these funds in a precarious position.

Israel is the largest economy in the region (its GDP in 1995, $94 billion, was larger than the sum of that of all its Arab neighbors); industrial, with a highly developed infrastructure; technologically advanced; extensively connected to world markets and financial centers, and distinctively a "steroid dependent economy," in which the government plays a dominant and decisive role in every aspect of the economy and society.

Peace is touted to hold promising benefits for the Palestinians in particular and for the Arabs in general. The "peace dividends" are presumed to derive from an increase in external aid, from the rebuilding of indigenous institutional capacities to guide economic and reconstruction efforts, from greater and more guaranteed access to the Israeli market and possibly other western markets, from an increased Palestinian command over domestic natural resources, from the expected increase in international tourism, from the decrease in military spending and from the reduction in political instability and general uncertainty that militated in the past against foreign investment in the region. The Israeli benefits are less discussed, but these, I fear, are far more important and certain than Arab benefits. In bargaining situations such as the one we are facing, it is the relative benefits that count. A balanced evaluation of the "dividends of peace" calls for an assessment of both sides of the ledger.

The alleged gains rest on some strong claims; they have to be examined and evaluated against the background and experience of the

Palestinians under occupation and against traditional economic analysis of evaluating opportunity costs and alternatives. I hasten to say that this calculus of peace is not only of interest to the Palestinians; it is also the concern of all the neighboring Arab countries who are watching the events closely and carefully. What is unfolding in the Occupied Territories is taken as a test case and as a precedent of what is likely to await the Arab economy at large. The more realistic, credible and visible the "benefits" of peace are, the less skeptical the neighbors will be. So far, the Arabs are highly skeptical.

The economic conditions and problems the Palestinians endured under occupation should provide a background and a yardstick for judging the promises and achievements of peace. Israeli occupation of the West Bank and Gaza was very costly for the Palestinians and the Arabs. These costs manifested themselves in a loss of control over water, loss of prime agricultural land, severance from traditional markets, constrained and limited industrial growth, disarticulated and precarious education, inadequate and insufficient investment in physical infrastructure, loss of the indigenous public sector that can protect and guide the process of development, subjugation of the Palestinian population to the occupiers' tax and import regimes, transfer of the Palestinian social surplus to Israel, the export of the local producers to either Israel or the Gulf, and political disruption and violence as people rebelled against the humiliating tyranny of their oppressors.

While the occupation may not be a strictly zero-sum game, Israel derived enormous gains from its occupation. These gains included tapping into Palestinian water, exploiting a captive export market, drawing on cheap labor whose income was spent primarily on Israeli products, confiscating prime agricultural land and skimming all the free rents derived from it, collecting tax revenues far in excess of the occupation and its administration costs, and scooping the large foreign exchange flows from Palestinian remittances from the Gulf and elsewhere.

It is natural to expect that under peace most of these negative factors will be eliminated, some positive gains will be realized and the Palestinians would be compensated for their losses and/or suffering. That is why it is imperative that we tally the Palestinian losses under occupation. It should not be unreasonable either to tally all the losses that the Palestinians suffered from the loss of Palestine in 1948 (see my "Economic Assessment"). Strangely, little mention of these enormous

The Arab Economy in Western Eyes: The Economics of Orientalism

losses surfaces when the economics of peace is discussed.

Under occupation, the West Bank and Gaza were forced into an economic union with Israel. A small, fragmented, disarticulated, poor, and labor-intensive economy was confronted with a relatively rich, advanced, capital-intensive, strategic, and highly centralized economy. Denied both the control over their most vital resource (water) and unimpeded access to the Israeli market or to their traditional Arab markets, agriculture—the mainstay of the pre-occupation economy and the largest employer of people—faltered.

Displaced from agriculture with no alternative employment in industry, labor from the territories moved to work in Israel generally at higher pay than in the Territories, but at the lowest end of the Israeli wage scale. Although they represented no more than 7 percent of total employment in Israel, they constituted the majority of workers in construction and a large share of agriculture labor. On the other hand, they represented over a third of all the employed residents of the Occupied Territories. Their earnings were about 25 percent of the GNP of the West Bank and 40 percent of Gaza's. This export of labor and the rise in labor costs in the Occupied Territories destroyed the possibility of developing domestic manufacturing production. Earnings in Israeli Sheckels went ultimately to buy Israeli goods. It is small wonder that Israeli net exports to the territories were over $500 million per year before the intifada.

Israeli manufacturing could have taken advantage of cheap, unemployed, and uprooted labor by locating in the territories. This did not happen. Some limited subcontracting of clothing and textile sub-activities occurred, but this was restricted to a limited subset of minor tasks generally performed by women. Some have argued that the security situation in the Occupied Territories and the general uncertainty about the future of the areas scared investment away (Kleiman). The insecurity during the intifada and the uncertainty about the future fate of the Territories may explain the lack of investment in the late 1980s, but what about the lack of investment between 1967 and 1987?

The communal pauperization of the Palestinians by denying them access to their resources and, ultimately, even their labor, cannot be dismissed as a pure accident of history or as an unintended and incidental effect of the occupation. Rather, it is part of a longstanding Israeli denial of the existence of the Palestinian as a people and a community capable of leading an independent national existence.

Improvement in the economic prospects of the Palestinians then requires their reconstitution as an independent national community. No amount of international aid can make up for the loss of land and water. In a primarily agrarian economy, water is the most critical economic factor upon which the Palestinian economy can be reconstructed, at least in the initial stages of reconstitution of the economy and society.

The financial requirements for development and reconstruction of the Palestinian economy are finite but massive. The list of urgent needs for sewers, roads, schools, hospitals, ports, airports, et cetera is long and dire. But finance without real resources will perpetuate the Palestinian economy's dependence on outside help and on the Israeli economy. Any large investments made now will go through the Israeli economy and would most likely not be sustainable. I come to this pessimistic view from reviewing the fate of the Arab economy in the 1980s, in which its GDP rate of growth fell far below other regions, including sub-Saharan Africa. Collectively the Middle East and North Africa grew at less than .5 percent a year between 1980 and 1990, whereas the Third World grew at an average rate of 3.4 percent a year during the same period.

Many underlying structural weaknesses in the Arab economy hamper its ability to adjust to global change, meet the challenges of "peace" and protect itself from adverse changes in the international economic environment. Over the 1970s and 80s, the Arab economy's "success" masked many structural problems.

The most fundamental problem afflicting the Arab economy is its heavy (if not exclusive) direct and/or indirect dependence on the natural resource of oil. This dependence has propagated an "Arab Disease" that raised the exchange values of most currencies in the region to the detriment of effective manufacturing exports, inflated costs of production, and undermined local industry and agriculture. It flooded domestic markets with cheap and large volumes of imports that ultimately compromised the balance of payments of even the richest states and engendered unsustainable high consumption patterns that are divorced from high production. The "Arab Disease" encouraged investments in large projects that often were unnecessary and unproductive and ultimately straddled the economy with large maintenance costs, bloated the domestic bureaucracies with overlapping rings of rent seekers, divorced income from production and exposed the domestic economies to the wide fluctuations of the world market for oil over which the Arabs had but little control. The "Arab Disease" is more fundamentally damaging than the "Dutch Disease" that afflicted Holland in the 1940s following the discovery and commercialization of natural gas. Holland had fertile land, abundant water, a highly skilled labor force, and a European infrastructure and market.

While it may be convenient to argue that the Arab economic difficulties in the 1980s can be explained by falling oil prices, the truth lies elsewhere. The fact that oil prices can affect so adversely all economic indicators of performance is itself revealing. In this respect the heavy dependence on oil rents is symptomatic of general economic failure.

The Arab economy today remains almost as undiversified as it was in the 1970s and 80s. Oil exports are still the exclusive economic engine of the region. Rentierism is a widespread phenomenon and is not restricted to the oil rich countries. There is now a "secondary dependence" on oil revenues throughout the region. Exports of manufactured renewable commodities and services contribute very modestly to the external sources of finance of all Arab countries.

Non-oil producing Arab countries have exported their producers to the Gulf and enjoy the convenience of remittances to the development of domestic exports. Manufacturing activity outside oil is limited, disarticulated, traditional, inward-looking, and technologically dependent on outside sources. Little or no technological capabilities are developed within the region. There is a strong preference for "turn key" projects. Expenditures on research and development are modest if not totally inconspicuous. Regional cooperation is a political slogan without any real economic transactions (until today exclusive of oil, Arab regional trade is only four percent of their total international trade). Most Arab countries are linking to non-Arab economic centers with little or no concern for their Arab neighbors. External indebtedness is massive and is beginning to sap the energies of the region. The Arab region is still gambling on "sunset" industries and old Fordist and smoke-stack manufacturing activities. There is little evidence of the new economy in the industrial structures of most Arab economies. Domestic savings are inadequate; they rarely finance investment. High and unproductive consumption habits have been staunchly ingrained in the operating systems of most Arab societies. Illiteracy is still excessively high. Mean years of schooling have increased but remain far below other successful developing countries.

Industrial policies are almost too stringent or absent altogether, with a tendency to adopt IMF peddled "policy fads" that are often inappropriate for Arab development and values.

In short, dependency on the rent from oil has reduced Arab incentives to diversify their economies, develop alternative manufacturing capacities, promote export-oriented industries, encourage domestic savings and anchor income on solid productivity grounds. Although large oil revenues brought about significant improvements in health, education, and infrastructure throughout the Arab world, they diminished the incentive to capitalize on these achievements. While the Palestinians urgently need external sources of finance, they must balance this urgency against the negative and disastrous dependency on precarious international charity. They simply do not need to repeat the Arab experience in the 1970s and 1980s, and should try to avoid contacting this crippling Arab disease.

While water issues are still to be negotiated, all the Agreements concluded so far do not augur for a reasonable Palestinian control over this vital resource. There is a lot of discussion about "unitizing" the management of this "common" resource. Indeed, there are efficiencies in managing jointly this resource, but before any joint management procedures are put in place, it is critical that "property rights" over this resource be established. Agreement (OSLO I) after Agreement (Paris Protocol and OSLO II) still treat Palestinian water as Israeli charity to the Palestinians. Israel raises the share of the Palestinians by a modest amount. This presupposes exclusive Israeli control and management of water. Peace will be credible and visible to the extent the Palestinians are able to reclaim their lost land and water. Even under Oslo II and in the last third phase of the Agreement, the Palestinians will have authority over only one third of their land and one fifth of their water.

Dismantling the occupation should allow the Palestinians to manage their economic affairs as they choose and to protect and guide their economy in the manner they see best serve their interests. The Paris Protocol[1] makes sure that this shall not be the case. The Palestinian economy is put under the Israeli import and tax regimes. Israel, fearing that the Palestinian economy may be used to smuggle duty-free goods (or act as a tax haven), moved very quickly to impose its own tariff regime (the same tariffs on all foreign goods in both Palestine authority territory and Israel). A few exceptions were allowed, as an afterthought to allow some latitude for the Palestinians over goods imported from countries that do not trade with Israel. But generally, the rule is that the

The Arab Economy in Western Eyes: The Economics of Orientalism

Palestinians must impose the same tariffs on imports as the Israelis. These tariffs have evolved to protect and promote the Israeli economy, they are not consistent with the interest of a fledgling economy with limited productive capacity. The Palestinians were promised smoother access to the Israeli market, but the price is greater integration with the Israeli economy. What the Palestinians have worked out is a sort of a mix between a "Custom Union" and a "Common Market" with the Israelis. Any such arrangement generally involves "trade creation" and "trade diversion." One wonders how giving the Israelis full and unimpeded access to the Palestinian market is good for their long-term prospects to build a diversified and productive economy. For all practical purposes, this Agreement perpetuates and legitimates the economic structures that emerged under occupation. Accepting the "Trade Diversion" implications of the Agreement simply means that the Palestinian Authority (PA) has tied its economic fortune to Israel rather than the Arabs. I wonder whether the Palestinian negotiators concluding this Agreement have thought carefully through all of its implications. I suspect not. It does not appear to be consistent with their interest in greater access to the Arab market.

Defenders of the Agreement often quote in its support the many advantages that economic theory generally predicts to follow from freer trade. The general economic belief is that smaller and poorer countries have the most to win from access to the market of richer partners. Much is missing from this argument. If this is really the case, how come we have depressed regions in most advanced economies (Appalachia in the United States, Newfoundland in Canada, and Sicily in Italy, et cetera)? Economists tend to exaggerate the benefits of free trade and underrepresent its "backwash effects" and adjustment costs.

Actually, bargaining theory is perhaps clearer and more realistic about the outcomes of bargaining among unequal partners. It predicts that the party with most options is likely to dictate its interests on the party with little or no options. It does not stretch the imagination much to suggest that all the Agreements concluded so far between the Israelis and Palestinians have been concluded between unequal partners and under duress and that little else but lopsided advantages to the Israelis could have been expected from them.

Many expect greater foreign investment to be attracted to the region as a result of the peace. That indeed is likely to be the case. But much, if not all, of this investment will likely go to the Israelis. Much of the foreign investment that is taking place today is of the tariff-jumping kind. The more custom unions the Israelis succeed in drawing in the region and the more clauses they eliminate from the Arab Boycott, the more foreign investment will come to them.

The Arab Boycott was very costly for the Israelis. Some estimates put the cost at $40 billion over the past four decades. I tend to believe that this cost may have been even higher, if one were to include in the estimate the amount of foreign investment that Israel could have attracted in its absence and if one were to adopt a real present value approach.

The Israelis have increasingly become concerned about the nature of their dependence on foreign aid from the United States. Foreign aid has been at the top of the chopping agenda, as the US has sought to balance its budget. Israel currently claims the lion's share of this aid, so its share will sooner or later be cut. Peace will give Israel a breathing space only. It will postpone the cutting but not the cut. Foreign investment on the order of $3–4 billion will be the only reliable alternative. Israel was not very successful in attracting foreign investment in the past ($200–300 million a year on average). No Arab Boycott and a few custom unions insuring unimpeded access to several Arab markets would change the picture dramatically. And Israel's gain here could easily be the Arab's loss.

Foreign investment in the Arab region has drastically declined from the high levels in the 1950s. Actually the share of the region in total world foreign investment is now less than 3 percent. Access to world markets, new technology, advanced management systems and large investments are almost the exclusive preserve of multinationals. The Palestinians will be ill advised not to take advantage of the current favorable international climate to host and attract foreign investment. But it is equally true that foreign investment is not necessarily beneficial to the host country.

Examples of multinationals that exploit the local market, wrestle substantial concessions that far outweigh their positive contributions, and provide little or no transfer of technology abound. It is invariably the case that positive net benefits from foreign investment were derived by enlightened governments that obstinately negotiated favorable terms from these multinationals that included product mandates, home base operations, and systematic transfer of technology. In the absence of a representative and free national government, the Palestinians are in a weak position to negotiate favorable terms. Besides, their chances of getting a respectable share of foreign investment could depend critically on their guaranteed access to the

The Arab Economy in Western Eyes: The Economics of Orientalism

wider Arab market. The more the Palestinians tie their economic fortunes to the Israelis, the less likely that they will be able to derive concessions from their Arab brethren in this regard.

Greece, which is an hour flying time from Palestine, attracts 12 million international tourists a year. Israel attracts no more than 2 million. With peace, international tourism is likely to increase rapidly. The Arab region is not well prepared for this influx. The Arab tourism infrastructure is limited and international linkages are almost absent. Lebanon used to have a competitive tourism infrastructure, but that was destroyed in the civil war. Today it is not even sufficient to meet the demand of returning Lebanese visitors. Egypt is the only Arab country with the capacity to benefit from the increased flow, but its share of the total is not certain.

The bottom line of tourism is length of stay. The longer tourists stay in a country the more they spend and the larger the benefits from tourism to the host country. Under the prevailing circumstances and if peace were to break out without sufficient planning and preparation, the rewards of tourism will be lost and may even involve diversion from traditional Arab tourist centers (tourists from Gulf states may visit Israel instead of Lebanon or Egypt).

The potential rewards from increased tourism are there. They would be more certain with pro-active preparation and planning. A concerted Arab tourism strategy is required to mount joint marketing and advertising campaigns and to connect tourism flows. In the absence of this pro-active planning and Arab coordination, Israel will get the tourists and would determine how long, how much, and where they spend their tourist dollars. The Arabs will get at most day-trippers. Most tourists will come to Israel and will make occasional short forays into Arab land. The Jordanians are already experiencing some of these negative effects.

For every dollar spent on education in the Arab world, $166 is spent on defense. If peace were to be just and enduring, there could be substantial savings in military wasteful expenditures. The Middle East has the dubious distinction of having the highest military expenditures shares in GDP than any other region in the world. Israel has already reduced her defense expenditures as a percentage of GDP from 22 percent of GNP before Camp David Agreement to 10 percent now. Israel will benefit far more than the Arabs from reallocation of resources away from the military, given the high differential average productivity of the resources in the military in Israel and in the Arab world.

Israeli exports correspond very closely to Arab imports. My own calculation of the Concordance Indices (indices of structural similarity of trade composition by commodity) show that the degree of Israeli concordance with Saudi, Iraqi, Syrian, et cetera trade is twice as large as the corresponding indices with Europe or the US. My estimates suggest a doubling of Israeli exports under peace. Geographical proximity is another advantage for Israel in the region. Using the Palestinians as her marketing agents can speed and raise the potential (see my *Economic Consequences*).

Israel has already gained from another trade angle that even the discussion of peace with the Palestinians brought about. In the past two years Israel had a booming trade surplus while Europe and the US were facing economic difficulties. The reason is increased trade with China, India, and Japan, countries that would not have dared to do business with Israel if the new arrangements with the Palestinians were not in place.

In sum, Israeli "peace dividends" are massive and real while Palestinian and Arab gains are conditional, precarious and highly illusive. Even when these gains are positive they are pale in comparison with those derived or to be derived by the Israelis. The peace agreements concluded so far guarantee Israel the economic benefits it derived under occupation, open new trade vistas, allow for the reduction of defense expenditures, dismantle the Arab boycott, attract new foreign investment, and new international tourism.

Conclusions

There is no level playing field between the Palestinians and the Israelis. The Agreements reflect the vertical organization of power and options in existence. What is concluded under duress cannot last. The interest of peace calls for the immediate and unconditional independence of the Palestinians. Only then can they be expected to conclude meaningful and lasting agreements. The Arabs are watching both the Israelis and the Palestinians. What they see now is not very encouraging.

While the rest of the Third World has one hegemon to contend with, the Arabs have two. The United States and Israel have combined their forces to shape and contain the Arab World. Perhaps more than any other region, the Arab World has suffered measurably from the forces and consequences of globalization. They lost heavily from the liberation of production from natural resources, which ushered in uncontrollable decline of oil prices; from the de-coupling of finance from the real economy, which drained their domestic economies from their high surpluses; from the dismantling of the Soviet Union, a technical and military supplier that moderated their strategic and technological imbalance with Israel, and from the transformation of east Europe from a cooperative region into a competitive one.

Islam has joined oil in deepening Arab strategic vulnerability. The West has reshaped and reoriented their strategic posture to emasculate the Arab world and repress its development. They have done so through blatant punishment of several of its states (Iraq, Libya, Sudan, Lebanon, Syria, Jordan, and Algeria) either through direct military action, political destabilization and/or through crippling embargoes and economic or military containment policies. They did so also by frustrating democratic transitions, preferring instead to deal with cost-effective or benefits-guaranteed despotic regimes.

Few countries in the Third World have suffered as much or in so many ways for their past non-compliance with the wishes of the hegemon. The Arabs appear to be singled out and they continue to pay. Orientalism has not only been a cultural phenomenon: at its heart are economics and strategic designs.

Notes
[1] Formally "Protocol on Economic Relations Between Israel and the PLO as Representing the Palestinian People." It is incorporated as Annex IV in the Cairo Agreement signed on 4 May 1994.

Works Cited
Adelman, M.A. "The Competitive Floor to World Oil Prices." *Energy Journal* 7: 4 (October 1986).
_____. "Oil Resource Wealth of the Middle East" *Energy Studies Review*, Vol. 4, No. 1, Pp. 7-22.
Ayoob, Mohammed. "The Security Problematic of the Third World." *World Politics* 43:2 (1991): 257–83.
Blair, J.M. *The Control of Oil*. London: Macmillan, 1977.
Al-Chalabi, Fadhil J. "Comment." *Energy Studies Review* 4:1 (1992):40–44.
Darmstadter, Joel, P.D. Teitelbaum and J.G. Polach. *Energy in the World Economy: A Statistical Review of Trends in Output, Trade and Consumption Since 1925*. Baltimore: John's Hopkins University Press, 1971
David, Steven R. "Why the Third World Matters." *International Security* 14 (1989): 50–85.
Drucker, Peter. "The Changed World Economy." *Foreign Affairs* 64: 4 (1986).

Fukuyama, Francis. *The End of History and the Last Man.* New York: Free Press, 1992.

Kleiman, Efraim. "The Economic Provisions of the Agreement Between Israel and the PLO." *Working Paper #300.* February, 1995. The Hebrew University of Jerusalem.

Kubursi, Atif. "An Economic Assessment of Total Palestinian Losses." *Palestinian Rights and Losses in 1948.* Ed. Sami Hadawi. London: Saqi Books, 1988:115–189.

Kubursi, Atif. *The Economic Consequences of the Camp David Accords.* Beirut: Institute for Palestine Studies, 1980.

Kubursi, Atif. *Oil, Industrialization & Development in the Arab Gulf States.* London: Croom Helm, 1985: 32–33.

Kubursi, Atif and K. Chan. *The Economic Implications of a Single European Market on Manufaturing in the ESCWA Countries.* 1994.

Lowenthal, Abe. *World Link* November/December 1994.

OPEC. *OPEC 1989 Annual Statistical Bulletin.* Vienna: OPEC, 1991.

Polyani, Karl. *The Great Transformation.* Boston: Beacon Press, 1957.

Radetzki, M. "The Middle East—Its Role in World Oil: A Survey of Issues." Energy Studies Review 4:1 (1992):1–23.

Safran, N. *Saudi Arabia: The Ceaseless Quest for Security.* Cambridge, MA: Harvard University Press, 1985.

Strange, Susan. *Casino Capitalism.* Oxford: Basil Blackwell, 1986.

Yergin, D. "Energy Security in the 1990s." *Foreign Affairs* 67 (Fall 1988): 110–132.

Yergin, D. *The Prize: The Epic Quest for Oil, Money and Power.* New York: Simon and Schuster, 1991.

Peace for Palestine: Building a More Humane Future

John Sigler

It was forty some years ago that I first walked into a graduate seminar on the Middle East. I had majored in international relations as an undergraduate and spent a year in international law on a Fulbright grant at the University of Grenoble in France. Then three years in the American Air Force during the Korean draft before returning to graduate work in international law. I had hoped to make a career with the UN, but my recent Air Force experience had included observing a White House dealing with a Middle East crisis over the Suez Canal. I realized at that time that I knew practically nothing about the Arab world, its history and culture, and even less about Islam, nor did most of the officials at the top of the US administration. I heard that there was a brilliant young Arab professor at Georgetown offering fresh insight on the Middle East, so I signed up for it as an elective. The material was entirely new, and presented in an intellectually stimulating and challenging way, far beyond dates, events, personalities, and structures. It was a total challenge: intellectual, cultural, and most of all moral. I have asked myself ever since how it was that I knew nothing about the Palestinian issue before that course, how could I have failed, as a specialist in international relations and international law, to have heard much about it, read about it, or become involved. Before too long, I changed my program to sign up for every seminar that Hisham Sharabi offered and began not only a lifelong friendship with that young professor but a lifelong commitment to doing whatever I could to learn and try to fill the yawning vacuum about the Arab world and Islam that characterizes so much of university education in North America. Had I been at Columbia, I would have found Edward Said, or Ibrahim Abu Lughod at Northwestern, Walid Khalidi at Harvard, Rashid Khalidi at Chicago, Naseer Aruri at Massachusetts, Fouad Moughrabi at Tennessee, or Elia Zureik at Queen's—and this list is only a partial one of the powerful Palestinian intellectuals who have had a profound effect on North American students. Certainly my life was totally changed, and I know

I speak for many others in acknowledging how important these individuals have been in modeling for their students and colleagues intellectual and social commitment.

Edward Said has provided us with invaluable insights on the relationship of culture to power, and why it has been so difficult to translate understanding and knowledge of the Palestinian position into greater public awareness and more informed and compassionate foreign policies, particularly in the United States, which took over the British imperial role in the Middle East after 1945. Americans have frequently identified with Israel out of a deep commitment to the American myth of a Chosen People exiled from Europe building a City on the Hill, a new Jerusalem, in the Promised Land of America. That Old Testament identification is found not only in the new religious right in the United States, but was shared by Biblically-oriented American presidents Wilson, Roosevelt, Truman, Johnson, Carter, Reagan, and Clinton.[1] Understanding the special relationship that exists between the United States and Israel certainly requires more than ethnic politics, electoral analysis, the influence of the lobby, and grand strategy, although it includes those as well. The seeming philo-semitism in some parts of American culture stands in stark contrast to the general Christian legacy of anti-Semitism in Europe to which political Zionism responded.

Said has also argued that the Palestinian case has been even harder to argue in the United States because of the Holocaust legacy, and the sympathy for the victims of one of the most cruelest persecutions in human history. As he argued in the *Question of Palestine*, "to be the victim of the victim" presents unusual difficulties for the Palestinian cause. All of us have encountered this when people know little of the origins of the Palestine question: sympathy for the victims of the Holocaust cannot be compromised by listening to any criticism of Israeli politics or pro-Israel lobbying. Perhaps Said's strongest contribution to understanding the cultural barriers to communication is his indictment of Orientalism, the deep prejudice against Arabs and Muslims in Western culture, which goes beyond the ethnocentrism common in all cultures, but reflects part of Western identity— whatever the West is, Islam is not, and vice-versa.

Reading *Orientalism* was one of the most important events in my life: after Georgetown, I had studied in the Islamic studies program at UCLA under Gustav von Grunebaum, and I remember constantly wondering why these great specialists in Islam seemed at the same time to be so hostile to it. Said's scholarship made all this much clearer as to how deep this bias ran in Western specialists on Islam. It was not my experience with Sharabi or with Jacques Berque, with whom I worked when he was a visiting professor at UCLA, so this entire argument about how civilizations learn from one another, articulated with brilliance in *Culture and Imperialism*, has been a major intellectual inspiration. In the doctoral seminar in international relations at Carleton, I used *Culture and Imperialism* as the main text, much to the concern of some of my colleagues about how and why I would use someone in the humanities as a source for teaching political science! Here again, Said was a major source helping me understand why I often felt so uncomfortable in the social sciences. In *Middle East Report* in July 1991, he talked about the responsibility of intellectuals. He noted what all of us have encountered in our university careers: a general reluctance of our colleagues to deal with the Middle East for all kinds of reasons. In my field of political science, his critique of American political science is particularly damning. He writes, "the US, as the last empire, has in the case of intellectuals internalized imperial rule" ("Intellectuals"). Like the earlier Orientalists of the British and French Empires, we prepare our students for positions of power. "Intellectuals today," he writes,

> do not challenge the prevailing consensus. They follow a Kuhnian research paradigm that guarantees consultancies, jobs, promotions and the like. American social science has been primarily oriented to social and economic, as opposed to overt military, control ("Prospects").

On that ground alone, one can find a substantial basis for collaboration between American and Israeli social scientists: the overall need for control of an unruly Arab presence.

The quick reorientation of American social science to every passing fad and research contract has only accelerated in the period of a globalized economy. The current emphasis on jobs has had very serious consequences for those of us in Middle East and African studies in particular. The jobs are in trade and investment, not in these "basket case" areas. Enrollments temporarily rise with dramatic episodes like Desert Storm, briefly revive with an Oslo peace process and the promise of trade and investment, and then fade as all the old problems resurface.

In all our graduate courses, we spend very little time on the question of the responsibility of intellectuals in this critical period ahead.

With his typical eloquence, Said has given us a charge:

> We need a return to a kind of old-fashioned historical, literary and above all intellectual scholarship based on the premise that human beings, men and women, make their own history. And just as things are made, they can be unmade and remade. That sense of intellectual and political and citizenry empowerment is what I think the intellectual class needs.
>
> There is only one way to anchor oneself, and this by affiliation with a cause, with a political movement... There has to be some identification, not with the powers that be... there has to be an affiliation with matters involving justice, principle, truth, conviction... For the American intellectual, that simply means, at bottom, in a globalized environment, that there is today one superpower, and the relationship between the US and the rest of the world, based on profit and power, has to be altered from an imperial one to one of coexistence among human communities that can make and remake their own histories together. This seems to me to be the number one priority—there's nothing else ("Intellectuals").

It is to this responsibility of the intellectuals that I want to return in my subtitle of "building a more humane future," but let me first take up that seemingly impossible theme in the first part of my title: Peace for Palestine. For many years, in accepting any invitation to speak about the Palestine question, to university audiences, to organizations, lunches, dinners I suggested the title: the Search for Peace in the Middle East, refusing the title Prospects for Peace, or now the misnomer, the Peace Process. Instead, I used the title of the study by the American Friends Service Committee—the search for peace in the Middle East. The choice of the word "search" remains an appealing one to me because it implies action and movement and responsibility and is therefore preferable to the neutral, observer tone of "outlooks" or "prospects," or even "obstacles." Additionally, "search" does not imply any inevitable success; the emphasis is rather on the difficulties involved in any worthwhile undertaking. The second term, "peace," is not obvious either, although much used and misused. Merely to wish for something is not sufficient to attain it; we require the intensive efforts of many minds to analyze the obstacles to peace, to propose through painstaking and careful research the means for attaining what is perhaps the most widely shared value on this planet.

Recent studies of children's views of the concept of peace have

Peace for Palestine: Building a More Humane Future

shown that it is a value that requires careful maturation and development. Children in their early years—and many of us in our more childlike moments in later years—conceive of peace as simply the absence of stimulus, of a void, of total quiet and withdrawal. Only as the individual matures does he or she develop the concept of peace as active, as an outreach to others, as integration, and in the ultimate sense, as love itself. If one wished to develop the thought, once could say, in the tradition of St. Augustine, born of a Roman father and a Berber mother on the shores of North Africa, that evil is rightly regarded as the absence of love, or in the sense talked of here, the absence of peace. What we really express in the search for peace is the longing shared by all of us for mutual respect and shared understandings.

Throughout his writings, which have often been surrounded by bitter political polemics, Edward Said has insisted on this view of peace: "unlike other peoples who have suffered a colonial experience, the Palestinians do not primarily feel they have been exploited but they have been excluded, denied the right to have a history of their own" ("On"). He has consistently argued as a political program: "We shall not submit to tyranny, we will resist, but we will do so in terms of a vision of the future—the Palestinian idea—based not on exclusivism and rejection, but upon coexistence, mutuality, sharing, and vision"("How to").

Although he was an early articulator of a two-state solution, he has always rejected the exclusivism inherent in nationalism, the core of Zionist thought. The question of Palestine, as it is still called on the UN agenda, has been carefully defined by Said:

> A national movement whose provenance and ideas were European took a land away from a non-European people settled there for centuries; that is a displacement, a conflict, a fact of history with which both Israelis and Palestinians live, and it is not something that rhetoric or drama can long conceal or prettify… that is what must be dealt with candidly and in detail ("Acre").

The Madrid and Oslo diplomatic process has refused to deal with this core question of the exclusive claim of Jewish nationalism. And neither Arab nationalism or Islamism has provided any effective answers to this problem other than to assert a counter-exclusivism. The sharp "we-they" distinctions so essential to all exclusivist discourse have been consistently targeted, in his critical analysis of Zionism, of Arab nationalism, Islamism, and now the "clash of civilizations" arguments of Sam Huntington. Where Said has often been used by proponents of the Arab cause for his critique of others, they have frequently ignored or abandoned him when his sharp analysis targets Arab and particularly Palestinian leadership for failing to affirm the universal values essential to his vision of peace and justice. He insists on the duality of this line of criticism:

> What seems intellectually required now is the development of a combination discourse, one side of which is concretely critical and addresses the real power situation inside the Arab world, and another side that is mainly about affection, sympathy, association, rather than antagonism, resentment, harsh religious fundamentalism, and vindictiveness ("Ignorant").

Said was an early critic of the Fatah policy choice of "armed struggle," inspired as it was by a romantic view of the Algerian fight for independence. The legacy of the FLN has proved a bitter one: a military regime which failed, despite its oil revenues, to develop economically, socially, or politically, and is today locked into a bitter internal struggle of the cruelest violence. From 1982 to 1991, Said tried to get Yasir Arafat to coordinate a massive human rights campaign in the United States, working with a broad international coalition including Israeli supporters of Palestinian rights. The PLO response was a bureaucratic and inept one, always looking for some high level access, harboring a faith in American power to change the situation if the PLO only had access. To get to Washington and the White House handshakes, Yasir Arafat was prepared to make incredible sacrifices in the Palestinian position. From the beginning, Edward Said rejected the Oslo agreements and has consistently and accurately predicted the course of the degradation of the Palestinian cause under this regime. He has insisted: "I am for peace. And I am for a negotiated peace. But this accord is not a just peace"(Shulman). Even the defenders of Oslo would not say it provides for a just outcome. A senior American diplomat expressed American policy clearly to Sara Roy:

> The Israelis are our allies and we are here to support them. The Palestinians are the weaker party and they will just have to take it on the chin. They have to do what we tell them. It's not fair, but that's the way it is (6).

Reading this passage I was reminded of Martin Buber's deep criticism of Zionist practice:

Peace for Palestine: Building a More Humane Future

> (We were) overrun by the consequences of the most frightful happening of modern history, the extermination of millions of Jews by Adolph Hitler.... (these new immigrants) saw in this land merely safety and security. But that hour in world history in which evil seemed to have become all-powerful, able to extirpate everything odious to it with impunity, also exercised a harmful inner influence. The most pernicious of all false teachings, that according to which the way of history is determined by power alone, insinuated itself everywhere into the thinking of people and their governments, while faith in the spirit retained only a mere phraseology.... In a part of the Jewish people...the false teaching continued to prevail even when the subhuman was overthrown. And here in Jewry, in an altogether special way, it meant the betrayal of faith ("Israel").

So in American imperial rhetoric and Israeli practice, power is set against justice, and it is difficult to see how this can ever provide peace in the sense defined above and long argued so eloquently by Edward Said. We are at a deep point of despair, but we may find allies in unlikely places.

For example, during all the years anti-nuclear activists tried to mobilize the Western public and Western leaders to the increasing dangers of hair-trigger deterrence systems and the threat of nuclear holocaust, none of us envisaged that this extensive body of argument and research would be taken up not in the West, but by a new Soviet leader, Mikhail Gorbachev, an intellectual conscious of the need for widespread change in superpower relations. Former Israeli Prime Minister Benjamin Netanyahu hastened the contradictions in the Zionist belief system and provoked a new opposition among Israeli intellectuals and even in the American administration, if we can believe some of the reports about a reluctant secretary of state who was not on speaking terms with the Israeli ambassador, and who has spoken publicly and most likely privately against the collective punishment of the Palestinians by repeated closures and the withholding of tax revenues.

For the first time we have an active post-Zionist movement among Israeli intellectuals (Newman). The new school says that rather than being a Jewish state in which Jews by definition are accorded preferential rights, Israel should be a state of all its citizens. The state cannot be Jewish and democratic at the same time. In the present state of ascendancy of the religious nationalists in Israel today, one could hardly argue that the post-Zionists can or will change much in terms of

Israeli policies in the near future. But a debate has begun. I was much taken by Marc Ellis's recent argument that a Jewish state that permanently oppresses another people means the end of Judaism.

These are not the arguments of *realpolitik*, that all that counts is the power to dominate, ubiquitous and important as that is in all human affairs. But we are caught again in a deep "is-ought" tension, the core of the humanities concern. We would be well advised to heed the advice and the practice of Edward Said in dealing with the challenge ahead. Don't join the naysayers or the pessimists, and most of all, don't withdraw or hide. Take up every invitation to speak out, to write, to argue, to contend, to continue to deal with the vital question of the future of Palestine, and the intellectual's major responsibility "to restore justice to the dispossessed." The issue here is not only to restore justice to this badly fragmented, scattered, and traumatized group of six million Palestinians, but as part of the larger question involved, as defined by Said:

> We need to reorient education so that central to the common awareness is not a paranoid sense of who is top or best, but a map of this tiny planet, its resources and environment nearly worn out, its inhabitants' demands for better lives nearly out of control. The competitive, coercive guidelines that have prevailed are simply no good anymore. To argue and persuade rather than to boast, preach, and destroy—that is the change to be made ("Ignorant").

Note

[1] Peter Grose developed this Biblical theme at some length in *Israel in the Mind of America* (New York: Knopf, 1982), although Said has emphasized that Grose does not tie these cultural factors to vested imperial interests as well. For an important analysis of the impact of this cultural identification with Israel on American presidents, see Leslie Ring's *By Heaven Designed: American Foreign Policy toward the State of Israel* (Master's thesis, Norman Paterson School of International Affairs, Carleton University).

Works Cited

Buber, Martin. "Israel and the Command of the Spirit." Quoted in Paul R. Mendes Flohr, ed. *A Land of Two Peoples*. London: Oxford University Press, 1893: 291–2.

Ellis, Marc. Paper presented to North American Coordinating Committee of NGOs on the Question of Palestine. United Nations. New York, 11 June 1997.

Newman, David. "Rethinking Zionism for the Next Half Century." *Globe and*

Mail 30 August 1997: D4.

Roy, Sara. "US Economic Aid to the West Bank and Gaza Strip: the Politics of Peace." *Middle East Policy* 4 (1996): 6.

Said, Edward. "The Acre and the Goat." *New Statesman* 11 May 1979. Rpt. In *The Politics of Dispossession*: Chapter 4.

———."How to Answer Palestine's Challenge." *Mother Jones* September 1988. Rpt. in *The Politics of Dispossession*: Chapter 14.

———."Ignorant Armies Clash by Night." *The Nation* 11 February 1991. Rpt. In *The Politics of Dispossession*: Chapter 28.

———."The Intellectuals and the War." *Middle East Report* July 1991. Rpt. in *The Politics of Dispossession*: Chapter 30.

———. "On Palestinian Identity: a Conversation with Salmon Rushdie." *New Left Review* December 1986. Rpt. In *The Politics of Dispossession*: Chapter 12.

———. *The Politics of Dispossession*. New York: Vintage, 1995.

———. "The Prospects for Peace in the Middle East." Open Magazine Pamphlet Series. Rpt. in *The Politics of Dispossession*: Chapter 17.

———. *Question of Palestine*. New York: Vintage, 1979.

Shulman, Ken. "Roots of the West's Fear of Islam." *International Herald Tribune* 11 March 1996.

EPILOGUE

Edward W. Said & His "Beautiful Old House": A Response to Weiner

Muhammad A. Shuraydi

Justus Reid Weiner's 1999 article, "My Beautiful Old House and Other Fabrications by Edward Said," in *Commentary* magazine reignites the venomous attacks waged in the 1980s by some Zionists and pro-Israeli sympathizers on this internationally renowned scholar and spokesperson of the Palestinian and other voiceless victims of oppression, apartheid, postcolonialism, and dictatorships. These slanderous attacks characterized Said as the "Professor of Terror" (Alexander), the "Bright Star of English Lit. and PLO " (Eder), and a source of "Palestinian Rage" (Krupnick).

Notwithstanding the fact that these despicable attacks failed to discredit Said's academic integrity or taint his political commitment, they did inflict immense psychological pain on Said and his family, as he himself acknowledged:

> My family and I lived with death threats; my office was vandalized and sacked; I had to endure libelous abuse about my people and cause—not only as a terrorist but also as a professor of terror, an anti-Semite, an accomplice to murder, a liar, a deranged demagogue, etc" (*Politics* xix).

The most recent wave of vilification against Said was led by the same right-wing magazine, *Commentary*, that targeted him a decade ago. Weiner's article spearheaded a series of articles maliciously deconstructing Said in prestigious newspapers, including the *London Daily Telegraph, The Wall Street Journal, The New York Times, The Boston Globe,* and *The Jerusalem Post.*

The new defamation campaign coincided with two significant events: the publication of Said's first volume of memoirs, *Out of Place,* and the approach of the final status negotiations between Israel and the Palestinian Authority. In this regard, it became of paramount significance for his opponents to undermine Said's moral authority as a staunch defender of the Palestinian people and their inalienable rights and a powerful narrator of their history of victimization, diaspora, and

Edward W. Said & His "Beautiful Old House": A Response to Weiner

suffering to the international community. Debunking the symbolism of Said to the Palestinian cause served Israel's interests especially vis-a-vis his vehement critique of the Oslo Accords and their failure to bring about a just lasting peace. To borrow Weiner's own labeling terminology, Said's "uncompromising politics," and "inflammatory term of reparations" embody long-term dangerous implications for Israel, particularly if we also add his concept of a secular binational state for both Israeli Jews and Palestinians. Hence, to Weiner, his financiers and collaborators, it was well worth it to travel over a three-year span to four continents and five countries conducting 85 interviews in order to "substantiate" his predetermined conclusion alleging that Edward Said has for the last thirty years been lying about his Palestinian identity and selfhood, childhood experiences and schooling, the departure of his family from Jerusalem, Palestine, and the ownership of his "beautiful old house" in Talbiya, Jerusalem. The project was principally funded by Michael Milken, a former junk bond dealer jailed in 1991 for insider trading. It required the insidious talents of a researcher of the caliber of Justus Reid Weiner, who prior to his joining the Jerusalem Center for Public Affairs, "was for 12 years an official in the Israeli justice ministry, one of whose tasks was to defend the security forces in the occupied territories from Amnesty International (Jaggi).

Weiner, who accuses Edward Said of a "typical disregard for facts" allows himself to "speculate" that Said was alerted of his research and, therefore, was forced to revise his previous autobiographical account. Two facts are totally distorted in this respect. First, that Said started writing his memoir in 1994, the time he started chemotherapy, at least two years prior to Weiner's research. Second, that Said's writing of his memoir was in response to his grief over the passing away of his mother as a cancer victim in 1989 (Jaggi).

Weiner compliments himself on his "Newtonian discovery," which consumed three years of a "columbo-like" investigative endeavor to corroborate the "truth" about Said's childhood. This achievement could have conveniently and fairly been verified by interviewing Edward Said in person, which by all measures is the most valid approach; or at least documenting that all avenues to do so were exhausted and failed. Weiner's ego-involvement in the research should have required him to do more than make "a request for an interview made through his (Said's) assistant, Zeineb Istrabadi, [which] met with no response" (29). Dr. Istrabadi swears this is a lie (Blume).

Weiner refers to Said's "nuclear family" at least three times in his article. He never places Edward Said within the proper broader context of the extended family, the Wadies and Boulos' together, which was the dominant family pattern in the region in the 1930s and 1940s. His cultural myopia is also apparent in his Western assertion that a family of ten members, both Wadie's and Boulos' could not be accommodated in an apartment consisting of four bedrooms because, "assuming two rooms were set aside for parents, this would have meant accommodating ten children in the remaining two bedrooms" (27). How culturally evident is Weiner's lack of awareness that in some Arab countries, including wealthy ones, some large-size families do live in one- or two-bedroom apartments, with children sleeping in the same room as the parents. In his pursuit to discredit Edward Said, Weiner and his collaborators have done a marvelous job of discrediting themselves. As Said puts it, "going to someone's childhood home to see how many family members they think could fit in it is something even the most extreme Stalinist commissar would have shied away from" (Jaggi).

In the Arab culture, a house is not a real estate affair in the same way it is in Western cultures, in at least two ways.

First, families in the Arab culture are not primarily preoccupied with title deeds or questions of ownership or even private matters in the same way as they are in the West. They are more concerned about helping each other manage their residential arrangements to maintain the warmth, support, and emotional ties of the extended family. In many cases, children marry and continue to reside with their parents or in-laws. Relatives live with other relatives according to their convenience or until they can secure their own residential arrangements. Wives, children, and other members of a family live with other relatives when their "bread-winners" are "officially" residing in other countries or places. A clear case in point is the fact that at the present many Lebanese, Egyptians, Syrians, Jordanians, and other Arab nationals work or own businesses in the Arab Gulf countries such as Saudi Arabia, Kuwait, and U.A.E., while other significant members of their families remain in their countries of origin. To equate a formal address or a blank space relating to a local address with true indicators of family secrets or deceptions, or to impute dishonest motives, as Weiner does, is methodologically erroneous to say the least. Double or multiple residences of a family in the same country or different countries were and still are a common and legally acceptable practice.

Second, symbolically and psychologically speaking, a house signifies

Edward W. Said & His "Beautiful Old House": A Response to Weiner

more than a title deed. In a symbolic interactionist perspective, according to George Herbert Mead, Herbert Blumer, and others, a house is an object that embodies a multiplicity of meanings or symbols. Childhood memories, recollections, and fantasies are an inseparable part of this symbolic representation. Edward Said's memories of his house in Palestine, as well as his other places of residence in Cairo, Egypt and Dhour el-Showeir, Lebanon, should be objectively evaluated as such. If childhood memories of places of residence are to be evaluated by title deeds only, then this procedure will surely deprive many children in the West of their childhood dreams and memories. After all, the banks in Western societies actually own a high percentage of houses belonging to families that falsely think and cognitively behave as if they really own their houses.

Just ask a sample of innocent children what comes to their minds when they think of "their house." I did this simple test with my nine-year-old daughter, who responded in writing in a five-minute interval without bothering to ask whether our house is fully paid for or if we own the title deed. Her responses were:

> When I think of my house I think of birds singing on trees, I think of buzzing bees, I think of kids screaming, I think of mommy and my two birds Night and Zana. But most of all I think of daddy doing his Ph.D. I think of that stupid dog barking, I think of happiness, I think of love, I also think of a white dove, I think of the fake eagle on the roof, I think of flowers, birds and bees, but most of all I think of you and me. You heard my story, now I get to hear you.

In sum, "my beautiful old house," connotatively carries more meanings and symbolism for Edward Said than the ridiculous simplistic identification with a title deed. In any case, Edward Said's father, Wadie, was a fifty-percent partner in the ownership of the house and property (Blume). His father's cousin, Boulos, owned the other fifty percent.

Only future history will reveal the significance of the traumatic memories of the Palestinian children who have for decades been living in refugee camps in the diaspora and in whose name Said is continuing the struggle for a just peace. In their book, *Palestinians Without Palestine: A Study of Political Socialization Among Palestinian Youth*, Kuroda and Kuroda empirically documented that, "you can take the Palestinians out of Palestine, but you cannot take Palestine out of the Palestinians." They had skillfully shown how Palestinian children born outside Palestine maintain their Palestinian national identification around which their sources of happiness or unhappiness are defined and anchored. Since human beings, unlike animals, function at a conceptual level that enables them to transcend the constraints of time, place, and even title deeds, should these children be deprived from identifying with Palestine because they were not born there? Should Edward Said be uprooted from his childhood memories about the displacement of his own people, the Palestinians, by the mere fact that he belonged to a prosperous family? Or, should he be denied empathy with their catastrophe (*Al-Nakba*), forced exodus, and diaspora, because of his upper class affiliation that sheltered him from directly experiencing the immediate suffering poorer Palestinians went through? Clearly no. He himself, in more than one place and on more than one occasion, stressed that he belonged to a privileged family and he did not first-hand experience the indescribable suffering of Palestinian refugees, a fact which certainly should not strip him of his championing the Palestinian cause. Not all the prominent scholars who have written powerfully about the horrors of Auschwitz were themselves Holocaust survivors.

Does the fact that Edward Said left Jerusalem permanently in 1947 rather than forcibly fled the next year undermine the indisputable fact that hundreds of thousands of Palestinians were dispossessed and forced to leave Palestine in 1948? The unforgettable reminders of this fact are not the statistical data scattered in dusty books but the millions of Palestinians still living under the most miserable conditions in refugee camps in the West Bank and Gaza, Jordan, Egypt, Lebanon and Syria.

As Israeli scholar Israel Shahak, himself a survivor of the inhuman Holocaust, properly puts it,

> The argument over how the Said family left did not affect Professor Said's status as a refugee. This is like saying Jews who escaped from Germany before the war were not kicked out. The main argument is that they were prevented from returning to their land. This is what it is about (Borger).

Should one accept Weiner's innuendo that Edward Said was in reality an Egyptian accidentally born in Jerusalem during a family visit there? Daniel Pipes, who makes a career out of championing Israel's agenda, explicitly and rather astonishingly declares that Said "falsely claims to be a Palestinian" because this serves as "a good career move." In fact, and paradoxically, Said's unsurpassed scholarship, expertise as a

Edward W. Said & His "Beautiful Old House": A Response to Weiner

literacy/cultural critic, and authoritative knowledge of the European classics preceded his political advocacy. It was precisely his scholarly prominence that contributed to his effectiveness in articulating the Palestinian cause.

With the approaching final status negotiations between Israel and the Palestinian Authority, Weiner does not forget to address the question of compensation or reparations. He asks why Edward Said did not file a claim for his lost property since he knows, "that the process is simplicity itself. All that is required is the completion of a two-page form that can be filled out in English, Hebrew, or Arabic" (30). Weiner's characterization of the Israeli legal system disregards its double standard of justice and projects a false image of Israel as the only democracy in the Middle East. Because Israel was founded and to this day functions as a state for all Jews and not for all its citizens, its judicial system is inherently discriminatory and racist. An illustrative example is the case of the village of Ikrit. Its Christian Arab natives are still deprived of returning to their village despite a ruling by the Israeli high court to this effect 51 years ago, and despite the fact that they have learned Hebrew and taken Israeli citizenship. As Neil MacDonald, the Middle East CBC correspondent in Jerusalem reported on September 22, 1999, Israel does not want the dispossessed villagers of Ikrit to have their village back, "because if the people of Ikrit can have their village back, what about all the other Palestinians who were forced out of their homes and off their lands to make room for the Jewish State?"

Said himself answers the question, in "Defamation, Zionist Style:

> ...Weiner says that we didn't try for reparations, thereby deliberately obfuscating two facts: that my father did in fact try to sue the Israeli Government for reparations and second, that by 1950 the law of absentee property passed by Israel had converted all Palestinian property, illegally of course. No wonder our efforts were unrewarded.... Weiner is a propagandist who, like many others before him, has tried to depict the dispossession of the Palestinians as an ideological fiction: this has been a constant theme of Zionist "information" since the 1930s. Weiner's polemic covers up the racism of Israel's Law of Return, which allows any Jew anywhere to emigrate to Israel, while no Palestinian, even someone born there, has any such right. If someone like Edward Said is a liar, runs the argument, how can we believe all those peasants who say they were driven off their land?" (Said, "Defamation")

Weiner's true political purpose is revealed at the end of his article when he urges his readers to generalize from the specific case of Edward Said to the entire Palestinian people (31). This dangerous extrapolation is not only scientifically and methodologically unacceptable, but it is a monstrous falsehood from someone pretending to unearth the lies of others.

One further note. Contrary to Weiner's completely false portrayal of Said as intransigent and uncompromising on the Arab-Israeli conflict, Said has been known since the middle of the 1970s and throughout the 1980s as a pioneer of the strategy of real reconciliation between Palestinians and Israeli Jews. His book, *The Question of Palestine,* is an essay on reconciliation. His original call for the recognition of Israel and a two-state solution was severely attacked within the PLO by both the mainstream Fatah and the leftist Popular Front for the Liberation of Palestine, in addition to many other Palestinian and Arab analysts. His conciliatory stand was reiterated in the "Declaration of Independence" which was adopted by Palestine National Council (the PLO's parliament-in-exile) in Algiers in 1988, and which Said both helped to formulate and translated into English. What now seems to infuriate Weiner and his collaborators is Said's change from "being a supporter of Yasir Arafat to a vociferous opponent, accusing the PLO Chairman of having betrayed 50 years of Palestinian aspirations by signing the Oslo agreements with Israel" (23).

The irony of history and of pragmatic politics is that Arafat, the despised terrorist of yesterday, has been ingeniously marketed as the brave peacemaker and Nobel prize winner of today. Edward Said, on the other hand, is depicted as a pathetic liar and an unreasonable, intolerant radical. Paradoxically, he has become the common enemy of both the Zionists and the leadership of the Palestinian Authority.

Said's rejection of the Oslo Declaration of Principles, which he called a "Palestinian Versailles" is not based on his rejection of peace with Israel or the denial of the legitimate rights of the Jewish people. Rather, he views Oslo's one-sided concessions, which undermine the national aspirations of the Palestinian people, as an obstruction to the attainability of a just peace. He emphasizes the fact that the Oslo Accords do not include any reference, not even a sentence, about the Palestinians' right to self-determination (*Peace* 173–4). Within the Israeli scheme, he notes, "self-rule is an extension of the occupation by other means." He asserts that, "for the first time in the twentieth century an anticolonial liberation movement had made an agreement to cooperate with a military occupation before that occupation had ended" (xxix).

Edward W. Said & His "Beautiful Old House": A Response to Weiner

In many interviews, Said maintained his rejection of the Oslo Accords as "skewed and unworkable," offering no adequate redress for Palestinian suffering. In *Al-Hayat* (3 October 1999) and *Al-Ahram Weekly* (September 30-October 6, 1999), Said reaffirms that view, unabashedly analyzing Arafat's successful attempts to diminish the democratic political participation of the Palestinian people. Furthermore, he stresses that, "There is little doubt that his (Arafat's) circumstances will compel him to sign what the Israelis and the US want him to sign."

Unambiguously stated, Said is definitely not against any genuinely just peace that equally takes into consideration the legitimate rights of both the Israeli Jews and the Palestinians. He certainly is against any capitulation nicely packaged in the name of peace or any domestication of the will of the Palestinian people cunningly marketed as a national victory.

The potential danger of Edward Said to the Zionists and pro-Zionists does not merely lie in his fierce opposition to the Oslo Accords, which have generated their own realities on the ground. His real threat inheres in his revised call (see "The One-State Solution") for a single secular democratic binational state for both Israeli Jews and Palestinians, based on the concept of citizenship with equal justice for each citizen guaranteed by the constitution. It carries with it unforeseen consequences for the survival of the State of Israel as an exclusivist Jewish state. This new concept is intentionally or unintentionally totally ignored by Weiner. Ironically, its profound implications would have come closer to justifying his expensive three-year investigation aimed at dismantling Said's unassailable international reputation and solidly growing popularity even inside Israel itself, as a committed scholar, a revered anti-colonial writer, and a defender of an honorable, true and lasting peace with equality, freedom, dignity, and justice for all.

Works Cited

Alexander, Edward. "Professor of Terror." *Commentary* 88: 2 (August 1989).
Anis, Mona. "A Preview of Said's Out of Place: A Memoir." *Al-Ahram Weekly.* 9–15 September 1999.
Arnold, Michael S. "A Different Voice." *Jerusalem Post* 29 March 1999.
Barsamian, David. "Interview with Edward Said." *The Progressive.* April 1999.
Blume, Harvey. "Edward Said Confronts His Future, Past and His Critics' Accusations." *Atlantic Monthly* September 1999.
Borger, Jolian. "Friends Rally to Repulse Attack on Edward Said." *The Guardian,* 23 August 1999.

Eder, Richard. "Edward Said: Bright Star of English Lit and PLO." *New York Times,* 22 February 1980.

Ibish, Hussein. "They Can't Will the Palestinians Out of Existence." *Boston Globe* 1 September 1999.

Jaggi, Maya. The Guardian Profile: Edward Said. *The Guardian,* 11 September 1999.

Krupnick, Mark. "Edward Said: Discourse and Palestinian Rage." *Tikkun* 4:6 (1989).

Kuroda, A.K. and Y. Kuroda. *Palestinians Without Palestine: A Study of Political Socialization Among Palestinian Youth.* Washington, D.C.: University Press of America, 1978.

Lehmann-Haupt, C. "Out of Place: A Voice for Palestinians Speaks Now for Himself." *New York Times*, 16 September 1999.

MacDonald, Neil. "Asked to Leave 51 Years Ago—Villagers Still Hoping for Return." CBC News, 22 September 1999.

Pipes, Daniel. "A Good Career Move." *The Jerusalem Post* 7 September 1999.

Said, Edward W. "Defamation, Zionist Style." 1999. © Edward W. Said

_____. "The One-State Solution." *The New York Times Magazine* 10 January 1999.

_____. *Out of Place: A Memoir.* New York: Alfred A. Knopf, 1999.

_____. "On Palestinian Identity." *New Left Review* 160 (1986): 74–75.

_____. "Paying the Price for Personal Politics." *Al-Ahram Weekly,* 30 September–6 October 1999.

_____. *Peace and Its Discontents: Essays on Palestine in the Middle East Peace Process.* New York: Vintage, 1995.

_____. "Reflections on Exile." *Granta* 13 (Winter 1984).

_____. *The Politics of Dispossession: The Struggle for Palestinian Self-Determination, 1969-1994.* New York: Pantheon Books, 1994.

_____. *The Question of Palestine.* New York: Times Books, 1979.

Scott, A.O. "Edward W. Said: The Palestinian Tory." *Slate.* 1 October 1999.

Smith, Dinitia. "Arafat's Man in New York—The Divided Life of Columbia Professor Edward Said." *New York Magazine.* 23 January 1989.

Sprinkler, Michael. "Edward Said: A Critical Reader." Cambridge, MA: Blackwell Publishers, 1992.

Weiner, Justus Reid. "My Beautiful Old House and Other Fabrications by Edward Said." *Commentary* 108:2 (1999).

Contributors

As'ad AbuKhalil is associate professor of political science at California State University, Stanislaus and research fellow at the Center for Middle Eastern Studies at the University of California, Berkeley. He received his B.A. and M.A. from the American University of Beirut, and his Ph.D. in comparative government from Georgetown University. His articles on Middle East politics have appeared in Arabic, English, German, and Spanish. He is the author of the *Historical Dictionary of Lebanon*.

Yasmeen Abu-Laban is assistant professor of political science at the University of Alberta. Her research interests center on the Canadian and comparative dimensions of ethnic, gender, and identity politics, nationalism and globalization, immigration policies and politics, and citizenship theory. Her publications include articles in *Canadian Public Policy, Canadian Ethnic Studies*, and *The Canadian Review of American Studies*.

Naseer Aruri is professor emeritus of political science at the University of Massachusetts, Dartmouth. His articles on American foreign policy, human rights, Islam, the Palestine question and political violence have appeared in such journals as *The Muslim World, Third World Quarterly*, the *Middle East Journal*, and the *Journal of Palestine Studies*. He has been writing on contemporary Middle East issues in newspapers and magazines such as *Middle East International, al-Hayat, al-Qabas*, and various Arabic newspapers for the past three decades. He has served on the board of directors of Amnesty International, USA for three consecutive terms and he presently chairs the Boston-based Trans-Arab Research Center. He is the author of *Jordan: A Study in Political Development*, and editor of several books, including Occupation: Israel Over Palestine. His latest book is *The Obstruction of Peace: The U.S., Israel & the Palestinians* (Common Courage, 1995).

Timothy Brennan is professor of cultural studies and comparative literature at the University of Minnesota. His essays on cultural theory, media politics, American intellectuals, race and imperialism have appeared in such journals as *Critical Inquiry, Transition, Public Culture, The Nation* and the *Times Literary Supplement*. He has worked as a journalist in Central America and as a radio commentator on WKCR in New York. He is the author of *Salman Rushdie and* the Third World: Myths of the Nation (Macmillan, 1989), *At Home in the World* (Harvard, 1997) and the forthcoming *Music in Cuba* (Minnesota, 2001). He is currently at work on a book on the Eurocentrism of theory, entitled *Avant Gardes, Colonies, Communists, and Culture.*

Deirdre David is professor of English and vice president of the faculty senate at Temple University in Philadelphia. She is author most recently of *Rule Britannia: Women, Empire, and Victorian Writing* (Cornell, 1996), and is currently at work on two books: the first a study of British Victorian writing about America, and the second, a sequel to *Rule Britannia* that examines cultural change in Britain after WWII, with a particular emphasis on the decline of imperial power.

Lennard J. Davis is professor and graduate director at the State University of New York at Binghamton. He is the author of two works on the novel—*Factual Fictions: The Origins of the English Novel* (Columbia U. Press, 1983. Rpt. University of Pennsylvania Press, 1996) and *Resisting Novels: Fiction and Ideology* (Routledge, 1987) and co-editor of *Left Politics and the Literary Profession*. His works on disability include *Enforcing Normalcy: Disability, Deafness, and the Body* (Verso, 1995) and *The Disability Studies Reader* (Routledge, 1996). His memoir *My Sense of Silence* about growing up in a Deaf family will be published by the University of Illinois Press in 2000, and an edition of his parents' love letters, *Shall I Say a Kiss: The Courtship Letters of a Deaf Couple, 1936–38* was published by Gallaudet University Press in 1999. He was a founding member of the Modern Language Association's Committee on Disability Issues in the Profession, is an active member of Children of Deaf Adults (CODA), and is on the editorial board of *Corporalities:* Discourses of Disability Series at the University of Michigan Press.

Marc H. Ellis is University Professor of American and Jewish Studies and director, Center for American and Jewish Studies at Baylor University. He has written extensively on Jewish and Christian affairs, concentrating on the topics of Holocaust, Israel/Palestine and the future of religious thought. Ellis has written many books, including *Toward A Jewish Theology of Liberation* and *Unholy Alliance: Religion and Atrocity in Our Time*. His latest book, *O'Jerusalem: The Contested Future of the Jewish Covenant*, addresses the future of Jews and Palestinians and the covenant so central to Jewish life and history. A collection of essays, *Revolutionary Forgiveness: A Jew Among Christians* and *Practicing Exile: A Memoir of Struggle and Hope* are forthcoming.

Richard Falk is Albert G. Milbank Professor of International Law and Practice at Princeton University. He represented Ethiopia and Liberia before the International Court of Justice and is honorary vice president of the American Society of International Law. He has written extensively on human rights, nuclear weapons, and international law. His most recent books are *Law in an Emerging Global Village and Predatory Globalization: A Critique*.

Atif Kibursi is professor of economics at McMaster University and president of Econometric Research Ltd., Economic Management Consultants. He has written seven books and over 150 articles and reports. He is a consultant to the United Nations and is president of the National Council on Canada Arab Relations. He is a long time activist, spokesperson, and media personality on issues related to the economy, the Middle East, and the Canadian Arab community.

Muhammad A. Shuraydi is associate professor of sociology, department of sociology and anthropology at the University of Windsor, Ontario. He taught at the University of Kuwait in 1975–1976 and 1988–1989, and at Wayne State University, 1979–1982, in the College of Education, Bilingual/Bicultural Program. A former president of the Canadian Arab Federation, he has organized and participated in many conferences, workshops, and seminars on the Arab world and the Arab-Israeli conflict. He was the chairperson of a two-day symposium on "Culture, Politics and Peace" honoring the scholarly contribution of Professor Edward Said, 19–20 September 1997, at the University of Windsor. His publications focus on the Palestinian question and the Arab world and on bilingual/bicultural education in the United States.

John Sigler is adjunct professor of political science and international affairs at Carlton University and the University of Ottawa, after retiring from fulltime status in 1997. He was the director of the Norman Paterson Graduate School of International Affairs at Carlton from 1977–1982. His special interest is US & Canadian policies in the Middle East. His articles have appeared in *International Journal, International Studies Quarterly, Etudes Internationales, Cholx*. He writes an annual chapter on conflict in the Middle East in the collection *Les Conflits dans Le Monde*, edited by Albert Legault and published by Laval University Press since 1982.

Index

A
Ab'ad (journal), 106
Abdel-Malek, Anouar, 100
'Abdur-Raziq, 'Ali, 113
abolitionist concerns, 32–34
abortion, 80
Abrams, Elliot, 42
Abu Lughod, Ibrahim, 159
Al-'Adhm, Sadiq Jalal, 101, 105, 106–9
affiliation, 96, 162
Adorno, Theodor, 3
After the Last Sky (Said), 87
Ahmad, Aijaz, 76
Ajami, Fouad, 102
Al-Azhar University, 112–14
Al-Hayat (newpaper), 110
Al-Ma'rifah (journal), 107–8
Althusser, Louis, 11
America. *See* United States
American Annals of the Deaf, 13
American Friends Service Committee, 162
American Israel Public Affairs Committee, 43
American Notes (Dickens), 35
'Amil, Mahdi, 106–9
Amnesty International, 171
Anderson, Benedict, 5–7
Anti-Defamation League, 43
anti-Semitism, 38–39, 42, 60–61
    John Cuddihy, 47–48
    Orientalism, 114
    vs. philo-Semitism, 160
    in Said's work, 61–65
apartheid, 52–53, 59, 122–23, 126, 129
Arab Boycott, 153–54
Arabic language, 103
Arabs, 110, 126–27
    oil-based economy, 141–46, 157
    on *Orientalism,* 100–115
    Orientalist views of, 134–57
    private property, 172–73
    racism toward, 94
Arafat, Yasir, xv–xvi, 120–33, 164, 176
Arkoun, Muhammad, 106

Aruri, Naseer, 159
Ash-Sharq Al-Awsat (newpaper), 110
Auerbach, Erich, 93

B
Al-Bahiyy, Muhammad, 113
Balfour, Arthur, 97
Balibar, Etienne, 5–6, 8, 10–11, 22, 81
Balta, Paul, 104
Barak, Ehud, 120–22, 128, 129
Baram, Haim, 126
Barbauld, Anna, 35
Barsamian, David, 124
Barthes, Roland, 3
Ba'thism, 109
Baynton, Douglas, 13
Becker, Carl Heinrich, 102
Begin, Menachem, 122, 128
Beginnings: Intention and Method (Said), 3, 90
Bell, Alexander Graham, 11
Bellow, Saul, 53
Benjamin, Walter, 21
Benvinisti, Meron, 125
Bernal, Martin, 99, 115
Berque, Jacques, 161
Bhabha, Homi, 5–6, 30
bi-nationalism in Israel, 123–26, 132, 159–66, 171–77
Bird, Isabella, 32
Bishara, Azmi, 124–25
Al-Bitar, Nadim, 105
Bloom, Alan, 102
Blumer, Herbert, 173
the body, 4–28
Bogdan, Robert, 18–19
Boyarin, Daniel, 59–61, 67
Boyarin, Jonathan, 44, 59–61, 67
Brass, Paul, 7–8
Britain
    Middle Eastern policies, 103–4
    views on America, 29–37
    western vs. eastern culture, 51–52
Buber, Martin, 53, 54, 164–65

Index

Burke, Edmund, 5, 29
Burton, Richard, 98

C
Cairo accords, 120
Cambridge Illustrated History of the Islamic World (Robinson), 102
capitalism, x–xi
Catholicism, 80
Chomsky, Noam, 44, 58, 64, 71–6
    Orientalism, 96
"Chomsky and the Question of Palestine" (Said), 71n6
Chrisman, Laura, 76
Christianity
    fundamentalism, 78
    Israel, 42
    Orientalism, 112–14
    Western culture, 75–79
The Chronicle of Higher Education, 90–91
circus culture and disabilities, 18–20, 27n9
citizenship for Palestinians, 124n6, 132
civilization, 80
civil liberties. *See* human rights
civil rights movement, Israeli, 58
The Clash of Civilizations and the Remaking of the World Order (Huntington), 79–84, 103, 164
"The Clash of Civilizations" (Huntington), 79
class issues
    British writing on America, 30–37
    disabilities, 14–20
    intelligence levels, 26–27n8
Clifford, James, 90–91
colonialism, 30, 81, 111–12
    disabilities, 26n3, 27–9
    Orientalism, 76, 101–3
Columbia University, 3–4
Commentary (magazine), 42, 170–77
Communism, 80
comparative literature, xi, 75
"Conciliation with America" (Burke), 29
The Condition of the Working Class in England (Engels), 16–17
conflict, xi
Connolly, William, xii

Connor, Walker, 5, 7
Conrad, Joseph, 90
Corbett, William, 35
The Country and the City (Williams), 90
Covering Islam (Said), 78–79, 87
Crone, Patricia, 104
cross-disciplinary study, 94–95
Cuddihy, John Murray, 44–70
cultural superiority of British writing on America, 30–37
Culture and Imperialism (Said), xiv, 32, 83, 106, 161
Cuvier, Baron Georges, 88

D
Davis, Lennard, 2–28
deaf culture, 4, 12–15
deafness, 2–28
debtor countries, 139
"Declaration of Independence," 176
"Defamation, Zionist Style" (Said), 175
dehumanization of the other, 75–79
Derrida, Jacques, 90
Descartes, René, xvi
Desloges, Pierre, 13–14
development
    Arab economy, 151–52
    Palestinians, 123, 150
    See also economic issues
de Vos, George, 9
diaspora
    of the Jewish people, 68
    of the Palestinians, 48, 65–70
Dickens, Charles, 34–35
Dictionary of Political Thought (Scruton), 77
difference, 54–61
    See also racism
disabilities, 2–28
displacement. *See* diaspora; exile
diversification of the Arab economy, 150–52
diversity, 82
Diyab, Muhammad, 114
Djait, Hichem, 106
domination vs. subordination, xiv
Duran, Khalid, 102
Durant, Will, 23

183

E

Early Empowerment, 120
East. *See* Middle Eastern culture
Eastern Europe, 139–40
Economic and Philosophical Manuscripts of 1848 (Marx), 4–5
economic issues, 134–57
    foreign aid, 139–40, 147, 154
    Gaza, 148
    military power, 137–38
    Third World, 134–36
education, 11–13, 26n6, 155
Edwards, Martha L., 18
Egypt, 155
Ellis, Marc, 166
empire. *See* colonialism
Enforcing Normalcy: Disability, Deafness, and the Body (Lennard), 2–28
Engels, Friederich, 16–17
Esposito, John, 80–81
essentialist thought, 54–61, 107, 163–64
ethnicity, 6–8
eugenics, 10–11, 17
European contexts, 29–37, 51–52, 88
    Orientalist studies, 101–2
    postcolonial studies, 90–91, 95
European Union, 81
exile, x–xi, xiii–xiv
    See also diaspora
the Exodus, 55

F

Fackenheim, Emil, 41–42, 71n3
Factual Fictions: The Origins of the English Novel (Lennard), 3
Faith or Fear: How Jews Can Survive in a Christian America (Abrams), 42
Fatah/FLN, 164, 176
FDR's Splendid Deception (Gallagher), 22
filiation, 96
Findley, Paul, 43–44
Finkelstein, Norman, 44
Flaubert, Gustave, 98
foreign aid, 139–40, 147, 154
foreign investment, 135, 153–55
foreign policy, 160
Foucault, Michel, xii, 3, 96, 98
    postcolonial studies, 89–91

Freak Show: Presenting Human Oddities for Amusement and Profit (Bogdan), 18–19
free markets, 137
French scholars
    Orientalism, 88, 101–2
    postcolonial studies, 90–91
Freud, Sigmund, 44–47, 54
Friedman, Thomas, 102
Front National, 83
Fruman, Rabbi Menachem, 126
fundamentalism, 78–81
    Islamic, 103, 111–14

G

Gallagher, Hugh, 21–24
Gaskell, Elizabeth, 33
Gaza, 148
Gellner, Ernest, 100–101
gender, 6, 16, 29–37, 76
Ghanem, Adel, 124
Al-Ghazzali, Muhammad, 112–14
Gibb, Sir Hamilton, 107
globalization, x–xi, xiv, xvi, 82–83
    anti-Semitism, 42
    Arab economies, 136–41
    investment, 139–40
    Orientalism, 91–92
Goldziher, Ignaz, 104
Gorbachev, Mikhail, 165
Gramasci, Antonio, 53
Great Britain. *See* Britain
Greenberg, Irving, 71n3
Groce, Nora Ellen, 10
Groom, Jane Elizabeth, 14
Gross Domestic Product (GDP) of Arab economies, 150
von Grunebaum, Gustav, 160
Guillaumin, Colette, 10
Gulf War, 103, 138, 161
    Arab economy, 134–35
    Arab neoconservatism, 110
Gunther, John, 25
Gwaltney, J., 18

H

Hanafi, Hasan, 105, 114–15
Harris, William, 103

Index

Hebron Agreement, 120
history, 6, 99
    of the Jewish people, 38–72
the Holocaust, 38–72, 160, 164–65, 174
Hourani, Albert, 101, 103–4
houses, 172–73
humanism, 75–79, 86
human rights
    Arab world, 78
    Palestinians, 53–54, 61–65, 124–25, 127–29, 164, 176–77
Huntington, Samuel, 74–75, 79–83, 103, 164
Hurgronje, Snouck, 102

I

"An Ideology of Difference" (Said), 55–56
Ikrit, Israel, 175
immigrants, 81–83
imperialism, 26n5, 161
    Orientalism, 76, 103
    postcolonial studies, 90, 97
"The Incivil Irritatingness of Jewish Theodicy" (Cuddihy), 47–48
indigenous Americans, 32, 82
industrialization and disabilities, 16–18
intellectuals, xii–xiii, xii–xv, 74–84, 100, 159–66
    Jewish, 38–39, 45–47, 50, 61–70
    literary, 93–94, 99
    Orientalism, 95–97
    Zionism, 102, 122, 132
internationalism. *See* globalization
International Monetary Fund, 137–41
Intifada, 44, 60, 127, 149
investment, 135, 139–40, 153–55
Irish immigrants, 32, 34–35
irrationality of Eastern culture, 75–79
Islam
    economic impact, 157
    fundamentalism, 78–81, 103, 112–14
    nationalism, 163–64
    Orientalism, 111
    secularism, 104
    the West, 75–79, 100–101, 136
Islam and the West (Lewis), 100–101
Islamic studies, 112–14
Al-Islam wa Usul Al-Hukm, 113

Ismael, Jacqueline S., 76
Israel, x–xi, xvi
    Arab neoconservatives' views, 110
    civil liberties for Palestinians, 53–54, 61–65, 124–25, 127–29, 164, 176–77
    economic issues, 146–56
    foreign aid, 147, 154
    future of Palestine, 160–66
    growth of power, 61–70
    judicial system, 175
    Labor Party, 122, 128, 130
    Lebanon, 44, 55–56, 96
    legitimacy, 53–54
    Likud Party, 122, 130
    nationalism, 165–66
    Orientalism, 77–79
    Oslo accords, 120–33, 170–71
    right wing rabbis, 125–26
    taxes, 152–53
    West Bank settlements, 120, 122, 127, 131
Issawi, Charles, 105
Istrabadi, Zeineb, 171

J

Jarvis, Edward, 17
Jerusalem, 121–22, 131, 174
Jewish people, x–xi, 11
    chosenness of, 54–61, 160, 166n.1
    culture of, 71n5
    future of, 38–72, 166
    political institutions, 43–45
    and power, 61–70
    See also Israel
Johnson, William Henry, 19–20
Jordan, 123, 155
Josselyn, John, 32
journalists, 86, 102

K

Kaplan, Chaim, 47–48
Kaplan, Robert, 112
Kedourie, Elie, 102
Kemble, Fanny, 33–35
Kennedy, John F., 21

Khalidi, Rashid, 159
Khalidi, Walid, 159
Al-Kharbutli, Ali Husni, 113
Khazanov, Anatoly, 103
Khomeini, Ayatollah, 110
Kubursi, Atif, vii–viii
Kuroda, A.K., 173–74
Kuroda, Y., 173–74

L

labor, 4–5, 137, 138
Labor Party (Israeli), 122, 128, 130
Lammens, Henri, 102
Lane, Edward, 98
language
    deafness, 7–15
    ethnicity, 13–14
    knowledge, 103
    literacy, 26n4, 151
    nationhood, 5–7
Law of Return, 124, 175
Lebanon, 155
    invasion by Israel, 44, 55–56, 96
legitimacy of Israeli policies, 61–70
Lévi-Strauss, Claude, 44–47, 54
Lewis, Bernard, 54–55, 76, 79, 102, 105, 108, 112
    Orientalism, 100–101, 104
liberation theology, 38–39
Likud Party (Israeli), 122, 130
literacy, 26n4, 151
literary criticism, 105
    Orientalism, 86–99
    vs. political thought, 93–94, 99
literature, xi
    British, on America, 29–37
    deaf culture, 9

M

MacDonald, Neil, 175
Mackey, Sandra, 102
Madrid process, 163
Magna Carta, 81
Mahdi, Muhsin, 100
Makiya, Kanan, 101–2, 106, 110–11
Malik, Charles, xv
Martin Chuzzlewit (Dickens), 35
Marx, Karl, 4–5, 44–47, 54, 108

Marxism, xii
Marxism, 106–9
"Marxism and the National Question" (Stalin), 6
Mead, George Herbert, 173
Mexico, 81–82
Middle Eastern culture
    Arab neoconservatives, 110
    power, 74–84
    vs. Western, xiv, 50–54, 62–65
    See also Arabs; *Orientalism*
military
    enforcement of economic policies, 137–38
    expenditures, 155–56
Milken, Michael, 171
Miller, Judith, 102
Mills, C. Wright, 92
Min-ha, Trinh, 7
minorities, 6
morality, 39–41, 43–45
Morris, Benny, 132
Moughrabi, Fouad, 159
Moynihan, Senator Daniel Patrick, 53
multidisciplinary scholarship, 74–76, 100
multiethnic culture, 68–70, 82
music, xi
Muslim Brotherhood, 114
Muslims. *See* Islam
Muslim women, 76, 103, 111–12
"My Beautiful Old House and other Fabrications by Edward Said" (Weiner), 170–77

N

narrative in *Orientalism,* 97
nationalism, 26n5, 101–2
    Arab, 106, 163–64
    Zionist, 163–65
nationality and disability, 2–28
The Nation (magazine), 4
native Americans, 32, 82
natural resources, 147–50
neoconservatism
    colonialism, 103–4
    Orientalism, 109–12
Netanyahu, Benjamin, 120–22, 128–30, 165
new anti-Semitism, 42

Index

New World Order, 134–36
New York Times Sunday Magazine, 90–91
The New York World (newspaper), 23
Nicholas Nickleby (Dickens), 35
1948 War, 55–56
1967 War, 40–41, 55–56
    Elie Weisel and, 71n.2
Nobel Peace Prize, 39, 176
non-marital cohabitation, 80
novels, 7

O

Occidentalism, 114–15
oil, 141–46, 150, 157
    production, 143–44, 143t, 145t
    reserves, 142–44, 143t, 145t
Olcott, Martha, 103
Oliver, Mike, 14–15
Oliver Twist (Dickens), 35
"Opening of the Indian and Colonial Exhibition by the Queen" (Tennyson), 29
oppressors, 60
The Ordeal of Civility (Cuddihy), 44–70
Orientalism, 74–84, 96–97, 101–2, 112–14, 160–61
    Israeli, 77–79
Orientalism (Said), 50–54, 75–79, 160–61
    American context, 87–99
    Arab views, 100–115
    new terminology, 96
    post colonial studies, xiv, 86–99
Oslo accords, vii, xv–xvi, 61, 71n7, 161, 163–65, 170–71, 175
    Arafat's role, 120–33, 164
    pluralism in Palestine, 120–33
    single-vs.-two-state approaches, 123–27
    water, 152
    See also Intifada
Out of Place (Said), xiii–xiv, xv, 170–71

P

Palestine
    future, 159–66
    single-vs.-two-state approaches, 120–33, 159–66, 171–77
    See also Oslo accords
Palestine Liberation Organization, 126
    See also Yasir Arafat
Palestinian Authority, 127–28, 170–71, 175
Palestinians, 3, 77–79, 111
    Arab neoconservatives, 109–10
    economic considerations, 146–56
    exile, 48–70
    human rights, 53–54, 61–65, 78, 124–25, 127–29, 164, 176–77
    independence, 127–28
    intellectuals, 159
    Intifada, 44, 60, 127, 149
    legitimacy of Israel policies, 61–70
    national identification of, 57–58, 173–74
    natural resources, 147–50
    Oslo accords, 120–33, 176–77
    as victims, 38–72
    Zionism, 103–4
"Palestinians without Palestine" (Kuroda & Kuroda), 173–74
Pappe, Ilan, 131–32
Patai, Raphael, 102, 112
Peace and its Discontents (Said), 71n7, 78
peace between Israel and the Palestinians
    economic considerations, 147–56
    role of intellectuals, 159–66
Peace Now, 56–57
Percy, Senator Charles, 43–44
Peres, Shimon, 128
Perlmutter, Nathan, 42–43
Pipes, Daniel, 102, 174
pluralism in Palestine/Israel, 120–33, 159–66
Podhoertz, Norman, 42
Poliakov, Sefei, 102–3
political correctness, xv, 112
political issues
    globalization, 138
    idealism, 35
    oil, 142
    water, 148, 150, 152
    See also power
political parties
    Israeli Labor Party, 122, 128, 130
    Israeli Likud Party, 122, 130

Palestinian parties, 130
political science, 79–80, 161
    vs. literary thought, 93–94, 98

The Politics of Disablement: A Sociological Approach (Oliver), 14–15
Polyani, Karl, 137–38
Popular Front for the Liberation of Palestine, 176
Porter, Dennis, 90–91
post-colonial studies, 89
    Orientalism (Said), 86–99
post-Zionism, 131–33, 165–66
power, xii, xiv, 35, 138, 160
    Israel, 44–46, 61–70, 71n3, 71n4
    Orientalism, 74–84
    Oslo agreements, 164
    Palestinians, 38–72, 58–59, 120
Princeton University, xv
Pryce-Jones, David, 102

Q

The Question of Palestine (Said), 50–54, 77–79, 87, 176
Qur'an, 104

R

Rabin, Yitzhak, 122, 128, 129, 130
race, 81
    Arabs, 94
    British writing on America, 32–37
    disabilities, 9–20
    Orientalism, 89–99
    Palestinians, 59–61
    See also anti-Semitism
Raritan (journal), 90
rationality of Western culture, 75–79
Ar-Rayyis, Muhammad Diya', 113
Reaganism, 88
The Real Antisemitism in America (Perlmutter), 42, 43
1993 Reith Lectures, xii
religiosity, 80
    Israel and the Palestinians, 38–42, 125–26
    Orientalism, 107–8, 112–14
    vs. secularism, xii
Renan, Ernest, 88, 98
reparations, 175
Representations of the Intellectual (Said), xii
research on the Arab economy, 151–52
right-wing rabbis in Israel, 125–26
Robinson, Francis, 102, 103
Rodison, Maxime, 101
Roman Catholics, 38–39
Romantic tradition, xvi
Roosevelt, Franklin Delano, 20–26
"The Roots of Muslim Rage" (Lewis), 79
Rothman, David, 15
Rouhana, Nadim, 124–25
Roy, Sara, 164
Rushdie, Salman, xii, 111
Rywkin, Michael, 102

S

Sadat, Anwar, 105
Safire, William, 122
Saghiyyah, Hazim, 110–12
Said, Edward, 3–4, 159, 170–77
    on cultural isolation, 31, 37
    future of Palestine, 159–66
    on the Jewish people, 48–70
    memoirs, 170–71
    Oslo accords, vii
    Palestinian civil rights, 132–33
    role in Palestinian government-in-exile, 105
    single-state solution for Palestine/Israel, 123–26
    See also titles of individual works
Samara, Adel, 124
Satanic Verses (Rushdie), xii
Saudi Arabia, 146
Schaw, Janet, 36
scholars. *See* intellectuals
Schwab, Raymond, 88, 98
Scruton, Roger, 77
"Secular Criticism" (Said), 87
secularism, xi–xvi, 88
    Islamic world, 104
    Israeli left, 125–26
    in a Palestinian/Israeli state, 132, 171
self-determination, 176

Index

separation. *See* two-state solution
"Seven Roads: Theoretical Options for the Status of the Arabs in Israel" (Rouhana), 125
Shahak, Israel, 58, 174
Shamir, Yitzhak, 122, 130
Sharabi, Hisham, 159, 161
Shararah, Wadah, 110–12
Sharm al-Shaykh agreement, 120
Sheleg, Yair, 126
As-Siba'i, Mustafa, 114
sign language, 12–13
single-state solution for Palestine/Israel, 123–26, 132, 159–66, 171–77
Sivan, Emmanuel, 105, 108
Sivan, Kenan, 114–15
Six-Day War. *See* 1967 War
social scientists. *See* political science
Soviet Union, 139–40, 157
Spivak, Hayatri, 30–31
Stalin, Joseph, 6, 12–13
Stasiulis, Daiva, 82
subjectivity, xvi
Sullivan, Earl L., 76
Swift, Jonathan, 90

T
Talmadge, Gene, 24
Taylor, Rupert, 79–80
technology, 137
Tennyson, Alfred, 29
Thackeray, William, 34
Third World economic issues, 134–36
Tibawi, A. L., 100, 112–14
Till the End of Time (film), 25
Time (magazine), 24
Tolmacheva, Marina, 103
tourism in the Middle East, 155
"Toward a Methodology of Beginnings" (Lennard), 3
traces of history, 99
transnational corporations, 137
"Traveling Theory" (Said), 87, 94
Trollope, Anthony, 34, 36
Trollope, Frances, 35
two-state solution for Palestine/Israel, 120–33, 159–66

U
United Nations, 42, 56, 139
United States
    Arab neoconservatives and, 110
    British writer's views, 29–37
    foreign aid, 139–40, 154
    foreign policy, xvi, 43–44, 120, 128–30, 160, 164, 166n1
    globalization, xiv, 134–36
    Gulf War, 138
    labor, 138
    "left" wing, 87–88
    oil, 141–42, 145–46
    Orientalism, 87–99
    political science, 79–80, 161
    politicians, 27n10
    Presidents, 20–26
    slavery, 32–37
    writings on the Civil War, 32–34, 36
US Agency for International Development, 139–40

V
Vatican Council II, 38–39
Vatikiotis, P.J., 103
Vico, Giambattista, 3
victims, 53–54, 60

W
Walby, Sylvia, 6
Wallerstein, Immanuel, 5–6, 10
Walzer, Michael, 54–61, 65, 67
Warsaw Diary (Kaplan), 47–48
water, 148, 150, 152
Watt, W. Montgomery, 104–5
Weiner, Justus Reid, 170–77
Weisel, Elie, 39–41, 60, 71n2, 71n3
Weizmann, Chaim, 51
Wensinck, A.J., 102
West Bank, 120, 122, 127, 131, 148
Western culture, 50–54, 63–65, 80–83, 103
    Jewish people, 38–72
    Mexico, 81–82
    vs. Middle Eastern, 62–65, 103
    Orientalism, 75–79, 100–105
    power, 74–84
    See also Orientalism
"The West Unique, Not Universal"

(Huntington), 79–80
White, Hayden, 5–6
Why I Am Not a Secularist (Connolly), xii
Williams, Patrick, 76
Williams, Raymond, 90
women, 80
    British writing, 30–37
    Muslim-, 103, 111–12
The World, the Text, and the Critic (Said), 68, 87–88, 93, 96
World Bank, 139
World Trade Organization, 137–41
Wye River memorandum, 120

Y
Yergin, David, 146

Z
Zaqzuq, Mahmud, 112–14
Zionism, 52–54, 56–57, 59, 62–63, 66
    after the Oslo peace accords, 131–33
    role in Palestinian dispossession, 103–4
    See also Israel; post-Zionism
Zuriek, Elia, 159